First World Wa

and Army of Occupation

War Diary

France, Belgium and Germany

17 DIVISION
51 Infantry Brigade
Sherwood Foresters (Nottinghamshire and Derbyshire Regiment)
10th Battalion
14 July 1915 - 31 March 1919

WO95/2008/2

The Naval & Military Press Ltd
www.nmarchive.com
Published in association with The National Archives

Published by

The Naval & Military Press Ltd

Unit 10 Ridgewood Industrial Park,

Uckfield, East Sussex,

TN22 5QE England

Tel: +44 (0) 1825 749494

www.naval-military-press.com

www.nmarchive.com

Contents

Document type	Place/Title	Date From	Date To
Heading	2008/2 51 Infantry Brigade 10 Battalion Sherwood Foresters		
Heading	17th Division 51st Infy Bde 10th Bn Notts & Derby Regt Jly 1915-Mar 1919		
Heading	51st Inf. Bde. 17th Div. 10th Battn. The Sherwood Foresters (Nottinghamshire And Derbyshire Regiment) July (14/27.7.15) 1915		
War Diary	Winchester	14/07/1915	14/07/1915
War Diary	Boulogne	15/07/1915	15/07/1915
War Diary	St. Omer	16/07/1915	16/07/1915
War Diary	Zudausques	16/07/1915	16/07/1915
War Diary	Ebblinghem	18/07/1915	18/07/1915
War Diary	Caestre	19/07/1915	21/07/1915
War Diary	Reninghelst	25/07/1915	27/07/1915
Heading	51st Inf. Bde. 17th Div. 10th Battn. The Sherwood Foresters (Nottinghamshire And Derbyshire Regiment). August 1915		
War Diary		01/08/1915	01/08/1915
War Diary	Ouderdom	02/08/1915	04/08/1915
War Diary	Reninghelst	06/08/1915	22/08/1915
War Diary	Trenches	23/08/1915	31/08/1915
Heading	51st Inf. Bde. 17th Div. 10th Battn. The Sherwood Foresters (Nottinghamshire And Derbyshire Regiment). September 1915		
War Diary		31/08/1915	23/09/1915
Heading	51st Inf. Bde. 17th Div. 10th Battn. The Sherwood Foresters (Nottinghamshire And Derbyshire Regiment). October 1915		
War Diary		01/10/1915	06/10/1915
War Diary	Eecke	07/10/1915	20/10/1915
War Diary	Near Ouderdom	21/10/1915	30/10/1915
War Diary		28/10/1915	28/10/1915
War Diary		04/10/1915	04/10/1915
Heading	51st Inf. Bde. 17th Div. 10th Battn. The Sherwood Foresters (Nottinghamshire And Derbyshire Regiment). November 1915		
War Diary		01/11/1915	30/11/1915
Heading	51st Inf. Bde. 17th Div. 10th Battn. The Sherwood Foresters (Nottinghamshire And Derbyshire Regiment). December 1915		
War Diary	Trenches	01/12/1915	11/12/1915
War Diary	Ramparts	11/12/1915	31/12/1915
Heading	17th Div 51st Bde 10th Sherwoods Vol 6 Jan 1916		
War Diary	Ouderdom	03/01/1916	10/01/1916
War Diary	Houlle	11/01/1916	29/01/1916
Heading	10th Notts & Derby's 17th Div (51) Vol 7 Feb 1916		
War Diary	Houlle	05/02/1916	29/02/1916
Miscellaneous	Detail of Assembly Trenches. Appendix No. 1		
Miscellaneous	Distribution of Grenades.		
Miscellaneous	2nd Bn. Suffolk Regt. Appendix No. 2	29/02/1916	29/02/1916

Miscellaneous	Preliminary Orders by G.O.C. 76th Infantry Brigade. Appendix No 3	24/02/1916	24/02/1916
Diagram etc	Distinguishing Marks. Black On Yellow.		
Operation(al) Order(s)	70th Infantry Brigade Operation Order No. 10. Appendix No. 4	27/02/1916	27/02/1916
Miscellaneous			
Heading	10th Notts & Derbys Vol 8 March 1916		
War Diary		29/02/1916	14/03/1916
War Diary	La Creche	14/03/1916	31/03/1916
War Diary	Trenches	01/04/1916	04/04/1916
War Diary	Armentieres	05/04/1916	16/04/1916
War Diary	Trenches	16/04/1916	20/04/1916
War Diary	Armentieres	20/04/1916	31/05/1916
War Diary	Houlle	01/06/1916	30/06/1916
Heading	51st Inf. Bde. 17th Div. War Diary 10th Battn. The Sherwood Foresters (Nottinghamshire And Derbyshire Regiment). July 1916		
War Diary		30/06/1916	26/07/1916
Heading	51st Brigade 17th Division 1/10th Battalion Sherwood Foresters August 1916		
Heading	War Diary 10th Sherwood Foresters August 1916 Vol 12		
War Diary		01/08/1916	30/09/1916
Heading	War Diary 10th Sherwood Foresters October 1916 Vol 14		
War Diary	Conteville	01/10/1916	02/10/1916
War Diary	Mezerolles	02/10/1916	03/10/1916
War Diary	Halloy	03/10/1916	04/10/1916
War Diary	Bayencourt	05/10/1916	06/10/1916
War Diary	Hebuterne	07/10/1916	09/10/1916
War Diary	Bayencourt	10/10/1916	19/10/1916
War Diary	Lucheux	20/10/1916	22/10/1916
War Diary	Mericourt	22/10/1916	26/10/1916
War Diary	Citadel Camp	28/10/1916	29/10/1916
War Diary	F. Camp	29/10/1916	29/10/1916
War Diary	Front Line	30/10/1916	31/10/1916
Heading	War Diary 10th Sherwood Forester November 1916 Vol 15		
War Diary	Front Trenches	01/11/1916	01/11/1916
War Diary	Mansel Camp	02/11/1916	04/11/1916
War Diary	Support Trenches	05/11/1916	05/11/1916
War Diary	Front Trenches	06/11/1916	06/11/1916
War Diary	Trenches	06/11/1916	09/11/1916
War Diary	H Camp	09/11/1916	14/11/1916
War Diary	Edgehill Station	15/11/1916	15/11/1916
War Diary	Hangest	15/11/1916	15/11/1916
War Diary	Picquigny	16/11/1916	12/12/1916
War Diary	Corbie	12/12/1916	20/12/1916
War Diary	Mericourt	23/12/1916	23/12/1916
War Diary	Carnoy (17 Camp)	24/12/1916	25/12/1916
War Diary	Carnoy (19 Camp)	25/12/1916	25/12/1916
War Diary	Guillemont	26/12/1916	26/12/1916
War Diary	Front Line	27/12/1916	29/12/1916
War Diary	Camp 19 Carnoy	30/12/1916	01/01/1917
War Diary	Front Line	02/01/1917	05/01/1917
War Diary	Camp 19 Carnoy	06/01/1917	06/01/1917

War Diary	Front Line	08/01/1917	10/01/1917
War Diary	Carnoy Meaulte	11/01/1917	11/01/1917
War Diary	Meaulte	13/01/1917	13/01/1917
War Diary	Maltz Horn & Bois Doree	26/01/1917	26/01/1917
War Diary	Bouleaux Wood	27/01/1917	27/01/1917
War Diary	Line	28/01/1917	28/01/1917
War Diary	Maltz Horn & Bois Doree	30/01/1917	30/01/1917
War Diary	Bronfay Camp 108	31/01/1917	31/01/1917
War Diary	Bronfay	01/02/1917	01/02/1917
War Diary	Bouleaux Area	02/02/1917	02/02/1917
War Diary	Line	03/02/1917	05/02/1917
War Diary	Maltz Horn	06/02/1917	06/02/1917
War Diary	Bouleaux Wood	08/02/1917	08/02/1917
War Diary	Line	09/02/1917	09/02/1917
War Diary	Maltz Horn	13/02/1917	13/02/1917
War Diary	Bronfay Camp	14/02/1917	16/02/1917
War Diary	Bouleaux Wood	16/02/1917	17/02/1917
War Diary	Line	17/02/1917	18/02/1917
War Diary	Bronfay Camp	19/02/1917	19/02/1917
War Diary	Bonnay	20/02/1917	21/02/1917
War Diary	Bronfay Camp	19/02/1917	19/02/1917
War Diary	Bonnay	21/02/1917	22/03/1917
War Diary	Rougefay	23/03/1917	28/03/1917
War Diary	Le Souich	31/03/1917	05/04/1917
War Diary	Maisnil St Pol	06/04/1917	06/04/1917
War Diary	Ambrines	07/04/1917	07/04/1917
War Diary	Habarcq	08/04/1917	08/04/1917
War Diary	Arras Area	09/04/1917	10/04/1917
War Diary	Arras Railway Triangle	12/04/1917	12/04/1917
War Diary	Battery Valley	13/04/1917	13/04/1917
War Diary	Brown Line	14/04/1917	17/04/1917
War Diary	Railway Triangle	18/04/1917	20/04/1917
War Diary	Brown Line	21/04/1917	22/04/1917
War Diary	Front Line	23/04/1917	24/04/1917
War Diary	Railway Triangle	25/04/1917	25/04/1917
War Diary	Grand Rullecourt	29/04/1917	01/05/1917
War Diary	Y Huts St Nicholas Camp	03/05/1917	03/05/1917
War Diary	Railway Cutting	10/05/1917	10/05/1917
War Diary	Lemon Trench	12/05/1917	12/05/1917
War Diary	Front Line	14/05/1917	19/05/1917
War Diary	Reserve Line	20/05/1917	20/05/1917
War Diary	St Nicholas Camp	21/05/1917	21/05/1917
War Diary	St Nicholas Camp To Black Line	22/05/1917	22/05/1917
War Diary	Black Line	26/05/1917	26/05/1917
War Diary	Green Line	27/05/1917	30/05/1917
War Diary	St Nicholas Camp	31/05/1917	31/05/1917
War Diary	Mondicourt	01/06/1917	21/06/1917
War Diary	St Nicholas Camp	22/06/1917	27/06/1917
War Diary	Front Line	29/06/1917	04/07/1917
War Diary	Black Line	05/07/1917	08/07/1917
War Diary	Front Line	09/07/1917	15/07/1917
War Diary	St Nicholas	16/07/1917	22/07/1917
War Diary	Green Line Now Called	23/07/1917	23/07/1917
War Diary	Gavrelle Switch	23/07/1917	27/07/1917
War Diary	Green Line	27/07/1917	30/07/1917
War Diary	Front Line	31/07/1917	08/08/1917

War Diary	St Nicholas Camp	08/08/1917	12/08/1917
War Diary	Gavrelle Switch	16/08/1917	23/08/1917
War Diary	Front Line	24/08/1917	31/08/1917
Operation(al) Order(s)	Operation Order No. 65 by Lieut Col. R.J. Milne Commanding Rose.	04/08/1917	04/08/1917
Miscellaneous	Special Instructions	04/08/1917	04/08/1917
Miscellaneous	Artillery Programme		
Miscellaneous	51st. Inf. Brigade No. G. 1895 19th. Sherwood Foresters	08/08/1917	08/08/1917
Miscellaneous	51st. Inf. Brigade No. G. 1900 10th Sherwood Foresters	08/08/1917	08/08/1917
Miscellaneous	51st. Infantry Brigade N G 1914 8th South Staffordshire Regt	09/08/1917	09/08/1917
War Diary	Front Line	01/09/1917	01/09/1917
War Diary	St Nicholas Camp	02/09/1917	02/09/1917
War Diary	Support Line	09/09/1917	16/09/1917
War Diary	Front Line	17/09/1917	23/09/1917
War Diary	Arras	24/09/1917	24/09/1917
War Diary	?Court	26/09/1917	26/09/1917
War Diary	Grand Rullecourt	27/09/1917	27/09/1917
Miscellaneous	Operation Orders by Lieutenant Colonel H.J. King Commanding 10th. Batt. Sherwood Foresters.		
Miscellaneous	Report On Raid.		
Miscellaneous	Headquarters R.A.M.	06/08/1917	06/08/1917
Miscellaneous	Left Patrol		
Miscellaneous	Centre Patrol		
Miscellaneous	Third Army No. G. 12/114 XVII Corps No. G. 48/10	13/09/1917	13/09/1917
Miscellaneous	51st Infantry Bde No. G 695 XVII Corps No G. 5/11	22/09/1917	22/09/1917
Miscellaneous	51st Infantry Brigade G 711 17th Division	24/09/1917	24/09/1917
Heading	10 Notts & Derby Rgt. Vol 26		
War Diary	Grand Rullecourt	01/10/1917	04/10/1917
War Diary	Grand Rullecourt To St Sixte	04/10/1917	04/10/1917
War Diary	St Sixte To Herzeele	05/10/1917	05/10/1917
War Diary	Herzeele	06/10/1917	07/10/1917
War Diary	Herzeele To St Sixte	08/10/1917	08/10/1917
War Diary	St Sixte To Harrow Camp To Support Line	09/10/1917	09/10/1917
War Diary	Support Line To Front Line	10/10/1917	10/10/1917
War Diary	Front Line	11/10/1917	13/10/1917
War Diary	Parroy Camp	14/10/1917	14/10/1917
War Diary	Dublin Camp	15/10/1917	15/10/1917
War Diary	Dublin Camp to Prattle Camp	16/10/1917	17/10/1917
War Diary	Prattle Camp	18/10/1917	20/10/1917
War Diary	Prattle Camp To Sanghen	21/10/1917	21/10/1917
War Diary	Sanghen	22/10/1917	24/10/1917
War Diary	Sanghen To Proven	25/10/1917	25/10/1917
War Diary	Proven To Boesinghe To Support Line	26/10/1917	26/10/1917
War Diary	Support Line	27/10/1917	29/10/1917
War Diary	Boesinghe to Proven	30/10/1917	30/10/1917
War Diary	Proven	31/10/1917	31/10/1917
Map	Map No. 241		
Miscellaneous	Message Pad.		
Map	Maps		
Operation(al) Order(s)	51st Infantry Brigade Order No. 204	11/10/1917	11/10/1917
Miscellaneous	H.Q. 51st Inf. Brigade. No. Q. 3673 10th Sherwood Foresters	15/10/1917	15/10/1917
Miscellaneous	7th Lincolnshire Regt	15/10/1917	15/10/1917
Miscellaneous	War Diary October 1917 10th Sherwoods.	18/10/1917	18/10/1917

War Diary	Proven To Zermezeele	01/11/1917	01/11/1917
War Diary	Zermezeele	02/11/1917	07/11/1917
War Diary	Zermezeele To Proven	08/11/1917	08/11/1917
War Diary	Prattle Camp	09/11/1917	10/11/1917
War Diary	Proven	11/11/1917	12/11/1917
War Diary	Elverdigne	13/11/1917	23/11/1917
War Diary	Oussel Camp B. 13.a	25/11/1917	30/11/1917
War Diary	Soult Camp Langemarck II Area	01/12/1917	03/12/1917
War Diary	Proven	04/12/1917	09/12/1917
War Diary	Sanghen	10/12/1917	11/12/1917
War Diary	Nordausques	12/12/1917	14/12/1917
War Diary	Barastre	15/12/1917	20/12/1917
War Diary	Line	21/12/1917	24/12/1917
War Diary	Havrincourt	25/12/1917	26/12/1917
War Diary	Butlers	30/12/1917	01/01/1918
War Diary	Front Line	03/01/1918	11/01/1918
War Diary	Hermies	12/01/1918	18/01/1918
War Diary	Phipps Camp	19/01/1918	24/01/1918
War Diary	London Trench	25/01/1918	28/01/1918
War Diary	Front Line	31/01/1918	01/02/1918
Miscellaneous	For War Diary January 1918 10th Sherwood Foresters		
War Diary		01/02/1918	13/02/1918
War Diary	K. 13.d.	14/02/1918	18/02/1918
War Diary	K. 9.c	19/02/1918	28/02/1918
Heading	51st Inf. Bde. 17th Div. 10th Battn. The Sherwood Foresters (Nottinghamshire And Derbyshire Regiment). March 1918		
War Diary	2 Coys & B.H.Q. Camp J. 34 d 2 Coys a32 K.32	01/03/1918	01/03/1918
War Diary	H.Q. K. 15.d.	02/03/1918	11/03/1918
War Diary	A Before	11/03/1918	19/03/1918
War Diary	Bertincourt	20/03/1918	20/03/1918
War Diary	Hermies	21/03/1918	22/03/1918
War Diary	Rocquiny	23/03/1918	23/03/1918
War Diary	Martin Puich	24/03/1918	24/03/1918
War Diary	Fricourt	25/03/1918	27/03/1918
War Diary	Bouzencourt	27/03/1918	31/03/1918
Heading	10th Sherwood Foresters diary March 1918		
Heading	17th Division. 51st Infantry Brigade War Diary 10th Battalion The Notts & Derby Regiment April 1918		
War Diary	In Front of Albert	01/04/1918	01/04/1918
War Diary	Warloy	02/04/1918	03/04/1918
War Diary	Mirvaux	04/04/1918	05/04/1918
War Diary	Millon Villers	06/04/1918	06/04/1918
War Diary	Domart	07/04/1918	10/04/1918
War Diary	Talmas	11/04/1918	11/04/1918
War Diary	Acheux	12/04/1918	13/04/1918
War Diary	Mesnil	14/04/1918	21/04/1918
Miscellaneous	10th Sherwood Foresters. Joined During Month Of April 1918		
War Diary	Mesnil	23/04/1918	30/04/1918
War Diary	Englebelmer	01/05/1918	18/05/1918
War Diary	Beauquesnes	20/05/1918	24/05/1918
War Diary	Acheux	25/05/1918	31/05/1918
War Diary	Auchon Villers	01/06/1918	17/06/1918
War Diary	P. 15 b. & d.	18/06/1918	22/06/1918
War Diary	Herissart	23/06/1918	07/07/1918

War Diary	Rubempre	07/07/1918	07/07/1918
War Diary	Herrissart	08/07/1918	09/07/1918
War Diary	Front Line	10/07/1918	10/07/1918
War Diary	Aveluy Sector	11/07/1918	14/07/1918
War Diary	Front Line	15/07/1918	28/07/1918
War Diary	Lothian System	29/07/1918	31/07/1918
Heading	51st Bde. 17th Div. 10th Battalion. Sherwood Foresters, August 1918		
War Diary	Martinsart	01/08/1918	06/08/1918
War Diary	Toutencourt	07/08/1918	08/08/1918
War Diary	Daours	09/08/1918	10/08/1918
War Diary	Vaux	11/08/1918	12/08/1918
War Diary	In The Line	13/08/1918	16/08/1918
War Diary	Fouilloy	17/08/1918	17/08/1918
War Diary	Vecquemont	18/08/1918	18/08/1918
War Diary	Herissart	19/08/1918	21/08/1918
War Diary	Hedauville	22/08/1918	24/08/1918
War Diary	Field	25/08/1918	31/08/1918
Miscellaneous	Casualties		
War Diary	Field	01/09/1918	01/09/1918
War Diary	Flers	02/09/1918	02/09/1918
War Diary	Rocquigny	03/09/1918	03/09/1918
War Diary	Line	04/09/1918	06/09/1918
War Diary	Rocquigny	07/09/1918	07/09/1918
War Diary	Vallulart Wood	08/09/1918	09/09/1918
War Diary	Line Q. 32	10/09/1918	10/09/1918
War Diary	Line	11/09/1918	11/09/1918
War Diary	Lechelle	12/09/1918	17/09/1918
War Diary	Line	18/09/1918	25/09/1918
War Diary	Manancourt	26/09/1918	05/10/1918
War Diary	Gouzeaucourt	06/10/1918	07/10/1918
War Diary	Hindenburg Line	08/10/1918	08/10/1918
War Diary	Mont Couvez Farm	09/10/1918	09/10/1918
War Diary	Montigny	10/10/1918	11/10/1918
War Diary	Inchy	12/10/1918	12/10/1918
War Diary	Line	13/10/1918	15/10/1918
War Diary	Montigny	16/10/1918	19/10/1918
War Diary	Line	20/10/1918	21/10/1918
War Diary	Inchy	22/10/1918	23/10/1918
War Diary	E 29a	24/10/1918	25/10/1918
War Diary	Beaumont	26/10/1918	26/10/1918
War Diary	Vendegies	27/10/1918	29/10/1918
War Diary	Inchy	30/10/1918	02/11/1918
War Diary	Poix-Du-Nord	03/11/1918	03/11/1918
War Diary	In The Field	04/11/1918	04/11/1918
War Diary	In Field	04/11/1918	06/11/1918
War Diary	La Tele Moir	07/11/1918	07/11/1918
War Diary	In Line at Limont Fontaine	08/11/1918	12/11/1918
War Diary	Locquignol	13/11/1918	13/11/1918
War Diary	Troisvilles	14/11/1918	07/12/1918
War Diary	Hermies	08/12/1918	09/12/1918
War Diary	Favreuil	10/12/1918	10/12/1918
War Diary	Albert	11/12/1918	11/12/1918
War Diary	Pont Noyelles	12/12/1918	12/12/1918
War Diary	Fourdrinoy	13/12/1918	13/12/1918
War Diary	Bailleul	14/12/1918	18/12/1918

War Diary	Epagnette	19/12/1918	28/03/1919
War Diary	Cocquerel	29/03/1919	31/03/1919

2008/2 51 Infantry Brigade

10 Battalion Sherwood Foresters

(Nottingham and Derbyshire Regiment)

17TH DIVISION

51ST INFY BDE

10TH BN NOTTS & DERBY REGT

LY 1915-MAR 1919

51st Inf.Bde.
17th Div.

Battn. disembarked
Boulogne from
England 15.7.15.

10th BATTN. THE SHERWOOD FORESTERS (NOTTINGHAMSHIRE AND DERBYSHIRE REGIMENT).

J U L Y

(14/27.7.15)

1 9 1 5

Instructions regarding War Diaries and Intelligence Summaries are contained in F. S. Regs., Part II. and the Staff Manual respectively. Title Pages will be prepared in manuscript.

10th Sherwood Foresters.

WAR DIARY
or
~~INTELLIGENCE SUMMARY~~
(Erase heading not required.)

Army Form C. 2118

10th Sherwood For: 8

Place	Date	Hour	~~Reference~~ Reference Maps. Sheet 27 & 28 BELGIUM & N.E. FRANCE. Summary of Events and Information	Remarks and references to Appendices
Winchester	July 14th		Left WINCHESTER for BOULOGNE via FOLKESTONE	
Boulogne	15th		Arrived at Rest Camp at 3.30 a.m & departed for PONT DES BRIQUES at 6 p.m	
St. Omer	16th		Detrained ST OMER soon after midnight	
Zudausques	16th		Marched to billets at ZUDAUSQUES arriving soon after 3 a.m. Two companies C & D going on to BOISDINGHEM.	
Ebblinghem	18th		Long march by day to EBBLINGHEM to billet for the night. Field Marshal Sir ~~GENERAL~~ FRENCH watched two companies march in – much impressed!	
Caestre	19th		Marched to billets between CAESTRE and EECKE by day	
	21st	3pm	Inspected by GENERAL PLUMER commanding IInd Army	
Reninghelst	25th		Marched by night to RENINGHELST arriving 2 a.m 26th.	
	27th		A Co. marched to trenches of 139th BRIGADE near HOOGE remaining till August 3rd and witnessed the loss of some trenches and the failure of a counterattack by the K.R.R.C. and R.B. Total casualties during their stay 14 Other Ranks wounded. Each company except D Company was able to send its men into the trenches for 24 hours instruction while on the OUDERDOM Road and at RENINGHELST fortunately without any casualties.	

GJP

1875 Wt. W593/826 1,000,000 4/15 J.B.C. & A. A.D.S.S./Forms/C. 2118.

51st Inf.Bde.
17th Div.

10th BATTN. THE SHERWOOD FORESTERS (NOTTINGHAMSHIRE AND DERBYSHIRE REGIMENT).

A U G U S T

1 9 1 5

Instructions regarding War Diaries and Intelligence Summaries are contained in F. S. Regs., Part II. and the Staff Manual respectively. Title Pages will be prepared in manuscript.

10th Sherwood [illegible] WAR DIARY or ~~INTELLIGENCE SUMMARY~~

(Erase heading not required.)

Place	Date	Hour	Summary of Events and Information	Remarks and references to Appendices
	August 1st		Marched by night to White Chateau near KRUISTRAAT arriving 3 a.m August 2nd.	
OUDERDOM	2nd.		Marched by night to huts on the OUDERDOM - VLAMERTINGHE roads.	
	4th.		M.G. section sent to take over two guns in trenches of 189th BRIGADE returning to RENINGHELST on August 16th. 1 O.R. wounded	
			Draft of 30 O.R arrived from Base.	
RENINGHELST	6th.		Marched by night back to RENINGHELST — a sudden move	
	12th.		1 O.R wounded while on working party.	
	15th.		Battalion marched to trenches to relieve 7th EAST YORKS in trenches U24, U25 and U26 and 1 Coy Bde Reserve at SCOTTISH WOOD 7th LINCOLNSHIRES on our right 2nd SUFFOLKS on our left	
	16th		1 O.R wounded, died of wounds next day.	
	17th		2. O.R. wounded.	
	18th		CAPT. GREGORY wounded in foot. 1 O.R. killed 2 O.R wounded.	
	20th		M.G. section rejoined the battalion.	
	21st		CAPT. OAKDEN hit in arm by rifle grenade.	
		6.50pm	German mine exploded followed by short bombardment on our trenches no damage.	
	22nd		CHATEAU LANKHOF bombarded from 1 - 2 p.m	

G.P.

1875 Wt. W593/826 1,000,000 4/15 J.B.C. & A. A.D.S.S./Forms/C. 2118.

Instructions regarding War Diaries and Intelligence Summaries are contained in F. S. Regs., Part II. and the Staff Manual respectively. Title Pages will be prepared in manuscript.

~~WAR DIARY~~ or ~~INTELLIGENCE~~ SUMMARY

(Erase heading not required.)

Place	Date	Hour	Summary of Events and Information	Remarks and references to Appendices
Trenches.	Aug. 23rd		4 O.R. wounded. Trenches on left taken over from SUFFOLKS by 6th SHERWOODS. Chateau shelled again.	
	24th		Small mine exploded West of our line near St ELOI in the evening. Magazine exploded at BEDFORD HOUSE by enemy's guns. New works in German parapets observed and reported. 4 O.R. wounded.	
	25th		2/LIEUT WILMOT & 4 O.R. wounded by a whizzbang.	
	26th		Small mine exploded at 6.55p.m. unknown direction. R.G. relieved by 7th EAST YORKS.	
	27th		New Gun opposite U 26. 4 O.R. wounded, two of whom died of wounds.	
	28th		Relieved by 7th EAST YORKS night 27th/28th arriving back in RENINGHELST in the morning. 2 O.R. wounded.	
	29th		3 O.R. wounded on a working party.	
	31st		Marched to trenches to join 9th Brigade, being detached from the 51st Bde & attd. 9th Bde. for a special purpose.	

G.J.P.

1875 Wt. W593/826 1,000,000 4/15 J.B.C. & A. A.D.S.S./Forms/C. 2118.

51st Inf.Bde.
17th Div.

10th BATTN. THE SHERWOOD FORESTERS (NOTTINGHAMSHIRE AND DERBYSHIRE REGIMENT).

S E P T E M B E R

1 9 1 5

Army Form C. 2118

Instructions regarding War Diaries and Intelligence Summaries are contained in F. S. Regs., Part II. and the Staff Manual respectively. Title Pages will be prepared in manuscript.

~~WAR DIARY~~

or

INTELLIGENCE SUMMARY

(Erase heading not required.)

10th SHERWOOD FORESTERS

Place	Date	Hour	Summary of Events and Information	Remarks and references to Appendices
			Refce. Map Belgium "B" Series Sheet 28 SEPTEMBER.	
			On the night 31/1st Septr the battalion marched into trenches in SANCTUARY WOOD in the 9th Bde. line being attached with the 7th BORDER REGT to that Bde for a special purpose.	
	Aug. 31st.	3.30pm.	Marched past GEN PLUMER cmdg IInd Army at road junction G. 35 c. 0. 7. on our way to the trenches.	
			Halted near White Chateau H. 23 a for two hours rest and tea	
			The relief of the trenches was complete at 11.30 p.m.: the 4th ROYAL FUSILIERS marching back to their billeting area: the night was fine.	
			The companies were posted as follows: D Coy. A4 – A7 both inclusive: A Coy. A8 – A11 both inclusive. B Coy in Strong Points R_2 & R_3 and C. Coy in reserve dugouts in S. end of SANCTUARY WOOD.	
	Sept.		The trenches were in good condition but were not revetted at all nor were the approach trenches boarded in most of their length. 36 hours rain on the 2nd & 3rd caused many of the trenches to fall in and made much of the approach trenches impassable. During our stay of 14 days much of this was remedied: the approach and reserve trenches were widened and revetted and duckboarding put down practically throughout: parapets were rebuilt and revetted.	
			A short bombardment of the enemy trenches to which they retaliated took place at about 4 o'clock each morning of the 2nd to 5th	

1875 Wt. W593/826 1,000,000 4/15 J.B.C. & A. A.D.S.S./Forms/C. 2118.

GJP

Instructions regarding War Diaries and Intelligence Summaries are contained in F. S. Regs., Part II. and the Staff Manual respectively. Title Pages will be prepared in manuscript.

or

INTELLIGENCE SUMMARY

(Erase heading not required.)

10th SHERWOOD FORESTERS

Place	Date	Hour	Summary of Events and Information	Remarks and references to Appendices
			Ref^ce. Map Belgium "B" Series Sheet 28 — SEPTEMBER.	
	September		On the 2nd the enemy bombarded SANCTUARY WOOD and ZOUAVE WOOD at 4.30 p.m and again at 7 p.m	
			On the 4th there was further heavy shelling by the enemy at 5 pm and again at 8 p.m. South of our trenches to which our guns replied.	
			Casualties 1st. 2 O.R wounded	
			2nd 1 O.R. killed 4 O.R wounded.	
			3rd 8 O.R wounded	
	2nd.		A draft of 50 men arrived at RENINGHELST on the 2nd from the Base and went from there to SCOTTISH WOOD. to work there.	
	3rd.		On the night of the ~~the~~ 3rd heavy transport was heard behind the German lines at 7.48 p.m. This was reported to the Artillery who shelled the roads at about that time the following nights.	
			The weather was then fine and continued so enabling us to put in good work on the trenches both by day and night.	
	6th 7th		A new C.T. called SHERWOOD ROAD was dug running through S: end of SANCTUARY WOOD and on to MAPLE COPSE	
			Casualties 5th 2/Lt. H.W. HOWARD wounded and 1 O.R. wounded	
			6th 2 O.R. Wounded	
			7th 1 O.R. Wounded.	

1875 Wt. W593/826 1,000,000 4/15 J.B.C. & A. A.D.S.S./Forms/C. 2118.

Army Form C. 2118

Instructions regarding War Diaries and Intelligence Summaries are contained in F. S. Regs., Part II. and the Staff Manual respectively. Title Pages will be prepared in manuscript.

WAR DIARY
or
INTELLIGENCE SUMMARY
(Erase heading not required.)

10th SHERWOOD FORESTERS

Place	Date	Hour	Refce Map. Belgium "B" series Sheet 28. Summary of Events and Information SEPTEMBER.	Remarks and references to Appendices
	September 8th		C. Coy relieved D. Coy in trenches A4 - A7, D Coy taking over the dugout in S. end of SANCTUARY wood.	
			2/LIEUT. J. HUTCHESON killed by sniper.	
	9th		B. Coy relieved A Coy in A8 - A11. A Coy taking over R_2 and R_3.	
			1 O.R. wounded.	
	11th		Working parties in reserve trenches were twice shelled with whizzbangs and also fire trenches. 4 O.R wounded.	
	12th		a little shelling of fire trenches 2. O.R. wounded.	
	13th		On the 13th the Germans shelled heavily in the morning between 7 am and 7.30 a.m. some directed against the fire trenches but more into SANCTUARY WOOD.	
			MAJOR A.W. YOONG killed 4 O.R wounded.	
	14th		On the night of the 14th/15th in slight drizzle but not enough to spoil the roads we were relieved by the 4th ROYAL FUSILIERS, the relief being complete at 10.45 p.m.	
	15th		Marched back by companies to old billets at RENINGHELST the first company arriving at 2.30 a.m. and the last at 5. a.m.	
			2 O.R. accidentally wounded, one of whom later died of wounds.	

GJP.

1875 Wt. W593/826 1,000,000 4/15 J.B.C. & A. A.D.S.S./Forms/C. 2118.

Army Form C. 2118.

WAR DIARY
or
INTELLIGENCE SUMMARY
(Erase heading not required.)

Instructions regarding War Diaries and Intelligence Summaries are contained in F. S. Regs., Part II. and the Staff Manual respectively. Title Pages will be prepared in manuscript.

10th SHERWOOD FORESTERS

Place	Date	Hour	Summary of Events and Information	Remarks and references to Appendices
			Refce. Map Belgium "B" Series Sheet 28 — SEPTEMBER	
	September		Fifteenth to Twentieth complete rest in old huts and dugouts near RENINGHELST. No working parties or fatigues – football and boxing in afternoons and evenings. Weather hot by day, cold by night.	
			On night 21st/22nd marched off at 3.45 p.m back to trenches to relieve 4th ROYAL FUSILIERS: halted as before at WHITE CHATEAU for rest and tea. Relief complete at 8.57 p.m: no casualties: a fine night, moon nearly full, roads very dusty.	
			Companies as follows: D Coy A4 – A7: A Coy A8 – A11, B Coy. R2 and R3, C Coy dugouts in wood.	
	22nd		1 O.R. wounded	
	23rd		R3 vacated and men put in support trenches behind D Coy.	
			On night 23/24th 1st LINCOLNSHIRES took over R3 and Reserve trenches behind A8 – A11 inclusive.	
	24th		Rain commenced on night 23rd/24th and heavy showers in afternoon 24th.	
			1 O.R. wounded on night 23rd/24th while on working party	
	23rd		Draft of 1 Officer 2/Lt A.G DENT and 45 men arrived at POPERINGHE from the base and marched to RENINGHELST to await further orders there.	
			GJP	

1875 Wt. W593/826 1,000,000 4/15 J.B.C. & A. A.D.S.S./Forms/C. 2118.

Instructions regarding War Diaries and Intelligence Summaries are contained in F. S. Regs., Part II. and the Staff Manual respectively. Title Pages will be prepared in manuscript.

~~WAR DIARY~~
or
INTELLIGENCE SUMMARY
(Erase heading not required.)

Army Form C. 2118.

10th SHERWOOD FORESTERS

Place	Date	Hour	Summary of Events and Information — Refce. Map. Belgium "B" Series Sheet 28 — SEPTEMBER	Remarks and references to Appendices
			On the night 24th/25th the new draft with 3 officers posted to us from Cadet School marched up and took their places with the Companies.	
			The attack near HOOGE began on morning 25th September, at 4.20 a.m. Our rôle was to protect the right flank of the attack by heavy rifle and machine gun fire. We were heavily shelled throughout the day and also on the 26th.	
			The attacking troops were unable to hold the captured trenches and our line remained unaltered.	
			On night 26th there was heavy gun fire and rifle fire by the enemy apparently started by a British bombing party — there was, however, no counterattack.	
			Our casualties were as follows:-	
			2/LIEUT. E.S. CHANDLER and 2/LIEUT. G.J. CHAPMAN slightly wounded.	
			7 O.R. killed 50 O.R. wounded and 1 O.R. missing.	
			On the night of the 27th we came under the orders of the 8th Brigade, who took over the sector from the 9th Brigade.	
			We reoccupied R.3. and took over new dugouts in the wood from LIVERPOOL SCOTTISH on the 28th.	G.J.P.

1875 Wt. W593/826 1,000,000 4/15 J.B.C. & A. A.D.S.S./Forms/C. 2118.

Army Form C. 2118

Instructions regarding War Diaries and Intelligence Summaries are contained in F. S. Regs., Part II. and the Staff Manual respectively. Title Pages will be prepared in manuscript.

~~WAR DIARY~~
or
INTELLIGENCE SUMMARY
(Erase heading not required.)

10th SHERWOOD FORESTERS

Place	Date	Hour	Summary of Events and Information	Remarks and references to Appendices
			Refce Map Belgium "B" Series Sheet 28. SEPTEMBER.	
			In the morning of the 28th B coy relieved A Coy in trenches A8-A11 A coy taking over R_2 and R_3. draft of 81 O.R arrived & joined us in trenches In the afternoon of the 29th the Germans exploded a mine under B4 and made an attack shelling SANCTUARY furiously. The immediate counter attack failed. On the night 29th/30th we were relieved by the 2nd ROYAL SCOTS the relief being cancelled and then later ordered. It was not complete till 1.10 a.m 30th. The bombers and Machine Gun and teams were ordered to remain behind to take part in the big counterattack on the 1st October. Some motor lorries met us at KRUISTRAAT and the first company arrived back at RENINGHELST at 4 a.m. the last at about 8 a.m. The road from SANCTUARY wood to KRUISTRAAT was extremely muddy – nearly knee deep in parts. Our M.G. returned on the night of the 30th but the bombers not till the following night. Total casualties during the month. Officers Killed 2 Wounded 3. O.R. Killed 10 Wounded 93 Missing 3.	

GJP

1875 Wt. W593/826 1,000,000 4/15 J.B.C. & A. A.D.S.S./Forms/C. 2118.

51st Inf.Bde.
17th Div.

10th BATTN. THE SHERWOOD FORESTERS (NOTTINGHAMSHIRE AND DERBYSHIRE REGIMENT).

O C T O B E R

1 9 1 5

Army Form C. 2118

Instructions regarding War Diaries and Intelligence Summaries are contained in F. S. Regs., Part II. and the Staff Manual respectively. Title Pages will be prepared in manuscript.

WAR DIARY

or

~~INTELLIGENCE SUMMARY~~

(Erase heading not required.)

10th SHERWOOD FORESTERS

Place	Date	Hour	Summary of Events and Information — Refce Maps Sheets 27 & 28 1/40,000 also Hooge 1/10,000 Trench Map. & VERBRANDENMOLEN 1/10000 — OCTOBER 1915.	Remarks and references to Appendices
	Oct 1st		Bombers returned from Sanctuary Wood after the endeavour by the 8th Bde to bomb the Germans out of Bu. They were quite exhausted but their spirit unimpaired. Their casualties were 5 O.R. wounded.	
	Oct 2nd		B & C. Coys moved into reserve dugouts near VERBRANDENMOLEN as brigade reserve to 51st Bde. H.Q. and A, B coys remaining at RENINGHELST as divisional reserve. The allotment of B & C Coys was as follows:- 1 Coy in Railway Embankment - ZILLEBEKE under 9th NORTHUMBERLAND FUSRS furnishing 2 Secns, 1 M.G. detachment in R7 and 1 Secn in R8 1 Coy in reserve huts in rear of Trench 33 under 8th S STAFFS furnishing 2 Secns., 1 M.G. detachment in R9	
	Oct 4th		These companies only remained there till Monday night Oct 4th/5th Casualties 1 O.R. wounded while the relief was taking place	
	Oct. 6th.		In the afternoon of Oct 6th the 8th R.W. Kent Regt took over our camp at RENINGHELST and the 51st Bde marched into billets near EECKE The march commenced at 6p.m and we were all in billets by 12 midnight between EECKE and CAESTRE. The roads were in excellent condition and the night dark and cold - all of which tended to make the march easier Most of the billets occupied were the same as those occupied in July but not in all cases and consequently the battalion was a good deal scattered. GJP	

1875 Wt. W593/826 1,000,000 4/15 J.B.C. & A. A.D.S.S./Forms/C. 2118.

Instructions regarding War Diaries and Intelligence Summaries are contained in F. S. Regs., Part II. and the Staff Manual respectively. Title Pages will be prepared in manuscript.

WAR DIARY
or
~~INTELLIGENCE SUMMARY~~
(Erase heading not required.)

10th SHERWOOD FORESTERS

Place	Date	Hour	Refce. Maps Sheets 27 & 28 1/40,000 and HOOGE Trench map 1/10,000. Summary of Events and Information OCTOBER 1915	Remarks and references to Appendices
EECKE	Oct 7th		We remained at EECKE for a fortnight waiting orders to move South which never came. Our days were spent in bombing, routemarching and in particular practising the attack, both as a battalion and also in conjunction with another battalion, in trenches over open ground and in adapting "enemy" trenches into use as fire trenches. The weather kept fine throughout our stay at EECKE and all ranks benefited by the rest.	
	Oct. 20th		On Oct. 20th very sudden orders were received to march that afternoon into billets near POPERINGHE as the 17th Division was to take over the line held by the 3rd Division. In spite of the fact that all companies had been for a long route march in the morning the march was a great success and we arrived in our new camp at H 13 d 6.6 Sheet 28 at 11.45 p.m. where we stayed for the night. The 1st GORDON HIGHLANDERS whose camp it was had had no orders on the subject and consequently refused to hand over the camp. Roads again good	
Near OUDERDOM	Oct. 21st		Sudden orders were received to march into trenches in SANCTUARY WOOD and the battalion marched out 925 strong all ranks, to take over trenches A12, B1, B2 and strong points R4, R5 from 7th K SHROPSHIRE L.I. the march beginning at 5 p.m.	

G.J.P.

1875 Wt. W593/826 1,000,000 4/15 J.B.C. & A. A.D.S.S./Forms/C. 2118.

Instructions regarding War Diaries and Intelligence Summaries are contained in F. S. Regs., Part II. and the Staff Manual respectively. Title Pages will be prepared in manuscript.

or

INTELLIGENCE SUMMARY

(Erase heading not required.)

10th SHERWOOD FORESTERS

Place	Date	Hour	Summary of Events and Information	Remarks and references to Appendices
			Refce. Maps. 28 1/40000 and HOOGE trench map 1/10.000 — OCTOBER 1915	
	Oct 21		The relief was complete at 10 p.m. but there was a good deal of confusion nor was there a proper handing over of stores. The companies were distributed as follows:-	
			A12, B1 and B2 were taken over by D Coy	
			R4 and R5 by C Coy who also had 2 platoons in dugouts in SANCTUARY WOOD	
			A & B Coys took over dugouts in SANCTUARY WOOD with the bombers and reserve M.G. detachment.	
			H.Q. were in dugouts in MAPLE CORSE.	
			This distribution was altered on the following day A Coy taking over B2 and 3 bays of B1 with 6 secns, which were relieved every 24 hours.	
			A12 was in fairly good condition but B1 & B2 were in a bad state even before the rain came.	
			An enemy sniper from the "bird-cage" in B3 claimed eight victims in B1 before this could be made safe. He was afterwards shot by Lieut. T.W. Daniel	
	Oct. 25th		On night 24th/25th the rain commenced and a relief of trenches was conducted on the afternoon of the 25th C Coy taking over from D Coy and B Coy from A Coy	

1875 Wt. W593/826 1,000,000 4/15 J.B.C. & A. A.D.S.S./Forms/C. 2118.

Instructions regarding War Diaries and Intelligence Summaries are contained in F. S. Regs., Part II. and the Staff Manual respectively. Title Pages will be prepared in manuscript.

WAR DIARY
or
~~INTELLIGENCE SUMMARY~~
(Erase heading not required.)

10th SHERWOOD FORESTERS

Place	Date	Hour	Refce Maps Sheet 28 1/40000 & HOOGE TRENCH MAP 1/10.000 — Summary of Events and Information — OCTOBER 1915.	Remarks and references to Appendices
			The woods being thinner than in summer nearly all work had to be done at night in the reserve line and communication trenches. Work was also handicapped by the lack of material.	
			The enemy was quiet during our stay and patrols failed to get any information except as to his wire which was found to be very strong and in two lines the first line being thickly barbed while the line nearer his trenches was plain French wire. Bands were heard playing in the enemy's line on two or three occasions but they were South of our sector and could not be located. The enemy artillery was active spasmodically and only once did any damage to our men when a direct hit on a dugout wounded five men one of whom died of wounds in Hospital. On two fine mornings the enemy aeroplanes were extremely active and dropped smoke bombs over some material lying in the open which was promptly shelled.	
	30th		On night Oct. 30th/31st the 9th NORTUMBERLAND FUSILIERS took over the sector the relief being complete at 10.5 p.m	

GJP

1875 Wt. W593/826 1,000,000 4/15 J.B.C. & A. A.D.S.S./Forms/C. 2118.

Instructions regarding War Diaries and Intelligence Summaries are contained in F. S. Regs., Part II. and the Staff Manual respectively. Title Pages will be prepared in manuscript.

or

INTELLIGENCE SUMMARY

(Erase heading not required.)

10th SHERWOOD FORESTERS

Place	Date	Hour	Summary of Events and Information	Remarks and references to Appendices
			Refce maps. Sheet 28 1/40.000 THOOGE Trench map 1/10.000 — OCTOBER 1915	
	30.		On night 30th/31st we marched back to the camp we had vacated on the 21st the first company arriving at 3 a.m. on 31st and the last ~~at~~ at about 4 a.m. It was fortunately a fine night but the road from SANCTUARY WOOD – KRUISTRAAT was extremely muddy and tiring.	
			During our ~~tour~~ our casualties were as follows:	
			CAPT. J. W. FISHER – wounded	
			1. O.R. Killed, 1 O.R died of wounds and 15 O.R wounded	
	28th		On the morning of the 28th H.M. the KING inspected a composite battalion of the Division. The 51st Bde. formed a composite company of which we supplied 1 Cpl 3 L/Cpls and 16 men. It rained very heavily for the inspection which was, however, in every other way satisfactory.	
	4th.		On Oct 4th LIEUT. J. N. KNIGHT was severely wounded at POPERINGHE and LIEUT. L. D. SAUNDERS slightly wounded: the latter remained at duty.	
			Total casualties during the month 3 officers wounded 1. O.R. killed 1 O.R. died of wounds 17 wounded and 4 accidentally wounded.	

GJP

1875 Wt. W593/826 1,000,000 4/15 J.B.C. & A. A.D.S.S./Forms/C. 2118.

51st Inf.Bde.
17th Div.

10th BATTN. THE SHERWOOD FORESTERS (NOTTINGHAMSHIRE AND DERBYSHIRE REGIMENT).

N O V E M B E R

1 9 1 5

WAR DIARY
or
~~INTELLIGENCE SUMMARY~~

(Erase heading not required.)

Instructions regarding War Diaries and Intelligence Summaries are contained in F. S. Regs., Part II. and the Staff Manual respectively. Title Pages will be prepared in manuscript.

10th SHERWOOD FORESTERS

Place	Date	Hour	Refce Maps. Sheet 28 1/40.000 Hooge Trench Map 1/10.000 — Summary of Events and Information — November 1915	Remarks and references to Appendices
	1st.		Two companies were employed as working party for 93rd. Fld. Coy R.E. on dugouts near KRUISTRAAT and the other two companies moved into huts at H.19 b. 7.8 where accommodation was better. Rain stopped their work soon after midday.	
	2nd.		Rain was too bad for similar working party and the day was spent in cleaning up. This rain continued throughout the next day	
	5th.		Two companies were employed as working party for 93rd Fld. Coy R.E. and the other two on the 6th: also 100 men as carrying party. On the night of the 5th orders were received that the battalion would relieve 9th Northumberland Fusiliers on night 7th/8th and that the machine guns and teams would go into trenches on the night 6th/7th.	
	6th.		The machine gunners marched for the trenches at 2.30 p.m. but a telegram was received from the Bde. at 3 p.m. cancelling the relief ordered the night before and a messenger was sent after them and brought them back.	
	7th.		Sunday a fine day on which the only work done was the early Church Parade.	

GJP

1875 Wt. W593/826 1,000,000 4/15 J.B.C. & A. A.D.S.S./Forms/C. 2118.

Instructions regarding War Diaries and Intelligence Summaries are contained in F. S. Regs., Part II. and the Staff Manual respectively. Title Pages will be prepared in manuscript.

WAR DIARY
or
INTELLIGENCE SUMMARY
(Erase heading not required.)

Army Form C. 2118

10th SHERWOOD FORESTERS

Place	Date	Hour	Summary of Events and Information	Remarks and references to Appendices
			Refce. Maps Sheet 28 1/40.000 Hooge Trench Map 1/10.000 — November 1915	
	9th		Battn moved off at 6.15, and marched up to Ypres in heavy rain, to relieve the 7th KRRC in the ramparts – position of Bde Reserve. HQ Coy, C Coy, & D Coy were in the Ramparts, A Coy in cellars, B Coy at L Farm on MENIN ROAD	
	10th		Bde HQ turned us out of our quarters, we moved to the neighbouring tunnels, still in the Ramparts. General cry for candles, as day & night are the same in the tunnels. A & B Coys shelled – 3 casualties in the latter.	
	11th		YPRES heavily shelled – Brigadier & BO nearly killed at MENIN GATE. Countless fatigues provided at night, carrying rations for LINCOLNS, stores for RE, and draining trenches. 70 men attached to Tunnelling Coy, as sapping work in this area is very critical	
	12th		Major General Pilcher inspected our tunnels, and talked about Electric light installations – a good idea. The same fatigues each night. Our quarters becoming more comfortable by the aid of a little successful looting	
	13th		Deserter reported that Huns intended to attack. 17th Div had a little strafe on its own, much to the terror of neighbouring units. A perfect hurricane blowed all day – one M. Gunner killed by falling wall, 5 of B Coy wounded. M.G. officer very busy with indirect fire.	
	14th		Huns still supposed to be going to attack. Considerable artillery activity. Winter frosts start. Lt Cuckow taken to hospital with Sciatica.	

[illegible]

1875 Wt. W593/826 1,000,000 4/15 J.B.C. & A. A.D.S.S./Forms/C. 2118.

Army Form C. 2118.

Instructions regarding War Diaries and Intelligence Summaries are contained in F. S. Regs., Part II. and the Staff Manual respectively. Title Pages will be prepared in manuscript.

WAR DIARY
or
INTELLIGENCE SUMMARY
(Erase heading not required.)

Place	Date	Hour	Summary of Events and Information (Refce Map Sheet 28 Hooge Trench Map.)	Remarks and references to Appendices
	15th		Regular frosts every night now. Battn & Bde HQ heavily shelled, but no damage done. Trenches reported to be waist deep in mud.	
	16th		Nothing to report from ramparts, except the arrival of waders for the Battn.	
	17th		Col. Banbury commanding the Bde, while the Brigadier is on leave. Lt Saunders RAMC leaves us for the 53rd F. Ambulance, Lt Murdoch reports in his stead. 2/Lieut Ebury joins the Battn, & is posted to C Coy.	
			Battn marched up to relieve 7th LINCOLNS (Trenches H13 - H19), starting from MENIN GATE at 5.15 PM; relief not completed till 11.20 PM. A & C Coys in firing line, B Coy at L farm, D Coy X1A.	
	18th		Hard frost. Trenches very bad, only one communication trench and that waist deep, no dug outs in firing line. Tremendous difficulty in getting rations and material up.	
	19th		Visited by Bde Staff at 5 AM, otherwise situation normal. A Coy one killed, B Coy one wounded, C Coy two wounded.	
	20th		German artillery very active. 2/Lieut A G Dent and 2 Cpls wounded on MENIN ROAD.	

1875 Wt. W593/826 1,000,000 4/15 J.B.C. & A. A.D.S.S./Forms/C. 2118.

Instructions regarding War Diaries and Intelligence Summaries are contained in F. S. Regs., Part II. and the Staff Manual respectively. Title Pages will be prepared in manuscript.

WAR DIARY

or

INTELLIGENCE SUMMARY

(Erase heading not required.)

Army Form C. 2118

Place	Date	Hour	Refer Maps. Sheet 28. Hooge Trench Map. Summary of Events and Information	Remarks and references to Appendices
	21st		Still very cold. First two cases of trench feet in battn. German Snipers accounted for two killed and one wounded. Trenches very exposed in places.	
	22nd		Thick fog and still colder. A noisy afternoon with trench mortars. Lt Cuckow rejoins, & 2/Lieut Milward arrives from 4th battn, & is posted to A Coy. Two more wounded.	
	23rd		7th BORDERS tried to take crater on our left, but failed to get through German wire. Heavy shelling all the afternoon. LINCOLNS ultimately relieved us, relief complete by midnight.	
	24th		Night of 23/24 spent in Ramparts. After resting battn moved back to rest billets on OUDERDOM - FLAMERTINGE road H13 d centre at 5.15 p.m. Total for the fortnight in trenches and reserve – 34 casualties, 35 sick, including 17 cases of trench feet.	
	25th		Next four days spent in the discomfort of "rest camp"! Bitterly cold, and the inevitable fatigues. 100 men & 2 officers to bury cable for OC Sigs 51st Bde every night, and daily loading party of 1 officer & 30 men at RE dump.	
			JMS.	

Instructions regarding War Diaries and Intelligence Summaries are contained in F. S. Regs., Part II. and the Staff Manual respectively. Title Pages will be prepared in manuscript.

WAR DIARY
or
INTELLIGENCE SUMMARY
(Erase heading not required.)

Army Form C. 2118

Place	Date	Hour	Summary of Events and Information	Remarks and references to Appendices
			Refce Map. Sheet 28 Hooge Trench Map.	
	29th		The Battn moved up into the trenches, H13–H19, to relieve 7th LINCOLNS. First Coy left Camp at 2 PM, relief not complete till after 11 PM. A very dark night, and great difficulty was encountered taking over orders from Bde HQ & fitting them on in the dark. Trenches worse than ever. Disposition A & C Coys in firing line, B Coy at L Farm, D Coy at X1A.	
	30th		Our 9.2's started firing on German saps, and kept it up all day, doing considerable damage to our trenches. Very heavy retaliation all over Battn area. Altogether a very trying day. Three men wounded.	

P. Vaux Shaw Lt. Act Adj.

Wt Sherwood Foresters.

1875 Wt. W593/826 1,000,000 4/15 J.B.C. & A. A.D.S.S./Forms/C. 2118.

51st Inf.Bde.
17th Div.

10th BATTN. THE SHERWOOD FORESTERS (NOTTINGHAMSHIRE AND DERBYSHIRE REGIMENT).

D E C E M B E R

1 9 1 5

Army Form C. 2118

Instructions regarding War Diaries and Intelligence Summaries are contained in F. S. Regs., Part II. and the Staff Manual respectively. Title Pages will be prepared in manuscript.

WAR DIARY
or
~~INTELLIGENCE SUMMARY~~
(Erase heading not required.)

10th SHERWOOD FORESTERS

Place	Date	Hour	Summary of Events and Information — Refce maps. HOOGE 1/10.000, Sheet 28 1/40.000 — DECEMBER 1915.	Remarks and references to Appendices
Trenches	1st		The enemy were very active with their artillery to which our guns replied suitably: casualties 2 O.R. killed and 7 wounded.	
	2nd.		Relieved companies in the evening after 48 hours: two days without sitting or sleeping and standing in knee deep mud and slush is quite enough for all ranks.	
	3rd & 4th		Two colourless days with no activity on either side	
			2/Lt. S. MELVILLE joined on 3rd & 2/Lt L. JACQUES on 4th.	
	4th		M.G. and bombers relieved on 4th.	
	5th		On the night 5th/6th the 7th LINCOLNSHIRES relieved the battalion which marched back to rest camp in H.9.b for one night: the last company did not arrive until 4.30 a.m. A very late relief caused by putting on and taking off thigh gum boots.	
	6th.		Battalion marched up to YPRES ramparts into Bde reserve there in pouring rain.	
			2/Lts. A.F. BENTLEY and G.R.T. THURLOW joined	
	7th to 11th.		These days were spent in recovering from night working parties involving the whole battalion working every night, in most of which it rained hard.	
			On the night 10th/11th there was very heavily shelling of the MENIN ROAD & working parties had to return early	

1875 Wt. W593/826 1,000,000 4/15 J.B.C. & A. A.D.S.S./Forms/C. 2118.

Army Form C. 2118

Instructions regarding War Diaries and Intelligence Summaries are contained in F. S. Regs., Part II. and the Staff Manual respectively. Title Pages will be prepared in manuscript.

WAR DIARY
or
INTELLIGENCE SUMMARY
(Erase heading not required.)

10th SHERWOOD FORESTERS.

Place	Date	Hour	Summary of Events and Information	Remarks and references to Appendices
			Refce Maps. HOOGE 1/10000 Sheet 28 1/40.000. DECEMBER 1915.	
Ramparts	11th		The shelling of YPRES and MENIN ROAD became so heavy that B. Coy in cellars near MENIN ROAD were ordered to stand to from 3.15 a.m. to 6.30 a.m.	
			On the night 11th/12th the battalion relieved the 7th LINCOLNSHIRES in H13 – H17 B & D Coys in firing line, A Coy in cellars in MENIN ROAD and C Coy in XIA.	
			Relief complete at 8.35 pm.	
			CAPT. J.W. FISHER rejoined battalion and resumed command of D Coy on the 12th.	
			At 10 pm. and again at midnight our artillery bombarded enemy Bn H.Q., dumps etc. but evoked no retaliation.	
	12th		H.E. shrapnel and crumps from direction of HILL 60 burst near Bn. H.Q. and R4 from 10.45 a.m. for about two hours. Two men were killed just outside H.Q. Signal dugout.	
	13th		An organised bombardment of enemy's trenches took place for 1 hour in the morning. Companies relieved in the evening and a patrol sent out reported considerable damage done to enemy parapet and wire. Retaliation by enemy resulted in 2 O.R. being killed.	

(G.J.P.)

1875 Wt. W593/826 1,000,000 4/15 J.B.C. & A. A.D.S.S./Forms/C. 2118.

Army Form C. 2118

Instructions regarding War Diaries and Intelligence Summaries are contained in F. S. Regs., Part II. and the Staff Manual respectively. Title Pages will be prepared in manuscript.

WAR DIARY
or
INTELLIGENCE SUMMARY
(Erase heading not required.)

10th SHERWOOD FORESTERS

Place	Date	Hour	Summary of Events and Information	Remarks and references to Appendices
			Refce Maps Sheet 28 HOOGE 1/10.000 1/40.000 — DECEMBER 1915.	
	13th		Reinforcements joined LIEUT. G.D.M. ABBOTTS and 2/LT. F.C. NODDER.	
	14th		An eventful day. The enemy began shelling casually from 10 a.m. until 1 p.m. when they began in earnest and bombarded for just over two hours the front line, R4 and battalion H.Q. being very heavily shelled. After 20 minutes every wire was cut except that to BORDER H.Q. who were also in same predicament. All dugouts in front line and many in second line were blown in. Companies in front line very badly shaken and so were relieved by B & D Coys who did excellent work in repairing, collecting and burying dead.	
			Casualties since last report. Lt. J.A. MEADS slightly wounded, 16 O.R killed and 25 O.R wounded a heavy toll.	
	15th.		Considerable artillery activity on both sides but no casualties were inflicted.	
	16th.		Six inch howitzers shot over right company from 1 pm to 3 pm. without much retaliation: on the whole a quiet day.	
			Companies were relieved in the evening.	
			No casualties.	

1875 Wt. W593/826 1,000,000 4/15 J.B.C. & A. A.D.S.S./Forms/C. 2118.

Army Form C. 2118

Instructions regarding War Diaries and Intelligence Summaries are contained in F. S. Regs., Part II. and the Staff Manual respectively. Title Pages will be prepared in manuscript.

WAR DIARY
or
INTELLIGENCE SUMMARY
(Erase heading not required.)

10th SHERWOOD FORESTERS.

Place	Date	Hour	Summary of Events and Information	Remarks and references to Appendices
			Refce. Maps HOOGE 1/10000 Sheet 28. 1/40.000. DECEMBER. 1915.	
	16th		There was considerable activity in artillery from 1pm. to 3pm but only occasional whizzbangs on front line: the wires were frequently broken back to Bde. H.Q.	
	17th.		A quiet day ideal for relief by 7th LINCOLNSHIRES. Relief complete at 7.30 p.m. then back to ramparts for one night. No casualties.	
	18th		Spent in ramparts before march back to rest camp at H.19.b. 1 O.R. previously reported wounded now died of wounds.	
	19th.		At 5.45 a.m. the C.O was awakened by sound of very heavy shelling and gave the alarm: the regiment was ordered to move up to YPRES: D Coy to X1A, C. Coy to the Horn Cellars on the East of the YPRES moat, A, B and H.Q Coys to the ramparts to act as brigade reserve. The last company marched off at 6.40 a.m. and everyone was in position by 8.40 a.m. On reaching YPRES the gas was so strong that men were compelled to wear smoke helmets. No casualties were due to gas	GJP

1875 Wt. W593/826 1,000,000 4/15 J.B.C. & A. A.D.S.S./Forms/C. 2118.

Army Form C. 2118

WAR DIARY
or
INTELLIGENCE SUMMARY
(Erase heading not required.)

Instructions regarding War Diaries and Intelligence Summaries are contained in F. S. Regs., Part II. and the Staff Manual respectively. Title Pages will be prepared in manuscript.

10th SHERWOOD FORESTERS

Place	Date	Hour	Summary of Events and Information DECEMBER 1915	Remarks and references to Appendices
19th			On arrival at YPRES it was found that the attack was North of our area and we were obliged to stand fast all day, marching back in the evening. Company and platoon commanders showed excellent judgment in taking their men through YPRES and the total casualties for the day were 1 O.R killed and 11 O.R wounded.	
20th			A quiet day in rest camp	
21st.			Orders were received on previous evening to "stand-to" from 5.45 a.m – 6.15 a.m. and the move up if it was considered necessary: fortunately it was a quiet morning.	
23rd.			On evening of 23rd the battalion marched up to the trenches to relieve the 7th LINCOLNSHIRES. Relief was complete at 8.50 p.m. Firing line was occupied by A Coy on right C Coy on left: D Coy at X1A & B Coy at cellars in MENIN ROAD. A quiet night for the relief.	

GJR

1875 Wt. W593/826 1,000,000 4/15 J.B.C. & A. A.D.S.S./Forms/C. 2118.

Army Form C. 2118

WAR DIARY

or

~~INTELLIGENCE SUMMARY~~

(Erase heading not required.)

Instructions regarding War Diaries and Intelligence Summaries are contained in F. S. Regs., Part II. and the Staff Manual respectively. Title Pages will be prepared in manuscript.

10th SHERWOOD FORESTERS

Place	Date	Hour	Summary of Events and Information	Remarks and references to Appendices
			Refer ~~Maps~~ Hooge 1/10000 Sheet 28 1/40.000 — DECEMBER 1915	
24th.			Early in the morning LIEUT. A.G. SHAW was shot dead by an enemy sniper while visiting his company R.I.P.	
			An enemy trench mortar opened fire on our front line trenches but failed to do any damage: retaliation by our 18 pounders proved very effective.	
25th.			Christmas day was a quiet day in the trenches: troops were warned against relaxing their vigilance and there was a little artillery activity	
			In the evening companies were relieved	
			1 O.R. was slightly wounded but remained at duty.	
26th.			Reinforcements of 3 officers and 91 O.R arrived but were kept at Rest Camp:- LIEUT. E.A TOLLEMACHE, 2/Lts. W.R.L DAVIS and R.A.C. ROTTLE the latter returning from England after his wound.	
			A quiet day in the trenches.	
27th.			The 6 inch. Howitzers shot on enemy front line trenches from 11 am. to 1 p.m. but appeared to do little or no damage. The enemy retaliated on front R4 Y near X1A for about an hour from 11.30 but not with any intensity G.J.P.	

1875 Wt. W593/826 1,000,000 4/15 J.B.C. & A. A.D.S.S./Forms/C. 2118.

Army Form C. 2118

Instructions regarding War Diaries and Intelligence Summaries are contained in F. S. Regs., Part II. and the Staff Manual respectively. Title Pages will be prepared in manuscript.

WAR DIARY
or
INTELLIGENCE SUMMARY
(Erase heading not required.)

7th SHERWOOD FORESTERS

Place	Date	Hour	Refce Maps Hooge 1/10.000 Shell 28 1/40.000. Summary of Events and Information DECEMBER. 1915.	Remarks and references to Appendices
	27th		Casualties 1 O.R. Killed 1 O.R wounded	
	28th		Trench mortars fired on enemy front line from 11 a.m. to which enemy replied with aerial torpedoes, whizzbangs and H.E Shrapnel but did no material damage.	
			At 2.10 pm a big gun from N.E fired for from 15 to 20 minutes on R4 and Bn H.Q. Fortunately this gun failed to make any direct hits.	
			Casualties 1 O.R. killed	
	29th		At 2.30 p.m. there were sounds of very heavy artillery activity some way south of our area: along our own front it was very quiet: at about 9 p.m. the enemy shelled MENIN ROAD with whizzbangs for about 15 minutes.	
			7th LINCOLNSHIRES relieved the battalion in the evening the relief being complete at 9.15 p.m. & the battalion marched back to rest camp at H19b for one night.	
	30th		In afternoon of 30th four companies moved over to camp at G.18.a. H.Q. remaining as usual at H.13d.	

1875 Wt. W593/826 1,000,000 4/15 J.B.C. & A. A.D.S.S./Forms/C. 2118.

Army Form C. 2118

WAR DIARY

or

INTELLIGENCE SUMMARY

(Erase heading not required.)

10th SHERWOOD FORESTERS

Instructions regarding War Diaries and Intelligence Summaries are contained in F. S. Regs., Part II. and the Staff Manual respectively. Title Pages will be prepared in manuscript.

Place	Date	Hour	Refce. Maps. Hooge 1/10000 Sheet 28. 1/40.000. Summary of Events and Information DECEMBER 1915.	Remarks and references to Appendices
	30th		2/Lt. S.C. DAY joined the battalion	
	31st.		MAJOR HALL BROWN joined the battalion being posted from No. 6. Entrenching battalion	
	30t 31st		These two days were spent in rest-camp.	
			Casualties for month of December.	
			LIEUT A.G. SHAW – Killed.	
			22. O.R. Killed.	
			38 O.R. wounded	
			9 O.R. wounded slightly at duty.	
			A very tiring and trying month for all ranks.	
			GJP	

1875 Wt. W593/826 1,000,000 4/15 J.B.C. & A. A.D.S.S./Forms/C. 2118.

17th Div

51st Bde

10th Sherwoods

Vol: 6

Jan 1916

Army Form C. 2118

WAR DIARY
or
~~INTELLIGENCE SUMMARY~~
(Erase heading not required.)

Instructions regarding War Diaries and Intelligence Summaries are contained in F. S. Regs., Part II. and the Staff Manual respectively. Title Pages will be prepared in manuscript.

10th SHERWOOD FORESTERS

Place	Date	Hour	Refce. Sheet 28. 1/40.000 Hazebrouck 5A. 1/100,000 — Summary of Events and Information — JANUARY 1916	Remarks and references to Appendices
OUDERDOM			Jan 1st & 2nd were spent in rest camp A New Years dinner was eaten on the 1st to the satisfaction of all ranks On 2nd a draft of ~~??~~ 57 O.R. arrived, mostly from 13th Battalion	
	3rd		Battalion marched to YPRES ramparts to relieve the 9th Northumberland Fusiliers: relief complete at about 6 p.m. delay being caused by N.F. gumboots being delayed by shelling of back area Machine Gunners and bombers relieved in trenches the former narrowly missing a shell on VLAMERTINGHE road.	
	4th.		Battalion relieved 7th Lincolnshire Regt. in trenches. A very dark night but the relief was complete at 7.50 p.m. both battalion knowing the trenches well During the night the enemy kept up persistent sniping both with rifle and machine gun fire and sent up fewer flares: it is thought that they may be fresh troops.	
	5th.		During the morning the enemy were very active with trench mortars: their ranging was bad ~~and~~ no damage was done. At 11.45 a.m. three very big shells burst near Bn. H.Q. It was thought enemy were registering with a new gun but no further shots were fired during this tour.	

G.J.P.

1875 Wt. W593/826 1,000,000 4/15 J.B.C. & A. A.D.S.S./Forms/C. 2118.

Army Form C. 2118

Instructions regarding War Diaries and Intelligence Summaries are contained in F. S. Regs., Part II. and the Staff Manual respectively. Title Pages will be prepared in manuscript.

WAR DIARY

or

~~INTELLIGENCE~~ SUMMARY

(Erase heading not required.)

10th SHERWOOD FORESTERS

Place	Date	Hour	Summary of Events and Information Refce Sheet 28 1/40.000 Hazebrouck 5A 1/100.000 JANUARY 1916	Remarks and references to Appendices
	6th.		A quiet day with a few odd shells scattered over our area. No. casualties.	
			The 12th Royal Fusiliers relieved the battalion: relief complete at 5 pm.	
			Battalion marched back for the night to rest camp at H19b.	
			Casualties during tour NIL.	
	7th	5.30 am.	Paraded for march to QUINTIN (near POPERINGHE) for train to ST OMER: transport moved off at 4 a.m.	
			Arrived QUINTIN 8 a.m. waited for train, and entrained at 9.15 a.m: trained moved off 10.45 a.m.	
			arrived ST OMER 1.50 p.m and marched to billets at HOULLE. arriving at 4.30	
			Lorries with blankets, left OUDERDOM at 9 a.m. and arrived HOULLE at 4 pm.	
			1 Coy billetted in MOULLE, two companies and H.Q. Coy at MALTERIE HOULLE, and 1 Coy in farms N.W. of HOULLE.	
	8th 9th		Rested and re-equipped, as much as possible	
	10th		10th Reinforcements 350.R joined battalion	

GJP

1875 Wt. W593/826 1,000,000 4/15 J.B.C. & A. A.D.S.S./Forms/C. 2118.

Instructions regarding War Diaries and Intelligence Summaries are contained in F. S. Regs., Part II. and the Staff Manual respectively. Title Pages will be prepared in manuscript.

WAR DIARY
or
~~INTELLIGENCE~~ SUMMARY
(Erase heading not required.)

Army Form C. 2118

10th SHERWOOD FORESTERS

Place	Date	Hour	Refce. Hazebrouck 5A. 1/100.000 Summary of Events and Information JANUARY 1916	Remarks and references to Appendices
HOULLE.	11th – 15th		Continued resting with short parades and marches and football games on each day.	
			Reorganised battalion as regards H.Q. company.	
			Officers & O.R. sent to Bde Schools for Machine Gun, & Signalling	
			Battalion Bombing School & Sniping School arranged and range at Quarries South of Calais Road prepared.	
	16th.		Training commenced. Company training and Musketry forming the first week's programme.	
	17th		Reinforcements 6. O.R. joined the battalion	
	18th.		Bde. marched passed Gen. Sir Herbert Plumer K.C.B., G.C.M.G., on Calais Road in column of route.	
			Battalion was in rear of Brigade followed by transport	
			Slight rain spoilt the day but march was satisfactory.	
	19th.		Battalion played 79th Bde. R.F.A. in Divisional Football League and were beaten by 2 goals to 1 on the home ground. The XI did not play up to expectations	
	20th – 31st		Continued training in Rest Billets at HOULLE: company training and Musketry forming programme.	
	29th		Reinforcements 20. O.R. joined battalion.	

GJP.

1875 Wt. W593/826 1,000,000 4/15 J.B.C. & A. A.D.S.S./Forms/C. 2118.

10th Notts &
Derby's
17th Div (51)
Vol. 7.

Feb 1916

26
3

Army Form C. 2118

Instructions regarding War Diaries and Intelligence Summaries are contained in F. S. Regs., Part II. and the Staff Manual respectively. Title Pages will be prepared in manuscript.

WAR DIARY
or
~~INTELLIGENCE~~ SUMMARY
(Erase heading not required.)

10th SHERWOOD FORESTERS.

Place	Date	Hour	Summary of Events and Information	Remarks and references to Appendices
			Refer Maps. Hazebrouck 5A. 1/100000 1/40.000 Sheets 27 & 28. FEBRUARY. 1916	
HOULLE.			Battalion remained at rest in HOULLE Feb. 1st to 4th with customary training. On the 4th reinforcements of 39 O.R joined the battalion.	
	5th.		Orders were received that the 17th Division were to relieve the 3rd Division in the trenches.	
			The battalion moved by rail as follows:-	
			A Coy with 1 Cooker from ST. OMER at 5.30 a.m on 6th. This company detrained at GODEWAERSVELDE whence it marched to POPERINGHE and from there to reserve dugouts near Canal at 1.33 a.	
			C Coy with 1 Cooker & remainder of transport for two companies from ANDRUICQ at 2.59 a.m on 6th. This company detrained at POPERINGHE from there marched to "A" Camp at H 31 b near OUDERDOM and from there the same day to reserve dugouts joining A Coy there.	
			A proportion of machine gunners, snipers and bombers from ANDRUICQ at 7.59 a.m. on 6th. This party detrained at POPERINGHE and from there were conveyed in busses to trench area and joined remainder in Reserve dugouts.	
			G.J.P.	

Instructions regarding War Diaries and Intelligence Summaries are contained in F. S. Regs., Part II. and the Staff Manual respectively. Title Pages will be prepared in manuscript.

WAR DIARY
or
~~INTELLIGENCE~~ SUMMARY
(Erase heading not required.)

Army Form C. 2118

10th Sherwood Foresters

Place	Date	Hour	Summary of Events and Information — Reference Map 1/40 000 Sheet 28. — FEBRUARY 1916	Remarks and references to Appendices
	6th.		These two companies were under Bde orders and furnished garrisons for fortins R10 and R11	
	8th		The remainder of the battalion entrained at ST. OMER at 5.39 a.m. on the morning of the 8th, detraining at GODEWAERSVELDE From there battalion marched via POPERINGHE to camp "A": on reaching OUDERDOM it was found that camp "A" had been taken over by another battalion and that camp "B" at 17 6 a was allotted. This was reached at dusk by a tired and footsore battalion.	
			2 O.R. were accidentally hurt on the march by a motor lorry which ran into the ditch	
	9th – 12th		Remained in rest camp	
	12th		Capt. H. Carpenter joined from England he returned to the 12th Battn. on the 14th.	
	13th		Marched up to trenches to relieve 7th Lincolnshire Regt. in trenches 29 – 32 immediately N. of Canal S.E. of YPRES Dispositions as follows: B Coy trench 29, crater & supports, A Coy 30 & supports, C Coy 31 & supports, D Coy 32 and supports. Bn H.Q. in dugouts on N. side of Canal bank	

(GJP)

1875 Wt. W593/826 1,000,000 4/15 J.B.C. & A. A.D.S.S./Forms/C. 2118.

Instructions regarding War Diaries and Intelligence Summaries are contained in F. S. Regs., Part II. and the Staff Manual respectively. Title Pages will be prepared in manuscript.

WAR DIARY
or
~~INTELLIGENCE~~ SUMMARY
(Erase heading not required.)

10th Sherwood Foresters.

Army Form C. 2118

Place	Date	Hour	Refce Map 1/40.000 Sheet 28. Summary of Events and Information FEBRUARY 1916	Remarks and references to Appendices
	13th.		Relief was complete at 8.50 p.m 2 O.R accidentally wounded slightly at duty. The night passed quietly with the exception of occasional H.E. Shrapnel.	
	14th		Casualties to 12 noon 1 O.R. killed, 7 wounded including 3 slightly at duty.	
			The following report by MAJOR J.C. KEOWN describes subsequent happenings.	
			"On the night 13th/14th Feb. the 10th Sherwoods relieved the 7th Lincolnshire Regt. in trenches F29, 30, 31, 32. All four companies occupied the front line and support trenches and there was no Battalion reserve.	
			"On the right of the battalion were the Lancashire Fusiliers extending from NEW YEARS trench inclusive and on the left were the S. Staffordshire Regt. occupying from Trench F33 inclusive. The night was comparatively quiet and at 7a.m I visited the trenches.	
			"At 8.30 a.m the enemy commenced an intermittent bombardment with trench mortars, rifle grenades and some guns, and in view of subsequent events this was apparently registering. This continued intermittently until 3.30 p.m when the enemy commenced a terrific bombardment on the front line	

1875 Wt. W593/826 1,000,000 4/15 J.B.C. & A. A.D.S.S./Forms/C. 2118.

Instructions regarding War Diaries and Intelligence Summaries are contained in F. S. Regs., Part II. and the Staff Manual respectively. Title Pages will be prepared in manuscript.

WAR DIARY
or
~~INTELLIGENCE SUMMARY~~
(Erase heading not required.)

Army Form C. 2118

10th Sherwood Foresters

Place	Date	Hour	Refce Map 1/40.000 Sheet 28 — Summary of Events and Information — FEBRUARY 1916	Remarks and references to Appendices
	14th		and support trenches. "At 3.40 p.m. a message was received at Bn H.Q. reporting heavy shelling in front line and supports. This was repeated to the Bde. and Artillery officers who were at Bn. H.Q. and as much retaliation was called for as could be obtained. "Communication with the front line was cut off very early but the shelling could be observed from H.Q. and constant messages were sent to the Bde. H.Q. reporting that the shelling was still very heavy. "The retaliation commenced at about 4 p.m. but was very inadequate and poor in comparison with that which was coming over and we had great difficulty in impressing the Artillery with the seriousness of the situation. At the very height of the bombardment a message was received 'Is that sufficient' "The Company Commanders although anticipating an attack, considered through information brought back to them by	

1875 Wt. W593/826 1,000,000 4/15 J.B.C. & A. A.D.S.S./Forms/C. 2118.

GJP

Instructions regarding War Diaries and Intelligence Summaries are contained in F. S. Regs., Part II. and the Staff Manual respectively. Title Pages will be prepared in manuscript.

WAR DIARY
or
~~INTELLIGENCE SUMMARY~~

(Erase heading not required.)

Army Form C. 2118

10th Sherwood Foresters

Place	Date	Hour	Summary of Events and Information — Refce. Map 1/40 000 Sheet 28 — FEBRUARY 1916.	Remarks and references to Appendices
	14th		officers Patrols, that it would be useless to send up any more men as the front trenches were battered to the ground and most of the original garrison incapacitated. "At 5.40 p.m a mine appears to have been exploded in trench 31 and almost immediately the bombardment lifted and was directed to reserve wood. "The Germans, preceded by a large number of bombers, who from some accounts were dressed in Khaki, with white bands on their right arms, jumped into our front line trenches as the guns lifted and must have been well across 'No man's land' before the bombardment lifted. "Finding little or no resistance in the front lines the enemy continued to advance both over the open and down the communication trenches, but were held up by our troops in the support trenches. "About this time (5.40 p.m) a messenger arrived at Bn HQ very exhausted and excited saying that the Germans	

GJP

Instructions regarding War Diaries and Intelligence Summaries are contained in F. S. Regs., Part II. and the Staff Manual respectively. Title Pages will be prepared in manuscript.

WAR DIARY
or
~~INTELLIGENCE~~ SUMMARY
(Erase heading not required.)

10th Sherwood Foresters

Army Form C. 2118

Place	Date	Hour	Summary of Events and Information — Refce Map 1/40.000 Sheet 28. FEBRUARY 1916.	Remarks and references to Appendices
	14th		were coming down the 'lane'. This was confirmed almost immediately by others so it was decided to occupy an old trench running from just below Bn. H.Q. across in the direction of CHESTER FARM, and a messenger was sent to the detachment of the 7th Lincolnshire Regt who were in SPOIL BANK DUGOUTS informing them of the situation. The two Companies were not under my command but at my invitation came up to reinforce the support lines. "I was then informed by the Bde that these two companies of the 7th Lincolnshire Regt and a company of 7th Border Regt were ~~at~~ being placed under my command for a counter attack; but I advised the Bde ~~to~~ send the whole Border Regt (which was done) as I considered that the enemy had had too much time to consolidate for the counter attack to be successful with so small a force. "To this they agreed and Lt Col Norrington arrived with the remainder of his battalion at about 10 pm and took over command of the sector." (Sd) J. C. Keown, Major 10th Sherwood Foresters	

Army Form C. 2118

Instructions regarding War Diaries and Intelligence Summaries are contained in F. S. Regs., Part II. and the Staff Manual respectively. Title Pages will be prepared in manuscript.

WAR DIARY
or
~~INTELLIGENCE SUMMARY~~
(Erase heading not required.)

10th Sherwood Foresters

Place	Date	Hour	Refce Map 1/40 000 Sheet 28. Summary of Events and Information FEBRUARY. 1916.	Remarks and references to Appendices
	14th		The counterattack was not successful.	
	15th		Half the men in trenches were relieved in the morning and the remainder in the evening, proceeding to reserve dugouts at I 33 a. 7th East Yorks took over	
			A counterattack with bombs was ordered for 9 p.m.	
			The battalion supplied 1 party consisting of Lt. Daniel, 8 bombers and 30 carriers under the orders of O.C. 7th Lincolnshire	
			A similar party of Cyclists came under C.O.'s orders. A carrying party of 12 men was supplied to carry bombs from R10 to a forward dump at end of HEDGE ROW.	
			This counterattack was also unsuccessful	
	16		On the night 16th/17th the remnants of the battalion was relieved by a portion of 2nd Suffolks and marched back to Camp "B" near Reninghelst. Busses for most of the men were available at Belgian battery corner. Last of battalion arrived back at about 2 a.m.	
			GJP	

Instructions regarding War Diaries and Intelligence Summaries are contained in F. S. Regs., Part II. and the Staff Manual respectively. Title Pages will be prepared in manuscript.

WAR DIARY
or
INTELLIGENCE SUMMARY
(Erase heading not required.)

Army Form C. 2118

10th Sherwood Foresters

Place	Date	Hour	Summary of Events and Information — Refce Map 1/40.000 Sheet 28 — FEBRUARY 1916	Remarks and references to Appendices
			Casualties during these operations were as follows.	
			Officers killed CAPT. G. P GOODALL, LIEUT. D. W. RAMSAY and 2/Lt. R. MILWARD. Wounded: CAPT. T.W. FISHER, LIEUT. P.E. CUCKOW, LIEUT. J.A. MEADS, LIEUT G.D.M. ABBOTTS, 2/LIEUT G.R.Y. THURLOW, LIEUT. T.W. DANIEL, 2/Lt. W.R.L. DAVIS; Missing CAPT E.T.R. CARLYON (wounded), LIEUT. P. KNOX SHAW, LIEUT. E.A. TOLLEMACHE, 2/Lt. W. EBERY, 2/Lt. E.S. CHANDLER, 2/Lt. H.C. MELVILLE.	
			Capt Fisher & Lt. Cuckow returned from C.C.S. on night of 17th	
			O.R. Killed 23 Missing 163 Wounded 148 including 31 remaining at duty.	
	17–29		Remained at "B" Rest Camp for reorganising and later for working parties.	
	26		Night of 26th orders were received to "stand to" and be ready to move at a moment's notice. Twenty minutes later an order came cancelling this order.	
			Reinforcements arrived as follows:	
	15th ~~14th~~ GJP		On ~~17th~~ 37 O.R. joined	
	17th		10 O.R. joined	

GJP

1875 Wt. W593/826 1,000,000 4/15 J.B.C. & A. A.D.S.S./Forms/C. 2118.

Instructions regarding War Diaries and Intelligence Summaries are contained in F. S. Regs., Part II. and the Staff Manual respectively. Title Pages will be prepared in manuscript.

WAR DIARY
or
~~INTELLIGENCE SUMMARY~~
(Erase heading not required.)

10th Sherwood Foresters

Army Form C. 2118

Place	Date	Hour	Refce Map 1/40.000. Sheet 28. Summary of Events and Information FEBRUARY 1916	Remarks and references to Appendices
	19th.		4 officers joined from 2nd Battalion LIEUT R.G. MILWARD, LIEUT. A.J.M. LANDER, LIEUT W.H.V. NELSON, and 2/Lt. R.A. PAGE.	
	20th		4 officers joined from 1st Battalion. LIEUT A.E. SPENCER, LIEUT. J.P. TUCKER, 2/Lt R.O. BROWN, 2/Lt. J.W. DAVIDSON.	
	23rd		2 O.R. reported accidentally wounded at TERDEGHEM grenade school.	
	25th		Bombing accident occurred resulting in following casualties 1. O.R. killed 1 died of wounds 7 wounded including 3 slightly at duty.	
	26th		2/Lt. F.W. HEWITT joined + 28 O.R.	
	27th		Four officers joined. CAPTN G.D. WALKER, LT. T.P.C. WILSON, 2/Lt. J.H. IDESON, 2/Lt. P.G. HARVEY.	
	29th		Orders to proceed to reserve Bde. dugouts received.	

GJP

1875 Wt. W593/826 1,000,000 4/15 J.B.C. & A. A.D.S.S./Forms/C. 2118.

DETAIL OF ASSEMBLY TRENCHES.

Ref:attached map 1/5,000.

2nd Bn. Suffolks.

3 Companies - approx. strength 400 men.

Length of trenches required 400 yards.

Trenches will be constructed approx. as shown on sketch.

2 C.T's will be constructed as shown.

The North C.T. for down traffic.

The South C.T. for up traffic.

Assembly slits will also be cut off both C.T's to take any possible overflow from the assembly trenches.

1 Company will assemble in PEAR TREE and 30 R.

Battalion H.Q. will be situated in the m.g. tunnels.

Battalion Aid Post in 172 Co. H.Q. dugout immediately W of GORDON POST.

Battalion Grenade Store for 2,000 grenades at Bn. H.Q.

For further stores see attached list.

Battalion S.A.A. reserve at Battalion H.Q.

10th Bn. R. W. F.

*In event of accomodation in GORDON POST being insufficient more than 200x of trenches must be dug in rear.

4 Companies - approx. strength 400 men.

*200 men will be accomodated in GORDON POST.

*200 yards of trenches will be dug in rear of GORDON POST as shown.

They will be joined by a C.T. to Gordon Post.

Battalion H.Q. will be in Gordon Post.

Battalion Aid Post will be immediately W of GORDON POST, close to Suffolk Aid Post.

Battalion Grenade Store for 1,000 grenades at Bn. H.Q.

S.A.A. reserve at Battalion H.Q.

8th Bn. King's Own.

4 Companies - approx. strength 600 men.

Length of trenches required 600 yards.

Trenches will be constructed as shown on sketch.

Actual length of new work required about 500 x

Following C.T's must be reclaimed so as to link up the assembly trenches:--

DAVIDSON LANE
Continuation of MAUD
BYDAND
WINGATE
MANSFIELD.

Battalion H.Q. will be constructed off HEDGE ROW.

Battalion Aid Post will be in dugouts constructed off MAUD as shown on sketch.

Battalion Grenade Store for 8,000 grenades in MAUD C.T. See also attached list.

Battalion S.A.A. reserve at Battalion H.Q.

1st Bn. Gordon Hrs. 4 Companies - approx. strength 600 men.

Length of trenches required 600 yards.

200 men will be assembled in 32 S and 33 S.

Trenches for 400 men will be constructed in rear of 32 S and 33 S as shown.

Battalion H.Q. will be situated in LOVERS LANE between 33 S and 33 R.

Battalion Aid Post will be in dugouts off DRIVE C.T. at about junction of 33 R and 32 R.

Battalion Grenade Stores - see attached list.

Battalion S.A.A. reserve at Battalion H.Q.

No.1 Support Bn. 1 Company in trench running S from MAUD across FIR LANE to point behind 30 R.

2 Companies in assembly trenches between MAUD and WINGATE.

1 Company in 32 R and 33 R.

Battalion H.Q. in dugouts at W end of HEDGE ROW.

Battalion Aid Post at Battalion H.Q.

Battalion Grenade Stores - see attached list.

Battalion S.A.A. reserve at Battalion H.Q.

No.2 Support Bn. In KINGSWAY DUGOUTS and dugouts in I.33.A.

Battalion H.Q. near Brigade H.Q.
Battalion Aid Post near Battalion H.Q.
Battalion Grenade Stores - see attached list.

Battalion S.A.A. reserve at Brigade H.Q.

Following C.T's to be constructed and reclaimed in addition to those already mentioned:--

C.T. from GORDON POST to PEAR TREE and from PEAR TREE to FIR LANE. to be partly reclaimed and partly redug.

PEAR TREE LANE to be repaired.

FIR LANE)
MAUD) slight repairs.
HEDGE ROW)
DRIVE)

WINGATE not to be reclaimed but to be drained.

New C.T. to join up N ends of assembly trenches between MAUD and WINGATE with HEDGE ROW.

C.T. joining new assembly trench to 30 R to be boarded and repaired.

WOOD ST to be drained.

LOVERS LANE to be repaired.

New C.T. to be dug parallel to DEESIDE from 33 R to 33 S.

Battalion H.Q. At least 4 dugouts for each H.Q.

There are already existing dugouts at all places selected except for the KING'S OWN H.Q.,which must be entirely built, other places will need attention.

In constructing assembly trenches attention must be paid to following points:--

1. They must be deep and boarded as troops have to spend at least 12 hours in them. For the same reason drainage is important.
2. Adequate arrangements must be made to enable the troops to leave the trenches. Steps and pickets for the men to pull themselves up by must be provided.
3. Where possible new work will be screened with branches &c
4. All C.T's to be boarded.
5. Bridges must be provided for crossing the assembly trenches.

Work will be undertaken in the following order:--

Suffolks trenches.

1/Gordons trenches.

No.1 Support Battalion.

R. W. F. trenches.

King's Own trenches.

The last named should be left until the last possible moment.

O.C., E Riding R.E. will supervise all the work.

G.O.C., 52nd Infantry Brigade has given permission for officers of the Staff and Battalions of 76th Infantry Brigade to supervise work generally.

Battalions will send up a responsible officer each day from the rest area to report fully to 76th Brigade H.Q. on the condition of the preparations and on any change noticable in the enemys defences.

A car will probably be available to carry officers to the trench area and to bring them back, arrangements will be made by Brigade H.Q. for this.

DISTRIBUTION OF GRENADES.

-:-:-:-:-:-:-:-:-:-:-:-:-:-

		Mills.	Rifle.
(1)	Suffolks H.Q. (battle)	2000	
(2)	Canal Bank(Brigade reserve) (about I.33 central)	14000	250
(3)	Maud C.T. (2 stores)	8000	
(4)	Fir Lane.	4000	
(5)	Pear Tree.	2000	200
(6)	R.11 (Gordon Post).	1000	
(7)	W end Hedge Row (2stores).	7000	
(8)	Hedge Row (between 32 R & 32 S).	1000	
(9)	32 S Right.	2000	400
(10)	E end of DRIVE C.T.	1000	
(11)	Lovers Lane (at R.line)	1000	200
(12)	Lovers Lane (Z.line)	1000	
(13)	Deeside (R.line)	500	
(14)	Rat Alley (R.line)	1000	
(15)	Deansgate (R.line)	1000	
(16)	In left sector(not available except in emergency)	5000	
(17)	To be carried by grenadier parties in assault.	9800	650
(18)	Carried by men of Battns - 2 per man.	6000	
(19)	At rifle grenade stands.		400
		67300	2100

Battalions will arrange for forward dumps to be made at points in the captured trenches and for this purpose will draw on the stores as follows. As far as possible they will draw on the stores nearest their H.Q.
These stores will be replenished from the Brigade Reserve under arrangements made by Brigade H.Q.

2nd Bn.Suffolk Regt.	No.1. No.5. No.4. No.6. No.3.
10th Bn. R. W. F.	No.6. No.1. No.5. No.4.
1st Bn. Gordon H'rs.	No.9. No.10.No.11.No.12.No.13.No.14.No.15.
8th Bn.King's Own.	No.3. No.7. No.8.
No. 1 Support Bn.	No.7. No.8.
No. 2 Support Bn.	Brigade Reserve (No.2)

8th Bn. K.O.R.Lancs. **SECRET.** Appendix No 2.
2nd Bn. Suffolk Regt.
10th Bn. R. W. F.
1st Bn. Gordon Highlanders.
7th Bn. Lincolnshire Regt.
10th Bn. Sherwood Foresters. ✓
52nd Infantry Brigade. } for information.
17th Division.

MOVE TO ASSEMBLY POSITIONS.

IN CONTINUATION OF O.O. No.10.

Battalions will move as follows on night of March 1st:

	Head of Battalion at CAFE BELGE.
7th Lincolns.	6 p.m.
10th R. W. F.	6.30 p.m.
1st Gordons.	7 p.m.
2nd Suffolks.	8 p.m.
8th King's Own.	9 p.m.

7th Lincolns will move into position by SANDBAG TRACK.

10th R. W. F. will move into position by LANKHOF - GORDON TERRACE - DUCKWALKS to GORDON POST.

1st Gordons will move into position by SANDBAG TRACK and up DRIVE C.T.

2nd Suffolks will move into position by LANKHOF - GORDON TERRACE - thence along N. edge of CANAL on South side of bank to GORDON POST.

8th King's Own will move into position by SANDBAG TRACK and HEDGE ROW C.T.

Battalions to report at once to Brigade H.Q. when their battalions are into the assembly positions.

Brigade H.Q. will open at GORDON TERRACE (I.33.A) at 7 p.m.

Battalion Commanders must carefully reconnoitre the routes to be taken by their battalions, in order that no delay may occur.

W La T Congreve

Captain,
29/2/16. Brigade Major, 76th Infty.Bde.

I. 24/2/16.

PRELIMINARY ORDERS
by
G.O.C. 76th INFANTRY BRIGADE.

SECRET.

appendix No 3

2nd Bn.Suffolk Regt.
8th Bn. K. O. R. L.
1st Bn.Gordon High'drs.
10th Bn. R. W. F.
7th Bn. Lincoln Regt.
10th Bn.Sherwood Foresters.
56 Field Coy. R.E.
East Riding R.E.
17th Division.)
51st Infty.Bde.) for information.
O.C.,T.M.Group.)

****

In confirmation of to-days conference O.C. Battalions will arrange the following details at once:-

1. Boots and putties will be worn and under no circumstances gum boots.

2. Leather jackets or fur jackets to be worn underneath the service dress jackets. If impossible for some men to wear the leather jackets or fur jackets underneath they will be worn above and discarded before the assault and left in the trenches.

3. Two smoke helmets will be carried.

4. As many steel helmets as possible will be procured and issued. Whether helmets or caps are worn, the chin straps will be down.

5. Distinguishing badges will be worn as per attached list. They must be sewn on to the jackets. All ranks must know the various marks.

6. Haversacks will beworn on the side and will contain the emergency rations. (Bully beef,biscuits and groceries).

7. Every man must carry his rifle cleaning kit.

8. Men carrying wire cutters will wear a piece of white tape on their shoulder straps.

9. Men detailed as R.E. working parties will wear a piece of yellow cloth on their right shoulder strap.

10. 120 rounds S.A.A. will be carried in the pouches.
10 rounds in the magazine.
1 bandolier of 50 rounds.

11. All water bottles will be filled.

12. Packs and greatcoats will not be carried.

13. Every man will carry a rolled waterproof sheet on his belt.

14. Every man will carry 3 sandbags tucked under his belt.

15. Entrenching tools will be carried.

16. Every man will carry 2 Mills grenades, one in each pocket. The pins will be carefully inspected before issue.

17. A large number of wire breakers have been asked for. These will be issued to Battalions on a scale according to the state of the wire they may be likely to meet, and will be fixed on to the rifles before moving into the assembly trenches.

18. A proportion of hedging gloves will be issued to all Battalions.

19. Every third man will carry a shovel slung on his back.

20. Bayonets will be dulled in every way possible.

21. If possible there will be one VERY pistol per platoon. The officer or N.C.O. carrying the pistol will carry a supply of cartridges in his pockets.

22. <u>Grenadiers</u>. Throwers will wear equipment without pack or entrenching tool. At least one and if possible 2 haver - sacks, waterbottle, bayonet, bludgeon (to be made under Battalion arrangements) 6 grenades.

<u>Carriers</u>. Same as for throwers except that they will carry rifle, waterproof sheet and 3 sandbags, 120 rounds S.A.A. and 25 grenades.

Acknowledge.

W. R. O'Congreve

Captain,
Brigade Major, 76th Infy. Brigade.

24/2/16

<u>DISTINGUISHING MARKS</u>.

<u>BLACK ON YELLOW</u>.

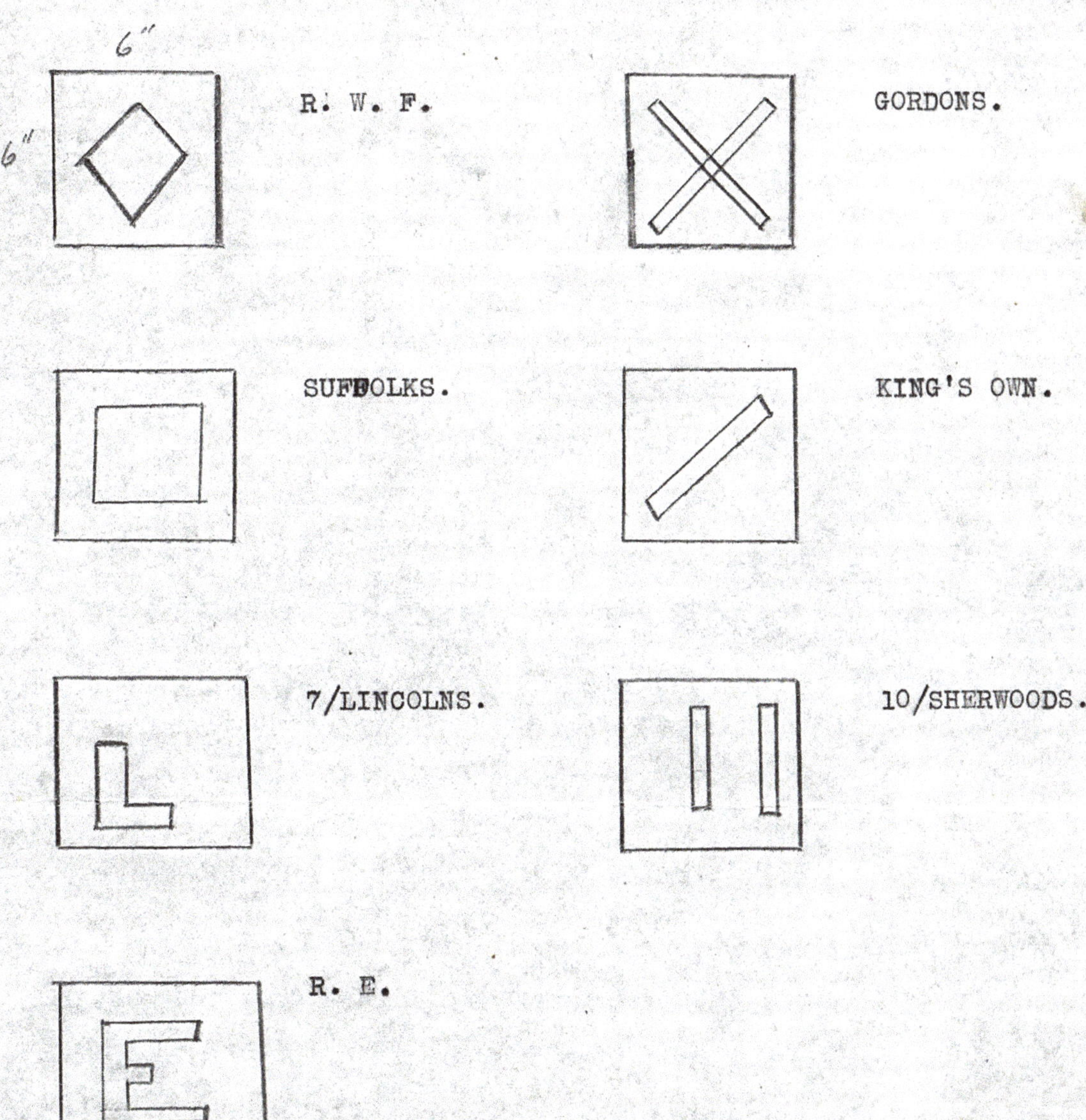

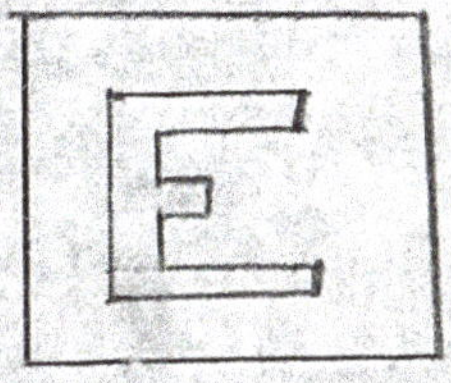

10/S.7.

SECRET appendix No 6

Copy No. 6

76TH INFANTRY BRIGADE OPERATION ORDER NO.10.

Ref: Special Map 1/5000 and 1/10000 Sheet 28.

1. The 76th Infantry Brigade with 2 Battalions of the 17th Division attached will attack the enemys front from the YPRES-COMMINES Canal to the RAVINE I.34.B.3.1, and will hold and consolidate the line as follows:--

Canal about 50 yards W. of Ruins O.4.A.6.9 - E. lip of BLUFF CRATERS - LOOP TRENCH - junction of 29 and 30 - S.W. corner of BEAN salient at I.34.C.9.4 - across the BEAN salient to a point halfway between I.34.D.1.7 and 2.6 - trench 32 about the C of "TRENCH 32" - trench 33 - head of RAVINE inclusive.

2. 17th Divisional Artillery with attached Batteries, the Heavy Artillery and Trench Mortars will bombard the front to be attacked from .... to .... At ....

Battalions will assault (Hours to be notified later).

All ranks must be made to realise the importance of their not overrunning the objective, the line of which must be consolidated without delay, and with unceasing energy.

3. Objectives are allotted to Battalions as follows:--

2nd Bn.Suffolk Regt. From CANAL - about 50 yards West of the Ruins at O.4.A.6.9 - E. lip of BLUFF CRATERS - LOOP TRENCH - junction of 29 and 30.

Consolidation of the BLUFF defences will be carried out as follows:--

(A) A new trench will be dug about 50 yards West of the Ruins extending from the second terrace of the Canal bank to the craters.

(B) NEW YEAR trench will be repaired.

(C) A C.T. will be constructed from WILLIAMS trench to the trench mentioned in para (A). THAMES ST. will be made use of if possible.

(D) The E. lip of the craters will be put into a state of defence and will then be held by 2 grenadier posts.

(E) LOOP TRENCH will be reclaimed.

(F) 29 trench will be reclaimed.

(G) ANGLE TRENCH and KING STREET will be reclaimed.

8th Bn. King's Own. From S.W. Corner of BEAN SALIENT at I.34.C.9.4 - across the BEAN to I.34.D.1.6.

A grenadier party will be detached at the junction of 31 and 30 and will capture trench 30 by bombing down to the junction of 29 and 30, where they will join up with the Suffolks.

Consolidation will be carried out as follows:--

(A) The old trench from the junction of 29 and 30 to I.34.C.9.4 will be repaired and held as a fire trench.

(B) A fire trench will be constructed from I.34.C.9.4 to I.34.D.1.6 taking advantage of the German system of trenches between these points.

(C) The main trench forming the Western edge of the BEAN will be reclaimed to act as a support trench.

(D) 31 will be reclaimed.

(E) 31 A will be reclaimed.

(F) 30 will be reclaimed.

(G) The 2 C.T's between 31 A. and the BEAN will be reclaimed.

1st Bn.Gordon Highlanders. From the point in BEAN SALIENT I.34.D.1.6 - a point about 20 yards East of I.34.D.1.7 - point in Trench 32 about O of "TRENCH 32 " - trench 32 - trench 33 - Eastern breastwork across the Head of the RAVINE.

Consolidation will be carried out as follows:--

(A) A fire trench will be constructed from I.34.D.1.6 to a point about 20 yards East of I.34.D.1.7 taking advantage of the German system of trenches between these points, and continuing the left of the King's Own.

(B) A fire trench will be constructed from a point about 20 yards East of I.34.D.1.7 to a point in trench 32 about the C of "TRENCH 32".

(C) Trenches 32 and 33 will be reclaimed.

(D) The Eastern breastwork across the head of the RAVINE will be reclaimed.

(E) The German C.T. which is in continuation of HEDGE RW. will be reclaimed.

(F) The continuation of WOOD ST from 32 S to 32 will be reclaimed.

(G) The C.T. running from a point in 33 S halfway between LOVERS LANE and DEESIDE to 33 will be reclaimed.

(H) The fire trench on the North edge of the RAVINE between the 2 RAVINE breastworks and in continuation of RAT ALLEY will be reclaimed, and a strong post constructed at the East end of this trench.

Areas for purposes of assembly have already been explained to Officer's Commanding Battalions.

4. Absolute silence will be maintained during the assault and bayonets will be dulled in every way possible.

5. Officer's Commanding Battalions and Company Commanders must thin out their lines at the first opportunity, keeping and bringing back as many men as possible in reserve.

6. 51st Infantry Brigade Machine-Gun Company is placed at the disposal of the 76th Infantry Brigade and will be issued with separate orders.

The Machine-Guns of the Battalion 52nd Infantry Brigade holding the trenches North of the RAVINE will co-operate in the assault by firing upon the German front trench I.34.B.4.0 - 5.1 - 6.3, and trenches in rear of this trench, and will be prepared to assist in repelling any hostile counter attack. The Machine-Guns South of the Canal are co-operating by firing upon the BLUFF during the final bombardment, and during the assault by firing upon the German trench O.4A.9.2 - 9.7 - 9.9 and trenches in rear of this trench.

N.F. Quad. 1 Pear Tree Farm Lane

1 32 S

1 33 8

L.F. 1 30.5.

2. 30 R

1. Griffiths Dennis (Gordons Post R.11)

They are also prepared to assist in repelling any hostile counter attack upon the BLUFF.

The Lewis Guns of the 10th Sherwoods will occupy the positions at present occupied by the Machine-Gunners of the 9th Northumberland Fusiliers, and will co-operate by firing upon the BLUFF, the enemy's trench from the junction of 29 and 30 to ANGLE TRENCH-CRATER TRENCH - Trenches 29 - 30- 31 A - 32 and 33 during the final stages of the bombardment. During the assault they will, where possible, fire over the heads of the assaulting troops and be prepared to repel any enemy counter attacks.

Assaulting Battalions Machine-Guns will come into action as follows:--

2nd Bn. Suffolks.

(A) One gun to be in position in the assembly trenches on the Canal bank. During the last few minutes of the final bombardment it will fire upon the German system of trenches opposite trench 28 on the South canal bank.

(B) One gun to take up a position on the South lip of the BLUFF CRATERS.

(C) One gun to take up a position in LOOP TRENCH.

(D) One gun to take up a position above BLUFF WYND from which it can cover the S. edge of the BEAN SALIENT.

8th Bn. King's Own.

(A) One gun to take up a position about I.34.C.9.4.

(B) One gun to take up a position at the junction of 31 and 30 from which it will flank the S edge of the BEAN and be able to fire over the trench which will be reclaimed from the junction of 29 and 30 to I.34.C.9.4.

(C) One gun to take up a position on the central BEAN C.T.

1st Bn.Gordon Highlanders.

(A) One gun to take up a position in trench 32 about the C of "TRENCH 32 ".

(B) One gun to take up a position at the point where the German C.T. leaves trench 32 at I.34.D.27.

(C) One gun to take up a position on the North side of the RAVINE, at the Eastern end of the trench which is in continuation of RAT ALLEY.

7. The trench mortars and stokes guns attached to the 76th Infantry Brigade will be divided into 2 groups - one South and one North of the Canal. They will be under the command of the 76th Brigade T. M. Officer,who has received separate orders.

8. The following R.E. are attached to the 76th Infty.Brigade:-

E. Riding R.E. 2 Sections.

56th Field Coy. R.E. 2 Sections.

They will be employed as follows:--

(A) 1 Section E.Riding R.E. will be attached to the 2/Suffolks and O.C.Suffolks will detail Infantry Working parties to work with this section in digging the C.T. mentioned in para. 3(C) (2/Suffolks), and on the reclaiming of ANGLE TRENCH and KING ST.

(B) 1 Section 56th Field Coy. R.E. will be attached to the 8/King's Own and O.C. 8/King's Own will detail infantry working parties to work with this section on reclaiming the trench from junction of 29 and 30 to I.34.C.9.4 and in opening up the C.T.s. mentioned in para 3 (G) (King's Own).

(C) 1 Section 56th Field Coy. R.E. will be attached to the 1/Gordons and O.C. 1/Gordons will detail infantry working parties to work with this section on the reclaiming of the C.T's mentioned in para 3 E.F.G.H.(1/Gordons).

(E) 1 Section E.Riding R.E. will be in Brigade Reserve in the E.Riding R.E. dugouts below GORDON POST.

The officers detailed to command the sections which are attached to Battalions will report to O.C., Battalions to whom they are attached after the Battalions have moved into their assembly positions.

Infantry detailed as R.E. working parties will wear a piece of yellow cloth on their right shoulder straps.

9. Grenadier squads will be given the following objectives:-

2nd Bn.Suffolks.

(A) Ruins O.4.A.6.9.

(B) 2 posts in E. lip of BLUFF CRATERS.

(C) Block in C.T. which joins CRATERS to German line.

(D) Clearing of WYND.

(E) Clearing of ANGLE TRENCH.

(F) Clearing of trench which runs from the junction of 29 and 30 to ANGLE trench.

One squad of 10/ R.W.F. will be attached to the Grenadiers 2/Suffolks and will clear ADAMSON ROAD.

8th Bn. King's Own.

(A) Clearing of trench 30.

(B) Block in the main trench which forms the S.edge of the BEAN.

(C) Blocks in the 4 C.T's of the BEAN.

(D) Clearing of the East end of HEDGE ROW.

1st Bn. Gordon Highlanders.

(A) Block in main trench which forms the North edge of the BEAN.

(B) Block in C.T. which is in continuation of HEDGE ROW.

(C) Block in C.T. running from trench 32 at I.34.D.2.7 to German lines.

(D) Block in C.T. running from trench 33 at the Craters to the German lines.

(E) Block in C.T. running from the trench on the North side of the RAVINE to the German lines.

that
O.C.Battalions will arrange/further squads are available to meet any contingency.

Squads which are detailed to form blocks will carry demolition charges to destroy the trench E of their blocks. All blocks formed will be at least 20 yards in advance of the line we are consolidating.

All Grenadiers will carry small black and yellow flags with them to show their position. Instructions in the use of these flags has already been issued.

10. (A) 10/R.W.F. will be in support to the 2/Suffolks, and will keep in constant communication with them. When GRIFFITHS trench is left unoccupied owing to the Suffolks advance, O.C. 10/R.W.F. will move forward one platoon and 2 grenadier squads to occupy it. GRIFFITHS trench must never be left unoccupied.

(B) 7/Lincolns will be in support as follows:--

1 Company to 2/Suffolks.

2 Companies to 8/King's Own.

1 Company to 1/Gordons.

O.C., 7/Lincolns will keep in constant communication with these battalions and will arrange to occupy the following trenches with a light garrison in event of their being left unoccupied:-

30 R. 30 S. 31 S. 32 S. 33 S.

Positions for assembly of 10/R.W.F. and 7/Lincolns have already been explained to Officers Commanding.

(C) The 10/Sherwoods will be in Brigade Reserve in KINGSWAY DUGOUTS.

(D) The left Battalion of the 52nd Infantry Brigade will be under the orders of the G.O.C., 76th Infantry Brigade and will continue to hold its present front.

11. Forward dumps of grenades, S.A.A. and VERY Lights will be formed as soon as possible at the following points. O.C., Battalions will detail special carriers for this work.

2nd Bn. Suffolks.

(A) N. end of NEW YEAR TRENCH.

(B) Junction of 29 with BLUFF CRATERS.

(C) Junction of LOOP TRENCH and 29.

8th Bn. King's Own.

(A) Junction of trenches 31 and 30.

(B) Point in BEAN Salient immediately opposite junction of trenches 30 and 31 where C.T. from 31 enters BEAN.

(C) Point where C.T. from the center of 31 enters the BEAN.

1st Bn. Gordon Highlanders.

(A) Point where C.T., which is in continuation of HEDGE ROW, enters the BEAN.

(B) Point where continuation of WOOD ST enters trench 32.

(C) Point where C.T. which runs from a point in 33 S half-way between LOVERS LANE and DYESIDE to 33 enters trench 33.

12. Positions and capacity of Grenade Stores and Brigade Reserve of Grenades have already been communicated to all concerned.

All stores will be labelled and also marked by a small black and yellow flag.

36 men will be detailed by O.C., 10/Sherwoods to be in charge of these stores, the B.G.O. will post these men.

O.C., 10th Sherwoods will also detail 70 men to act as carriers from the Brigade Grenade Reserve, B.G.O. will post this party.

13. Brigade Reserve of S.A.A. and VERY Lights will be at Brigade Head Quarters.

There will also be 100 boxes S.A.A. and boxes of VERY lights at the Head Quarters of each of the assaulting Battalions.

14. A reserve of rations has been placed at CHESTER FARM for use in case of emergency.

Application for these must be made to Brigade Head Quarters.

15. Traffic in C.T's will be regulated as follows:--

1. Duckwalks along N side of canal bank between PEAR TREE FARM and CHESTER FARM for UP traffic only.

2. GORDON POST C.T's (A) North. DOWN.
   (B) South. UP.

3. PEAR TREE LANE - DOWN.

4. FIR LANE - UP.

5. MAUD - DOWN.

6. HEDGE ROW - UP.

7. DRIVE - DOWN.

8. LOVERS LANE - UP.

C.T's not mentioned above may be used for traffic in both directions.

Grenadiers, grenade carriers, and orderlies may use C.T's in both directions. if bore in right direction.

O.C., 10/Sherwoods will post 2 sentries at the E and W end of all the above mentioned C.T's to regulate traffic as ordered.

He will also detail 6 men to act as Wardens of each of the above mentioned C.T's and O.C., E.Riding R.E. will detail one sapper to work with these parties.

Their duty will be at once to clear any part of the C.T. that may be blown in.

16. All Signal communications will be checked every hour.

17. All watches will be set correct time which will be given by the Brigade Signal Office at an hour to be notified later.

18. Depots of R.E. Stores will be established at

(3) (A) PEAR TREE FARM.

(1) (B) N. end of HEDGE ROW.

(2) (C) CHESTER FARM.

19. There will be a visual signal station at the W end of HEDGE ROW and a wireless station at the KING'S OWN HEAD QUARTERS. Both stations being in direct communication with Brigade Head Quarters.

Prisoners will be sent under Battalion escorts to WOODCOTE HOUSE where they will be handed over to Divisional escort. Battalion escorts will, after handing over, at once return to their units. Battalion Commanders will arrange, if possible, for German speaking men and N.C.O's to form a part of the escort. Escorts must be as small as possible.

21. There will be 300 petrol tins, containing water, placed in the assembly trenches.
200 tins will be at each of the forward R.E. Dumps and a further reserve at CHESTER FARM.

22. No documents or maps, which may be of any use to the enemy, will be carried.

23. A Dressing Station will be formed at BEDFORD HOUSE. Positions of Battalion Aid Posts have been already notified to all concerned.
The 2 trench railways will be used for stretcher cases. Walking cases will move down the trench railways and down SANDBAG TRACK.

24. O.C., 10/R.W.F. will detail a party to carry out a raid on the German trenches on the canal bank at O.4.A.?.7, with the object of discovering and destroying a suspected mine shaft. The hour at which the raid will be carried out and further orders concerning it will be issued later.

25. The O.C., 172 Tunnelling Coy. has detailed 4 parties each of one officer and 4 men to accompany the attack. One party will be attached to each assaulting Battalion and the fourth party to the R.W.F.
Officers in charge of these parties will report to O.C.s 2/Suffolks, 8/King's Own, 1/Gordons and 10/R.W.F., after the Battalions have moved into their assembly positions.
The parties have already received their orders from the O.C., 172 Tunnelling Company.

26. If the wind is favourable smoke barrages will be formed on either flank of the attack.

Neighbouring Divisions and Corps are also arranging demonstrations of various kinds and their artillery are co-operating in every possible way.

27. Artillery Liason Officers will be at the Head Quarters of the assaulting battalions. They will not go in front of Battalion Head Quarters unless the Battalion Commander considers it essential that they should do so, in which case he will give them the necessary orders.

28. Orders as to equipment; ammunition; grenades; very lights and rifle grenades stores - distinguishing marks etc have been already issued under a separate order to all concerned.

29. Brigade Head Quarters will be at the West end of the Canal bank in dugouts I.33.A.

17th Division Headquarters will remain in RENINGHELST.

Captain,

27/2/16. Brigade Major, 76th Infantry Brigade.

Copies to:--

No.1. 8th Bn. K.O.R.Lancs..
2. 2nd Bn. Suffolk Regt..
3. 10th Bn. R. W. F.
4. 1st Bn. Gordon Highlanders.
5. 7th Bn. Lincoln Regt..
6. 10th Bn. Sherwood Foresters..
7. Bn.
8. 17th Division.
9. 51st Infantry Brigade.
10. 52nd Infantry Brigade.
11. 17th Divisional Artillery.
12. East Riding R.E.
13. 93th Field Coy. R.E.
14. O.C., Trench Mortars.
15. 51st Brigade M.G.Coy.
16. O.C., 172nd Tunnelling Coy.

17

10th Notts & Derbys

Vol 8

March 1916

Instructions regarding War Diaries and Intelligence Summaries are contained in F. S. Regs., Part II. and the Staff Manual respectively. Title Pages will be prepared in manuscript.

WAR DIARY
or
~~INTELLIGENCE SUMMARY~~
(Erase heading not required.)

Army Form C. 2118

10th SHERWOOD FORESTERS

Place	Date	Hour	Summary of Events and Information Refce Maps Sheet 28. 1/40.000 & Sheet 36. 1/40.000 — MARCH 1916	Remarks and references to Appendices
Feb	29th.		Battalion marched to Bde Reserve dugouts I 33 a taking over from 10th LANCASHIRE FUSILIERS. Fortins R9 and R10 were relieved: also guards on Bridges 18 & 19, Ecluse No 8 and barricade on YPRES – LILLE Road where it crosses canal. As relieved battalion were finding working parties all that night relief was rather confused and late. As soon as relief was complete (11.45 p.m) the whole battalion was used for carrying material from WOODCOTE HOUSE to forward dumps.	
March	1st		A short bombardment of the enemy trenches and support lines took place at 4.30 a.m and lasted for 45 minutes and brought considerable reply. Casualties to 12 noon 6 O.R wounded including 3 slightly at duty. At 5 p.m. a demonstration was made, as though about to attack, by the 9th Northumberland Fusiliers and 9th WEST RIDING REGTS. holding the trenches. An intense bombardment took place and rapid rifle and machine gun fire: enemy replied vigorously and established two barrages as on Feb 14th — one behind Reserve Wood and one across from Canal Bank in front of CHESTER FARM	(G.P)

1875 Wt. W593/826 1,000,000 4/15 J.B.C. & A. A.D.S.S./Forms/C. 2118.

Army Form C. 2118

Instructions regarding War Diaries and Intelligence Summaries are contained in F. S. Regs., Part II. and the Staff Manual respectively. Title Pages will be prepared in manuscript.

WAR DIARY
or
~~INTELLIGENCE SUMMARY~~
(Erase heading not required.)

10th SHERWOOD FORESTERS

Place	Date	Hour	Summary of Events and Information	Remarks and references to Appendices
			Refce Maps. Sheet 28 1/40.000 Special BLUFF Map 1/5.000 Sheet 36 1/40.000 MARCH 1916	
	1st		76th Inf Bde took over command of sector, establishing their headquarters in Reserve dugouts I 33 a.	
			Bns. under command of 76th Inf Bde. took up position in assembly trenches in accordance with "detail of assembly trenches" & "move to assembly trenches" *	* Appendix Nos. 1 & 2
			Dress & distinguishing marks were worn in accordance with Preliminary Orders †	† Appendix No. 3.
	2nd		At 4.20 a.m. in accordance with Operations Orders ‡ the attack was launched.	‡ Appendix No 4.
			There was no preliminary bombardment immediately before the attack, a desultory ~~bom~~ shelling having taken place throughout the night to prevent the enemy carrying out repairs to wire etc.	
			The attack was in every way a success	
			The trench wardens supplied by battalion found great difficulty in coping with their task of keeping the trenches in repair and eventually it was to all intents abandoned	

1875 Wt. W593/826 1,000,000 4/15 J.B.C. & A. A.D.S.S./Forms/C. 2118.

Instructions regarding War Diaries and Intelligence Summaries are contained in F. S. Regs., Part II. and the Staff Manual respectively. Title Pages will be prepared in manuscript.

WAR DIARY
or
~~INTELLIGENCE SUMMARY~~
(Erase heading not required.)

Army Form C. 2118

10th SHERWOOD FORESTERS

Place	Date	Hour	Summary of Events and Information Refce Maps. Sheet 28 1/40.000 Sheet 36 1/40.000. MARCH 1916	Remarks and references to Appendices
	2nd		As soon as the assault and burst of shelling was over, what remained of the battalion after supplying the guards, wardens etc was utilised in carrying up ammunition and material to the forward dumps. This continued all day and most of the night,	
	3rd		and following morning - the latter under heavy shell fire. Bn. bombers were utilised to occupy posts in front line and did good work under Lieut. HOYTE. The orders for battalion to be relieved on night 3rd/4th by 7th Kings Shropshire Light Infantry were received in the early afternoon. This relief was a long and tedious process and was not complete till 3.45 a.m. The companies were able to get away before that time. The Bn. marched back to camp B - a long march but recompensed by the sleep that followed. Casualties during two days. CAPT. J.W. FISHER, 2/Lt. A.F. BENTLEY wounded + CAPT N.H. PRATT slightly at duty all on 3rd. O.R. Killed 17 Wounded* 76 Missing 3 * includes ~~??~~ 27 at duty	GJP

1875 Wt. W593/826 1,000,000 4/15 J.B.C. & A. A.D.S.S./Forms/C. 2118.

Army Form C. 2118

Instructions regarding War Diaries and Intelligence Summaries are contained in F. S. Regs., Part II. and the Staff Manual respectively. Title Pages will be prepared in manuscript.

WAR DIARY
or
~~INTELLIGENCE~~ SUMMARY
(Erase heading not required.)

10th SHERWOOD FORESTERS

Place	Date	Hour	Summary of Events and Information	Remarks and references to Appendices
			Refce Maps Sheet 28 1/40.000 Sheet 36. 1/40000 — MARCH 1916	
	4th.		Reinforcements of 48 O.R. joined battalion.	
	5th.		Orders received to march following day to billets near LA CRECHE. Billeting Party sent off.	
	6th.		Marched to new area: commenced 9.30 a.m. arrived 1.15 p.m. Sun for first half of march and snow for remainder. Two busses for sore feet men enabled battalion to arrive together.	
			News received LIEUT. E.A. TOLLEMACHE reported "missing" 14/2/16 now reported "prisoner of war."	
			Reinforcements 149 O.R. joined battalion.	
	7th.		Brigades Courses in M.G. and sniping commenced. Also battalion training of bombers, machine gunners.	
			Orders received to be ready to assemble at LA CRECHE at two hours notice.	
			Snow and sleet continue to fall heavily at intervals and hard frost at night.	

Army Form C. 2118

Instructions regarding War Diaries and Intelligence Summaries are contained in F. S. Regs., Part II. and the Staff Manual respectively. Title Pages will be prepared in manuscript.

WAR DIARY
or
~~INTELLIGENCE~~ SUMMARY
(Erase heading not required.)

10th SHERWOOD FORESTERS

Place	Date	Hour	Summary of Events and Information	Remarks and references to Appendices
			Refce Maps Sheet 36. 1/40.000 MARCH 1916	
	8–10th		Continued training in rest billets	
	10th		Reinforcements 67 O.R. joined battalion in the evening.	
	12th		1 O.R. previously reported killed + 1 O.R. previously reported missing 14/2/16 now reported "prisoners of war"	
			Reinforcements 3 O.R. joined battalion.	
			CAPT E.R. OAKDEN rejoined the battalion from 13th battalion	
			Weather warmer and continued	
	13th		2/Lt A.F. BENTLEY reported wounded 3/3/16 reported "died of wounds" 11/3/16 by O.C. No.1 Red Cross Hospital, Le Touquet	
			2/Lt R. MILWARD previously reported killed in action 14/2/16 now reported "prisoner of war"	
	~~14th~~		Reinforcements 36 O.R joined battalion	
	14th		The G.O. Commanding 2nd Corps inspected the battalion in field near H.Q. billet in Mass. After inspection he made a short speech welcoming battalion to new Corps and encouraging men to forget the hard times behind	
			The sun shone brilliantly and the inspection was quite success ful	G.J.P.

1875 Wt. W593/826 1,000,000 4/15 J.B.C. & A. A.D.S.S./Forms/C. 2118.

Instructions regarding War Diaries and Intelligence Summaries are contained in F. S. Regs., Part II. and the Staff Manual respectively. Title Pages will be prepared in manuscript.

WAR DIARY
or
~~INTELLIGENCE~~ SUMMARY

(Erase heading not required.)

Army Form C. 2118

10th SHERWOOD FORESTERS.

Place	Date	Hour	Summary of Events and Information Refce Maps Sheets 28, 36 1/40.000 ~~DECEMBER~~ MARCH 1916.	Remarks and references to Appendices
LACRECHE	14th	–18th	During these days the battalion continued training in rest billets	
	18th		Advanced party sent off to take over billets in ARMENTIERES 1 O.R. accidentally hurt by motor cycle: evacuated	
	19th		Marched to billets in Armentieres: last company marched off at 5.30 a.m. Battalion arrived in billets all correct at 8.30 a.m. A fine morning with roads comparatively clear of traffic. Transport & officers cobs at NIEPPE. "M" group billets taken over	
	20th		Battalion moved at 9.30 a.m. to "E" group billets: move anticipated by 9th N.F. who arrived just before us. Orders were then received to stand by for the matter to be adjusted: next order was to move into "B" group, which was reported vacant. On arrival 10th Lancashire Fusiliers were found in possession. They were moved into "M" group and we eventually took over at 1 p.m. Reinforcements 2/Lt T.B. WILLIAMSON, 11 O.R and Armourer Sergeant arrived	

1875 Wt. W593/826 1,000,000 4/15 J.B.C. & A. A.D.S.S./Forms/C. 2118.

Army Form C. 2118

Instructions regarding War Diaries and Intelligence Summaries are contained in F. S. Regs., Part II. and the Staff Manual respectively. Title Pages will be prepared in manuscript.

WAR DIARY
or
~~INTELLIGENCE SUMMARY~~
(Erase heading not required.)

10th SHERWOOD FORESTERS

Place	Date	Hour	Summary of Events and Information — Refce Map Sheet 36 1/40.000 — MARCH 1916	Remarks and references to Appendices
	19th.	7pm	Took over 8 bridge and road guards from 8th Somerset L.I	
			One company out on working party 7.45am–3 p.m on front line trenches.	
	21st.		Three companies out from 6.30 p.m. – 3 a.m.	
			Same working parties as above 4 Bridge guards relieved	
	22nd		One company on day working party	
	23rd		One company only by night	
			2/Lts A.W. BRITTAN and R.A. BARKER and 58 O.R. joined battalion	
	24th		Two platoons by day and 1 company by night working.	
	25th.		Two platoons by day and two companies by night.	
			2/Lt P.G. HARVEY wounded and 1 O.R	
			CAPT. E.T.R. CARLYON previously reported "wounded and missing" now reported "wounded and prisoner"	
	26th.		Two platoons by day and two companies by night working.	
	27th.		Casualties to 12 noon 1 O.R. wounded	
			LIEUT. P. KNOX SHAW previously reported "missing believed killed" now reported "wounded and prisoner"	

1875 Wt. W593/826 1,000,000 4/15 J.B.C. & A. A.D.S.S./Forms/C. 2118.

Army Form C. 2118

Instructions regarding War Diaries and Intelligence Summaries are contained in F. S. Regs., Part II. and the Staff Manual respectively. Title Pages will be prepared in manuscript.

WAR DIARY
or
~~INTELLIGENCE SUMMARY~~

(Erase heading not required.) 10th SHERWOOD FORESTERS

Place	Date	Hour	Summary of Events and Information Refce Map Sheet 36 1/40.000 WEZ MACQUART. 1/10,000 MARCH 1916	Remarks and references to Appendices
	27th		Relieved 7th LINCOLNSHIRE REGT in trenches 67, 68 and 69 Bombers, Lewis Gunners and Snipers relieved in the morning and remainder of battalion at night. Relief complete at 9.25 pm. Dispositions were as follows: B Coy hold 67 & ½ 68 and close support trenches D Coy ½ 68 and 69 and close support 8 Lewis guns in the firing line 4 belonging to LINCOLNSHIRES. The guns remain always, the regiment in the line finding the gun detachments. A Coy with 2 Platoons in LILLE POST & 2 in right subsidiary line. C Coy holding left subsidiary line H.Q in houses opposite Square Farm on CHAPPELLE D'ARMENTIERES road. The night was very dark and it was raining hard: generally a bad night for a relief. 7th Border Regt on left: 34th Division (First Army) on right with battalion of TYNESIDE SCOTTISH	

1875 Wt. W593/826 1,000,000 4/15 J.B.C. & A. A.D.S.S./Forms/C. 2118.

Army Form C. 2118

Instructions regarding War Diaries and Intelligence Summaries are contained in F. S. Regs., Part II. and the Staff Manual respectively. Title Pages will be prepared in manuscript.

WAR DIARY
or
~~INTELLIGENCE~~ SUMMARY
(Erase heading not required.) 10th SHERWOOD FORESTERS

Place	Date	Hour	Refce Map WEZ MACQUART 1/10.000 Sheet 36. 1/40.000 — Summary of Events and Information	Remarks and references to Appendices
	28th		A quiet day without casualty; working parties kept busy. 2/Lts. A.G DENT & A.G. BOWRING joined H.Q. having arrived on night 27th. also 1. O.R. joined 27th	
	29th		Another quiet day. Reinforcements 23 O.R joined the battalion	
	30th		There was considerably more activity on the part of the enemy; eight observation balloons in all were observed and desultory shelling which appeared to be registration was carried out	
	31st		Companies in the firing line were relieved in the morning A Coy taking over from B Coy, C Coy from D Coy.	
			Casualties during the month	
			Officers: Died of Wounds 2/Lt A.F. BENTLEY; wounded CAPT. J.W. FISHER, 2/Lt P.G. HARVEY and CAPT. N.H. PRATT (slightly at duty)	
			O.R. Killed, 17	
			wounded, 78 including 27 at duty	
			Missing. 3.	

GJP

1875 Wt. W593/826 1,000,000 4/15 J.B.C. & A. A.D.S.S./Forms/C. 2118.

Instructions regarding War Diaries and Intelligence Summaries are contained in F. S. Regs., Part II. and the Staff Manual respectively. Title Pages will be prepared in manuscript.

WAR DIARY
or
~~INTELLIGENCE~~ SUMMARY
(Erase heading not required.)

Army Form C. 2118

XVII

10th SHERWOOD FORESTERS Vol 8

Place	Date	Hour	Refce Maps. Sheet 36 1/40.000 WEZ MACQUART. 1/10.000 — Summary of Events and Information — APRIL 1916	Remarks and references to Appendices
Trenches	1		The day was marked by aeroplane activity on both sides. Bombs were dropped near Bn. H.Q. and also a few H.E. shrapnel but no damage was done. 68s & 69.s were shelled between 11.30 & 12 noon by light Field guns.	
	2.		Machine & Lewis guns had an organised shoot at about midnight firing 500 rounds per gun at enemy wire and parapets. One or two delays were caused by jams but on the whole the shoot was successful and produced little retaliation Casualty by day 1 O.R. wounded.	
	3.		at 1p.m the brigade on our right had a shoot with guns and machine guns. This produced considerable retaliation a little of which was in our area. H.E. burst in CHARDS FARM and light Field guns over 67s & LILLE POST. Casualties 3 O.R. wounded	
	4.		A quiet day. In the evening the 7th LINCOLNSHIRES relieved the battalion which marched back to billets in Armentières Relief complete at 8.30 p.m. Casualties during tour 4 O.R. wounded	

GPP

1875 Wt. W593/826 1,000,000 4/15 J.B.C. & A. A.D.S.S./Forms/C. 2118.

Instructions regarding War Diaries and Intelligence Summaries are contained in F. S. Regs., Part II. and the Staff Manual respectively. Title Pages will be prepared in manuscript.

WAR DIARY
or
~~INTELLIGENCE SUMMARY~~
(Erase heading not required.)

Army Form C. 2118

10th SHERWOOD FORESTERS

Place	Date	Hour	Summary of Events and Information Refce Maps Sheet 36 1/40.000 WEZ MACQUART 1/10.000 APRIL 1916	Remarks and references to Appendices
Armentières	5 -12		Period spent in rest billets in ARMENTIERES Working parties of two companies were sent out nightly to work on the C.T.s and support line	
	8.		Reinforcement 2/Lt. W.J.P. Mc COMBE joined the battalion	
	6		1 O.R. wounded.	
	9		1 O.R. wounded	
	10		1 O.R. wounded.	
	12		1 O.R. wounded: man wounded on 6th died of wounds Battalion relieved 7th Lincolnshires in the trenches A Coy on right, C Coy in left: B Coy in LILLE POST, D Coy SQUARE FARM Relief worked smoothly both battalions knowing the line	
	13.		A fairly quiet day with no casualties.	
	14		A little hostile shelling with practically no damage done 2 O.R. wounded reinforcements 19 O.R. joined battalion	
	15.		A quiet day An aeroplane was heard over our lines at 10.42 p.m making for Armentieres. It returned about 10.55 p.m and exchanged signals with enemy lines.	
	16.		Enemy rifle grenade wounded 7 O.R including 1 slightly at duty & 2 who subsequently died of wounds. There was also some shelling between 8.30 & 8.40 a.m and between 5.50 and 6 p.m G.J.P.	

1875 Wt. W593/826 1,000,000 4/15 J.B.C. & A. A.D.S.S./Forms/C. 2118.

Instructions regarding War Diaries and Intelligence Summaries are contained in F. S. Regs., Part II. and the Staff Manual respectively. Title Pages will be prepared in manuscript.

WAR DIARY
or
~~INTELLIGENCE~~ SUMMARY
(Erase heading not required.)

Army Form C. 2118

10th SHERWOOD FORESTERS

Place	Date	Hour	Refce Maps. Sheet 36. 1/40.000 WEZ MACQUART. 1/10.000 — Summary of Events and Information — APRIL 1916	Remarks and references to Appendices
Trenches	16.		Inter company relief was carried out & dispositions taken up as follows. B Coy right front. D Coy left front, A Coy LILLE POST and C. Coy left subsidiary line.	
	17.		Reinforcements 8 O.R. arrived	
	17–20		Quiet days with practically no shelling and with no casualties. Aeroplane activity was apparent on the latter of these days	
Armentières	20.		Battalion was relieved by 7th Lincolnshire Regt and marched back to billets in Armentières. Relief complete at 8.45 p.m	
	22		Reinforcement 2/Lt. R.C WILMOT rejoined the battalion	
	21 – 26		Remained in rest billets in Armentières sending out usual working parties of two companies nightly. No casualties.	
	26		During the afternoon an organised bombardment of the enemy lines was carried out and produced considerable retaliation. In the evening the battalion carried out a practice reinforcement of the subsidiary line across the open. This was successfully carried out without casualty. The working parties remained in the line	

[initials]

Instructions regarding War Diaries and Intelligence Summaries are contained in F. S. Regs., Part II. and the Staff Manual respectively. Title Pages will be prepared in manuscript.

WAR DIARY
or
~~INTELLIGENCE SUMMARY~~
(Erase heading not required.)

10th SHERWOOD FORESTERS

Army Form C. 2118

Place	Date	Hour	Summary of Events and Information Refce Maps Sheet 36. 1/40.000 WEZ MACQUART 1/10.000 APRIL 1916	Remarks and references to Appendices
	27		A quiet day with working parties as usual In evening there was a gas alarm which appeared subsequently to have been unfounded. Australians on right were very active.	
	28		Relieved 7th LINCOLNSHIRE REGT in trenches: A Coy on right, C Coy on left, B Coy in LILLE POST, D Coy at Square Farm. Relief complete at 8.40 pm. A quiet night with no casualties.	
	29		A quiet day with an occasional shell bursting in the area. In evening LILLE POST and right subsidiary line was taken over by 28th Battalion Australian I.F. relief complete at 8.40 pm. B Coy took over part of subsidiary line from new boundary north of LEITH WALK as far as LOTHIAN AVENUE. Casualties in the evening. 2/Lt. T.A.S. NICHOLLS, 2/Lt. S.C. DAY both slightly wounded at duty. 1 O.R. wounded. At 11.45 pm. a telegram was received stating that an attack was expected to the North and might spread to our front. At 1.40 ~~pm~~ a.m. a second telegram was received saying that a gas attack had been delivered on 5th Corps front.	GJP

1875 Wt. W593/826 1,000,000 4/15 J.B.C. & A. A.D.S.S./Forms/C. 2118.

Army Form C. 2118

Instructions regarding War Diaries and Intelligence Summaries are contained in F. S. Regs., Part II. and the Staff Manual respectively. Title Pages will be prepared in manuscript.

WAR DIARY

or

~~INTELLIGENCE~~ SUMMARY

(Erase heading not required.)

10th SHERWOOD FORESTERS

APRIL 1916.

Place	Date	Hour	Summary of Events and Information Refce Maps. Sheet 36. 1/40.000 QUEZ MACQUART. 1/10.000	Remarks and references to Appendices
	30th		a quiet morning with no casualties. Reinforcements 3 O.R. joined from hospital during the week. Casualties during the month. 2/Lt. T.A.S. NICHOLLS & 2/Lt S.C. DAY wounded slightly at duty. O.R. wounded ~~16~~ 15 includes 1 slightly at duty died of wounds 3 OR. GJP	

1875 Wt. W593/826 1,000,000 4/15 J.B.C. & A. A.D.S.S./Forms/C. 2118.

Army Form C. 2118

XVII

Instructions regarding War Diaries and Intelligence Summaries are contained in F. S. Regs., Part II. and the Staff Manual respectively. Title Pages will be prepared in manuscript.

WAR DIARY
or
~~INTELLIGENCE~~ SUMMARY
(Erase heading not required.)

10th SHERWOOD FORESTERS Vol 9

Place	Date	Hour	Refce Maps 1/40000 Sheet 36 Hazebrouck 5A.9 1/20000 Sheet 27A SE — Summary of Events and Information — MAY 1916	Remarks and references to Appendices
	Ap. 30th		On the night 30th/1st May, A Coy in CHARDS FARM locality was relieved by a company of 7th Australian Bde and on completion of relief took over the MUSHROOM locality from 7th BORDER REGT, one platoon occupying FIVE DUG OUTS.	Min Brown (2)
			Both reliefs were carried out without any hitch and were complete by 9.15 p.m.	
			At 11 p.m. a telegram was received reporting gas attack N. of PLOEGSTEERT but an hour later a second telegram reported "false alarm".	
			Reinforcements 33 O.R. joined battalion	
			Instructions were received that during tour in trenches very high pressure was to be brought on to troops to deal with the enormous amount of work needed on the line	
MAY	1st.		Marked by moderate artillery activity on the part of the enemy who shelled LOTHIAN AVENUE, close support trenches and support line. No casualties were, however, sustained	L 10
			At night 1 O.R was killed while out on a wiring party. The corpse was successful brought in	GJP

1875 Wt. W593/826 1,000,000 4/15 J.B.C. & A. A.D.S.S./Forms/C. 2118.

Instructions regarding War Diaries and Intelligence Summaries are contained in F. S. Regs., Part II. and the Staff Manual respectively. Title Pages will be prepared in manuscript.

WAR DIARY
or
~~INTELLIGENCE SUMMARY~~
(Erase heading not required.)

Army Form C. 2118

10th SHERWOOD FORESTERS

Place	Date	Hour	Summary of Events and Information	Remarks and references to Appendices
			Refce. Maps 1/40000 Sheet 36 Hazebrouck 5A & 1/20000 Sheet 27A SE. MAY 1916	
	2nd		There was considerable enemy artillery activity CHAPPELLE D'ARMENTIERES being shelled from 9.30 a.m to 11 a.m at intervals with H.E. and again at 12.10 p.m (for ten minutes) Otherwise a quiet day.	
	3rd		Marked by heavy shelling with Shrapnel and H.E on support line and LOTHIAN AVENUE from 11 a.m to 12.30 p.m also about 20 small H.E shrapnel on MUSHROOM LOCALITY. Casualties 1 O.R killed 5 O.R. wounded includes 1 slightly at duty.	
	4th		A quiet day freed from incident	
	5th		A little shelling both on front and support line early in the day. Casualties 1 O.R killed on wiring party & 2 O.R. wounded includes 1 slightly at duty by hostile shelling. In the afternoon there was very heavy shelling away on our left for about an hour. At 7.30 p.m. a gas alarm was taken up from the South, & gongs sounded. As soon as it was ascertained	

GPP

1875 Wt. W593/826 1,000,000 4/15 J.B.C. & A. A.D.S.S./Forms/C. 2118.

Army Form C. 2118

WAR DIARY
or
~~INTELLIGENCE SUMMARY~~
(Erase heading not required.)

Instructions regarding War Diaries and Intelligence Summaries are contained in F. S. Regs., Part II. and the Staff Manual respectively. Title Pages will be prepared in manuscript.

10th SHERWOOD FORESTERS

Refer Maps 1/40000 Sheet 36 Hazebrouck 5A & 1/20000 Sheet 27 A.S.E.

MAY 1916

Place	Date	Hour	Summary of Events and Information	Remarks and references to Appendices
	5th		that there was no gas on our front, helmets were taken off and work was resumed in its normal course.	
			1 O.R was wounded slightly at duty.	
	6th.		A quiet day.	
			In the evening the battalion was relieved by 7th Lincolnshire Regt. and marched back to billets in ARMENTIERES.	
			Relief was complete at 9.40 pm.	
	7th –13th		In billets at ARMENTIERES.	
			Working parties of 2 coys were sent out for first three nights but afterwards reduced to 2 platoons for one night and then cancelled altogether.	
			Small marches were carried out to harden the mens feet for the march to R Training area.	
			at 11.30 pm on night 13th/14th the battalion marched into billets at ESTAIRES arriving ~~at~~ into billets at 4 a.m.	
	14th		A short rest at ESTAIRES & battalion marched with 7th BORDER REGT to a camp between HAZEBROUCK and MORBECQUE arriving in camp at 7.30 pm	

GJP.

1875 Wt. W593/826 1,000,000 4/15 J.B.C. & A. A.D.S.S./Forms/C. 2118.

Army Form C. 2118

Instructions regarding War Diaries and Intelligence Summaries are contained in F. S. Regs., Part II. and the Staff Manual respectively. Title Pages will be prepared in manuscript.

WAR DIARY
or
INTELLIGENCE SUMMARY

(Erase heading not required.) 10th SHERWOOD FORESTERS

Place	Date	Hour	Summary of Events and Information — Refce Maps Hazebrouck 5A 1/100000 and 1/20000 Sheet 27A S.E. — MAY 1916	Remarks and references to Appendices
	15th		Remained in Camp at MORBECQUE waiting for remainder of the Brigade who were a day behind.	
	16th		Moved off at 10 a.m to billets at COMPAGNE – brigade HQ being at WARDRECQUES, arriving in billets at 3.50 p.m.	
	17th		Marched into Training Area at HOULLE: march started at 9.30 a.m. and arrived in billets at 2.45 pm	
	18th		Rest and baths for men who were quite tired after their long march with heavy kit. CAPT. A.H PRATT accidentally hurt on Staff ride but remained at duty	
	19th		Intensive training commenced	
	21st		1 O.R. accidentally wounded by revolver	
	27th		358 O.R. & 6 officers inoculated by new serum	
	30th		Divisional Day	
	31st		Report received 1 O.R. died of wounds reported wounded on 3rd Casualties during the month 4 O.R. killed or died of wounds 8 O.R. wounded includes 3 slightly at duty and 1 accidentally. A quiet month.	

G.P. [initials in circle]

1875 Wt. W593/826 1,000,000 4/15 J.B.C. & A. A.D.S.S./Forms/C. 2118.

XVII

10th Notts & Derbys

Army Form C. 2118

Vol 10

Instructions regarding War Diaries and Intelligence Summaries are contained in F. S. Regs., Part II. and the Staff Manual respectively. Title Pages will be prepared in manuscript.

WAR DIARY
or
~~INTELLIGENCE SUMMARY~~

(Erase heading not required.) 10th SHERWOOD FORESTERS

Place	Date	Hour	Refce Maps Hazebrouck 5A 1/100.000 Amiens 17 1/100.000 — Summary of Events and Information — JUNE 1916	Remarks and references to Appendices
HOULLE	1st to 12th		Continued intensive training in vicinity of DIFQUES and INGLINGHEM. Break in weather rendered training more difficult and less continuous. Following reinforcements arrived	
	2nd		29 O.R. a very inferior draft : old and weak.	
	5th		2/Lt. D F. PARR and 2/Lt. J.B. JOYCE joined battalion.	
	12th		Entrained at AUDRUICQ for LONGUEAU	
			Transport and advanced coy. moved off from billets at 4 a.m. remainder of battalion at 6 a.m. reaching AUDRUICQ at 9 a.m where tea was served. Forty minute halt at ABBEVILLE enabled more tea to be served. Arrived LONGUEAU at 7 p.m and reached camp all correct at 9.50 p.m. Camp was entirely new, consisting merely of tents put up by billeting party.	
	14th		A & B Coys sent out in busses for three days cable laying near BOIS DE TAILLES bivouacing in the wood.	
	15th		Reinforcements consisting of CAPT J.W. FISHER. D.S.O. (rejoined), CAPT. J.F.S. CROGGON, 2/Lt R.H.D. BLEAKLEY and 49 O.R. joined battalion Also 4 O.R rejoined from Hospital.	
	17th		Reinforcement 2/Lt H.E. HODDING joined the battalion	
			4 O.R. accidentally wounded ~~while~~ detonating bombs includes 3 slightly at duty	

1875 Wt. W593/826 1,000,000 4/15 J.B.C. & [illegible] D.S.S./Forms/C. 2118.

Army Form C. 2118

Instructions regarding War Diaries and Intelligence Summaries are contained in F. S. Regs., Part II. and the Staff Manual respectively. Title Pages will be prepared in manuscript.

WAR DIARY
or
~~INTELLIGENCE~~ SUMMARY
(Erase heading not required.)

with SHERWOOD FORESTERS

Place	Date	Hour	Summary of Events and Information	Remarks and references to Appendices
			Refce Maps 1/100.000 Amiens 17. 62D. 1/40.000 — JUNE 1916	
	19th		Reinforcements 2/Lt. R.B. LINDSAY and 8 O.R. joined the battalion	
	25th.		Reinforcements 98 O.R. joined battalion	
	26th		Reinforcement 10 O.R. joined battalion. Orders received to strike camp and march to HEILLY on the morning of the 27th. 2 O.R. att R.G.C. wounded.	
	27th		Marched from ALLONVILLE to HEILLY under canvas. Weather fine for striking camp at ALLONVILLE: heavy showers during march: camp at HEILLY very wet and very few tents available. March commenced 9 a.m: arrived in new camp 1.30 pm.	
	#		Two working parties sent out: 1 Officer & 30 O.R. to cut wire in front of third line & to make gaps: 1 Officer & 50 O.R. to unload trucks.	
	28-30		Remained in tents at HEILLY: a very wet and muddy camp, impossible to drain and with very scanty accommodation.	
	30		R.S.M. OLDERSHAW promoted Lt QrMr 11th Labour Battn. Royal Berkshire Regt. left for England.	
			Casualties during month. 6 O.R. wounded: include 4 accidentally 3 of which slightly at duty	

1875 Wt. W593/826 1,000,000 4/15 J.B.C. & A. A.D.S.S./Forms/C. 2118.

51st Inf.Bde.
17th Div.

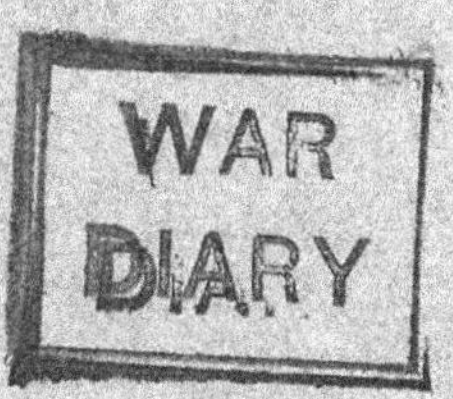

10th BATTN. THE SHERWOOD FORESTERS (NOTTINGHAMSHIRE AND DERBYSHIRE REGIMENT).

J U L Y

1 9 1 6

July Vol 11

Army Form C. 2118.

17/51

Instructions regarding War Diaries and Intelligence Summaries are contained in F. S. Regs., Part II. and the Staff Manual respectively. Title Pages will be prepared in manuscript.

WAR DIARY
or
~~INTELLIGENCE~~ SUMMARY
(Erase heading not required.)

10th SHERWOOD FORESTERS

Place	Date	Hour	Refer Maps Montauban [illegible] 62D. [illegible] — Summary of Events and Information — JULY. 1916	Remarks and references to Appendices
	June 30th		The billets marched to billets at MORLANCOURT leaving camp at HEILLY at 10 p.m and arriving in billets at 2.30 a.m on the morning of the 1st JULY.	
JULY	1st		Gun fire tea 5 a.m after which tools, S.A.A bombs etc to be carried under Table A were drawn from Divisional Dump near Crucifix at K4 d. Breakfasts 9 a.m on completion of which battalion stood by for orders to move. These orders were received at 4.00 p.m and the battalion marched to the dump at S.W. corner of BECOURT WOOD to pick up bombs and water, leaving prison guard company, transport etc at MORLANCOURT After picking up these stores MAJOR T. HALL BROWN with battalion bombers A and D Coys moved off to BECOURT VILLAGE and the remainder of the battalion to BONTE REDOUBT, arriving at about 5.30 a.m. for a short rest in the trench.	
	2nd		The original plans were for A & D Coys to move in support of the 7th Lincolnshires and 8th S. STAFFS in an attack on FRICOURT which had resisted all efforts to capture it on the previous day. Information was, however, received from patrols that the enemy had retired from the village and a later order was received to pass through FRICOURT, make good FRICOURT WOOD, and capture RAILWAY ALLEY from BOTTOM ALLEY inclusive to LOZENGE WOOD exclusive. Order of battle: 7th Lincolns on right, 8th S. Staffs on left, with the 10th Sherwood Foresters in support. B & C Coys were sent forward as right support, A & D Coys as left support	

1875 Wt. W593/826 1,000,000 4/15 J.B.C. & A. A.D.S.S./Forms/C. 2118.

Instructions regarding War Diaries and Intelligence Summaries are contained in F. S. Regs., Part II. and the Staff Manual respectively. Title Pages will be prepared in manuscript.

WAR DIARY
or
~~INTELLIGENCE SUMMARY~~

(Erase heading not required.)

Army Form C. 2118

10th SHERWOOD FORESTERS

Place	Date	Hour	Summary of Events and Information — Refce Map MONTAUBAN 1/20,000 — JULY 1916	Remarks and references to Appendices
	July 2nd		The advance began at 12 noon, but with the left of B.C. Coys on the line WELL LANE – RED LANE and remainder of battalion in vicinity of KONIG ~~TRENCH~~ SUPPORT the advance was held up. No definite information could be obtained as to the cause of the delay from troops in the front line and communication with Bde HQ at F8a.5.3 was a matter of difficulty.	
			The advance was eventually pushed on through FRICOURT WOOD as far as the line of its Northern edge at about 5 p.m. At this point the advance was again held up, RAILWAY ALLEY being strongly held and the wire uncut. On the left the advance was more successful and LOZENGE ALLEY from FRICOURT FARM exclusive was in the hands of the S. STAFFS.	
			On the night 2nd/3rd July A Coy were sent forward to make a bombing attack along trench leading from FRICOURT FARM Eastwards. The attack commenced at 11.30 p.m and with the help of the battalion bombers 170 yds. of this trench was captured. At this point a stop held up the advance; accordingly a stop was built and the position gained consolidated. The wire on the S of the trench was cut away in gaps to enable troops to pass through from direction of FRICOURT WOOD. At the same time D Coy sent forward a bombing attack up the C.T. from FRICOURT WOOD to RAILWAY ALLEY to the East of FRICOURT FARM, and gained some 200 yds of this trench.	
	July 3rd		This latter attack was continued in the morning and the whole of this C.T. was made good	

1875 Wt. W593/826 1,000,000 4/15 J.B.C. & A. A.D.S.S./Forms/C. 2118.

Army Form C. 2118

Instructions regarding War Diaries and Intelligence Summaries are contained in F. S. Regs., Part II. and the Staff Manual respectively. Title Pages will be prepared in manuscript.

WAR DIARY
or
INTELLIGENCE SUMMARY
(Erase heading not required.)

10th SHERWOOD FORESTERS

Place	Date	Hour	Summary of Events and Information (Refce Map MONTAUBAN 1/20000) JULY 1916	Remarks and references to Appendices
	July 3rd		A section of STOKES GUNS assisted in these attacks and two guns were installed in the C.T. to bring enfilade fire on RAILWAY ALLEY.	
			On the morning of the 2nd orders for an attack on RAILWAY ALLEY at 9 a.m were received: 7th BORDER REGT to attack with 7th LINCOLNS in Support and 10th SHERWOOD FORESTERS in Reserve.	
			The attacking troops were late in arriving and the result was only a partial success the right flank pushing through RAILWAY ALLEY and penetrating BOTTOM WOOD. The bombers of A Coy 10th SHERWOOD FORESTERS assisted the attack by bombing down the trench from the West and the line from X 28 c 8.6 to FRICOURT FARM inclusive on the left was made good.	
			A further attack was ordered at noon by C & D companies of the SHERWOOD FORESTERS. B Coy were disposed as under: 1 Platoon in WILLOW TRENCH and remainder of company at N.E. corner of FRICOURT WOOD building a strong point there. From these three platoons 1½ platoons had been sent forward as reinforcement to 7th BORDER REGT. A Coy was holding the line from X 28 c 8.6 to FRICOURT FARM inclusive.	
			Immediately before D Coy had withdrawn into position along the edge of the wood the 7th LINCOLNS who had held up their attack decided to push forward. The result was that the right attack consisting of 7th LINCOLNS and C Coy pushed on before the left attack by D Coy was ready. This company advanced some 15 minutes later.	

1875 Wt. W593/826 1,000,000 4/15 J.B.C. & A. A.D.S.S./Forms/C. 2118.

Instructions regarding War Diaries and Intelligence Summaries are contained in F. S. Regs., Part II. and the Staff Manual respectively. Title Pages will be prepared in manuscript.

WAR DIARY
or
~~INTELLIGENCE~~ SUMMARY
(Erase heading not required.)

Army Form C. 2118

10th SHERWOOD FORESTERS

Place	Date	Hour	Summary of Events and Information	Remarks and references to Appendices
			Refce Map MONTAUBAN 1/20,000 — JULY 1916	
	July 3rd		The attack, however, was in every way successful and the casualties comparatively slight. Meanwhile A Coy on the left brought heavy fire to bear on the trench 200 yds N.E. of FRICOURT FARM and on CRUCIFIX TRENCH. The garrison of the former of these trenches soon shewed the white flag and surrendered, and our troops pushed on to CRUCIFIX TRENCH, and occupied it. A mixed bombing squad was pushed down the C.T. leading from this trench and the result was the surrender of an entire battalion — the 3rd Batth. 186th Regt. — including the commanding officer. A small patrol pushed forward, found RAILWAY COPSE unoccupied.	
			At 7 p.m. orders were received to take up the line of the hedge from the N.W. corner of BOTTOM WOOD to N.E. corner of SHELTER WOOD; SHERWOOD FORESTERS on the right, S. STAFFS on the left, an approximate frontage of 400 yds each. The companies were disposed as follows: B Coy on right, D Coy on left; A Coy in Support and C Coy in reserve on the reverse slope of the hill. 7th Division were on the right. Bn. H.Q. established in a dugout in RAILWAY COPSE.	
			The night was spent in consolidating and patrol work, the latter considerably hampered by a sniper and a Machine Gun neither of which could be definitely located.	G.J.P.

1875 Wt. W593/826 1,000,000 4/15 J.B.C. & A. A.D.S.S./Forms/C. 2118.

Army Form C. 2118

Instructions regarding War Diaries and Intelligence Summaries are contained in F. S. Regs., Part II. and the Staff Manual respectively. Title Pages will be prepared in manuscript.

WAR DIARY
or
INTELLIGENCE SUMMARY
(Erase heading not required.)

10th SHERWOOD FORESTERS

Refer Map MONTAUBAN 1/20,000 Sheet 62D 1/40000 — JULY 1916

Place	Date	Hour	Summary of Events and Information	Remarks and references to Appendices
	July 4th		Rain seriously interfered with work during the afternoon of the 4th and guns shooting over N.W. corner of BOTTOM WOOD were hitting our forward line which was withdrawn to the line of the hedge. The movement of the enemy pointed to a counterattack but this did not materialise - due in all probability to British Field Guns which kept up a steady and effective fire on QUADRANGLE TRENCH. Our troops were anxious to capture that trench but orders were received for a relief by 52nd Bde. who had been given that task. This relief was carried out in pitch darkness and was complete at 12.30 a.m. the attack being timed to start at 12.45 a.m. On relief the companies marched independently to camp at VILLE marching from battle positions during a heavy bombardment by our guns on QUADRANGLE TRENCH. The following booty was captured during these operations. 2 Field Guns, 4 Machine Guns with 9 spare barrels, 1 artillery periscope, numerous rifles bayonets and other equipment including 25000 rounds SAA many maps and documents. Casualties: Lieut. A.E. SPENCER Killed 2nd; CAPT. E.R. OAKDEN, 2/Lt. A.G. BOWRING, 2/Lt. J.W. DAVIDSON (attd. 51 T.M. Batty) wounded 2nd. LIEUT. W.H.V. NELSON wounded slightly at duty 2nd. 2/Lt. J.H. IDESON wounded 3rd. O.R. Killed 13 Missing 8 Wounded 103 includes 11 slightly at duty	

1875 Wt. W593/826 1,000,000 4/15 J.B.C. & A. A.D.S.S./Forms/C. 2118.

Army Form C. 2118

Instructions regarding War Diaries and Intelligence Summaries are contained in F. S. Regs., Part II. and the Staff Manual respectively. Title Pages will be prepared in manuscript.

WAR DIARY
or
~~INTELLIGENCE SUMMARY~~
(Erase heading not required.)

10th SHERWOOD FORESTERS

Place	Date	Hour	Summary of Events and Information	Remarks and references to Appendices
			Refce Maps. 62D 1/40.000 MONTAUBAN 1/20.000 — JULY 1916	
	July 5th		The battalion arrived at CAMP at VILLE from 2am till 4am had tea and a sleep. Baths were available at the MILL and each man obtained a clean set of underclothes. Day spent reorganising and reequipping as far as possible.	
	6th		Remained in camp. Orders to be ready to move at a moments notice were received at 10.30 a.m., but further information was received later that no movement was to be made that day. Major G.D. Walker & Lieut R.G. Milward were sent forward in the afternoon for reconnaissance work but both these officers were unfortunately wounded. In the evening preliminary orders were received to be ready to move up at half an hours notice from 6 a.m the following morning.	
	7th		At 4 a.m orders were received to be in position on line of original British Front Line trench by 9 a.m with right of battalion resting on cross roads F9a 5.3. Tools, Lewis Guns, Signallers kit and M.O. Stores were sent on in advance and dumped at these cross roads. The battalion moved off from camp at 6.30 a.m. and was in position as ordered by 9 a.m A & D Coys in front line, B & C Coys in support BORDER REGT. on the right. On arrival a message was received that a preliminary attack on QUADRANGLE SUPPORT undertaken by 52nd Bde had failed and that attack was being renewed at 8 a.m	

1875 Wt. W593/826 1,000,000 4/15 J.B.C. & A. A.D.S.S./Forms/C. 2118.

Instructions regarding War Diaries and Intelligence Summaries are contained in F. S. Regs., Part II. and the Staff Manual respectively. Title Pages will be prepared in manuscript.

WAR DIARY
or
INTELLIGENCE SUMMARY

(Erase heading not required.)

Army Form C. 2118

10th SHERWOOD FORESTERS

Place	Date	Hour	Summary of Events and Information	Remarks and references to Appendices
			Refce Map. MONTAUBAN 1/20000 — JULY 1916	
	July 7th		At 9.30 a.m. an order was received to move to neighbourhood of LONELY COPSE. These new dispositions were taken up by 10.35 a.m. the battalion being in old disused trenches near WELL LANE and LONELY TRENCH. Bn. HQ established at F3 b. 2.6.	
			At 11.20 a.m. the following message was received: "You are to move forward into QUADRANGLE TRENCH with a view to relieving 52nd I.B. AAA On no account commit yourself to an attack without orders AAA Report your new position by bearer ...."	
			At this time there was a certain amount of shelling along the RAILWAY ALLEY – LONELY COPSE and the rain had begun to fall.	
			Accordingly companies were sent forward independently with orders to reorganise in valley S.W. of hedge between BOTTOM WOOD and SHELTER WOOD. On arrival at this point C & D Coys were sent forward to QUADRANGLE TRENCH, A & B Coys were retained near Bn HQ which was established in a shell hole at X28d 3.3 by 12.15 p.m.	
			The following situation report was dispatched at 12.20 p.m.	
			"C & D Coys in QUADRANGLE TRENCH where there are also representatives of three battalions of 52nd Bde AAA Trench seems crowded AAA A & B Coys SHERWOOD FORESTERS in support near Bn HQ AAA Portions 52nd Bde also in dugouts in C.T. from RAILWAY ALLEY to CRUCIFIX TRENCH AAA O.C. MANCHESTERS passed by me 20 minutes ago stating he had orders to organise details of 52nd Bde in QUADRANGLE TRENCH for fresh attack on QUADRANGLE SUPPORT AAA My Adjutant [illegible]	

1875 Wt. W593/826 1,000,000 4/15 J.B.C. & A. A.D.S.S./Forms/C. 2118.

Army Form C. 2118

Instructions regarding War Diaries and Intelligence Summaries are contained in F. S. Regs., Part II. and the Staff Manual respectively. Title Pages will be prepared in manuscript.

WAR DIARY
or
INTELLIGENCE SUMMARY

(Erase heading not required.) 10th SHERWOOD FORESTERS

Place	Date	Hour	Summary of Events and Information — Refce Map MONTAUBAN 1/20 000 — JULY 1916	Remarks and references to Appendices
	July 7th		"informed in QUADRANGLE TRENCH by an officer of 52nd Bde that QUADRANGLE SUPPORT was in our hands AAA not yet verified statement AAA barrage heavy in vicinity of RAILWAY COPSE to the North"	
			The shelling in the valley became more intense and several casualties both to officers and men were incurred: A & B Companies were therefore moved to the right in shell holes and trenches near BOTTOM WOOD	
			At 5 p.m orders were received to relieve all units of 52nd Bde in QUADRANGLE TRENCH, to clear up situation in PEARL ALLEY and to prepare for an attack on QUADRANGLE SUPPORT, details to be notified later	
			During the shelling 4 Lewis Guns were either buried or destroyed but subsequently two of these were recovered	
			A patrol sent to clear up situation in PEARL ALLEY found this trench not in our hands: further Quadrangle Trench from the point where it bends Northwards was little more than a ditch and in full view of CONTALMAISON (still in the enemy's hands) and sniping was active. A bombing squad was however sent down this trench and made PEARL ALLEY good almost as far as the CEMETERY	
			By this time Bn HQ had been reestablished in dugout in RAILWAY COPSE and the rain had stopped. The ground, however, was very heavy and extremely difficult to move over	

1875 Wt. W593/826 1,000,000 4/15 J.B.C. & A. A.D.S.S./Forms/C. 2118.

Instructions regarding War Diaries and Intelligence Summaries are contained in F. S. Regs., Part II. and the Staff Manual respectively. Title Pages will be prepared in manuscript.

WAR DIARY
or
INTELLIGENCE SUMMARY

(Erase heading not required.)

Army Form C. 2118

Place	Date	Hour	Summary of Events and Information Refce Map MONTAUBAN 1/20,000 — JULY 1916	Remarks and references to Appendices
	July 7th		At 6.45 p.m. orders were received to attack QUADRANGLE SUPPORT at 8 p.m. after 30 minutes bombardment. An attack on CONTALMAISON was also to be delivered by 3rd Corps on the left at the same time. This latter attack was not launched. The time allowed for the organisation of the attack was not sufficient and consequently the necessary advantage could not be taken of the bombardment, and the attack was lagged. The attack was launched but Machine Gun Fire from both flanks, rifle and Machine Gun Fire from the objective and an enemy barrage prevented the troops from advancing over the heavy ground, and a withdrawal was ordered, and carried out in excellent style. The men were wet through and cold. The ground was extremely heavy and both flanks were in the air. At about 9 p.m. orders were received that the 7th BORDER REGT were to relieve the battalion and on relief the battalion to proceed to area WILLOW TRENCH and RED COTTAGE. This relief was a difficult matter and it was not till 2 a.m. that the relief was complete. A, C & D Coys took up positions near FRICOURT TRENCH and B Coy in LONELY TRENCH. Bn HQ under the crucifix at F3b central	

1875 Wt. W593/826 1,000,000 4/15 J.B.C. & A. A.D.S.S./Forms/C. 2118.

Instructions regarding War Diaries and Intelligence Summaries are contained in F. S. Regs., Part II. and the Staff Manual respectively. Title Pages will be prepared in manuscript.

WAR DIARY
or
~~INTELLIGENCE SUMMARY~~
(Erase heading not required.)

10th SHERWOOD FORESTERS

Army Form C. 2118

Place	Date	Hour	Summary of Events and Information	Remarks and references to Appendices
			Refce Map MONTAUBAN 1/20 000 JULY 1916	
	July 8th	3am	Rations, including an issue of Rum were fortunately available and the troops were enabled to have a meal and sleep.	
			A quiet day as far as the battalion was concerned remaining at rest in positions taken up in the early morning	
	July 9th		Remained in same positions	
			An order was received at 10.15 a.m to stand by from 12 noon to relieve a battalion in the front line. No further news being received the battalion stood down at 1p.m. Again at 5.30p.m. an order was received "Be prepared to move up to the line of hedge at short notice after 9p.m"	
			From this time the battalion was ordered to provide carrying parties to the front line – bombs, Very lights, S.A.A. &c and 64 men to carry rations for S.STAFFS.	
			At 8.35p.m following order was received "Two companies are required to take over line from S.STAFFS tonight AAA please send an officer per company to report to H.Q. S STAFFS at 10.30p.m tonight the companies to follow fifteen minutes behind AAA COL. BARKER will give the officers instructions as to where he wishes the companies to go" A & D Coys were sent up for this work, moving off at 10p.m.	
	July 10th		At 2a.m a sudden order was received to send up remainder of battalion with as much S.A.A as could be carried: officers to be sent on ahead for instructions for COL BARKER as before.	

1875 Wt. W593/826 1,000,000 4/15 J.B.C. & A. A.D.S.S./Forms/C. 2118.

Instructions regarding War Diaries and Intelligence Summaries are contained in F. S. Regs., Part II. and the Staff Manual respectively. Title Pages will be prepared in manuscript.

WAR DIARY
or
INTELLIGENCE SUMMARY

(Erase heading not required.) 10th SHERWOOD FORESTERS

Army Form C. 2118

Place	Date	Hour	Summary of Events and Information (Refce Map MONTAUBAN 1/20.000) JULY 1916	Remarks and references to Appendices
	July 10th		The companies were immediately stripped out, drew bombs & S.A.A. from the dump near LONELY COPSE and went up to reinforce. Meanwhile A & D Coys had been ordered to occupy QUADRANGLE TRENCH during the S STAFFS attack on QUADRANGLE SUPPORT.	
			On arrival at RAILWAY ALLEY, B & C Coys were also ordered to proceed to QUADRANGLE ~~[illegible]~~ TRENCH and also the battalion bombers. Bn H.Q. was shared with 8th S STAFFS in dugout in RAILWAY COPSE	
			The attack of the S.STAFFS was at first successful but their flanks were left in the air and they were compelled to withdraw after holding QUADRANGLE SUPPORT for over three hours	
			~~Bef~~ By dawn the whole of the S.STAFFS REGT had been withdrawn and QUADRANGLE TRENCH taken over by SHERWOOD FORESTERS in the centre with 7th LINCOLNSHIRES with three companies holding part of [illegible] and the left of QUADRANGLE TRENCH and one company holding the extreme right of that trench	
			An advance on MAMETZ WOOD was observed on the right and patrols were pushed forward to see if this advance would cause the defenders of QUADRANGLE SUPPORT to retire This did not prove to be the case and the patrol was fired on and the trench found well occupied.	
			At 4.40 p.m. orders were received that the brigade was being relieved by 110th Bde and that positions to be taken up would be notified later	

1875 Wt. W593/826 1,000,000 4/15 J.B.C. & A. A.D.S.S./Forms/C. 2118.

Army Form C. 2118

WAR DIARY
or
INTELLIGENCE SUMMARY

(Erase heading not required.)

Instructions regarding War Diaries and Intelligence Summaries are contained in F. S. Regs., Part II. and the Staff Manual respectively. Title Pages will be prepared in manuscript.

10th SHERWOOD FORESTERS

Place	Date	Hour	Refer Map MONTAUBAN 1/20.000 — Summary of Events and Information — JULY 1916	Remarks and references to Appendices
	July 10th		These orders were sent up to the companies in the line. At 6.50 p.m. however a message was received that the enemy were retiring from QUADRANGLE SUPPORT under our fire and ordering patrols to be pushed forward into that trench. Shortly after this news was received of the capture of CONTALMAISON and with it an order to push forward and occupy QUADRANGLE SUPPORT in conjunction with the 7th LINCOLNSHIRES. After consulting C.O of that regiment, Lt Col W.E. BANBURY, C.M.G, ordered the attack to be delivered at 9.45 p.m. Lewis Gunners and patrol to be pushed forward to the ridge in front of QUADRANGLE TRENCH at 9.30 p.m. The attack commenced promptly at 9.45 p.m. and two companies of 8 STAFFS immediately occupied the trench left by the assaulting troops, which had been fairly heavily shelled for some time. Bn. Battle HQ was formed in QUADRANGLE TRENCH but telephonic communication to the rear was broken fifteen minutes before a wounded runner brought back the news that QUADRANGLE SUPPORT was captured and that as yet there was no news of the attacks on right and left by 7th LINCOLNS. This information was sent back at 10.30 p.m. the enemy barrage in QUADRANGLE TRENCH and immediately South of it still being heavy. At 11 p.m. information was received that 7th Lincolnshires in the line had received no orders to move forward: they were immediately sent forward to assist in holding the captured trench	

1875 Wt. W593/826 1,000,000 4/15 J.B.C. & A. A.D.S.S./Forms/C. 2118.

Instructions regarding War Diaries and Intelligence Summaries are contained in F. S. Regs., Part II. and the Staff Manual respectively. Title Pages will be prepared in manuscript.

WAR DIARY
or
~~INTELLIGENCE SUMMARY~~

(Erase heading not required.) 10th SHERWOOD FORESTERS

Army Form C. 2118

Place	Date	Hour	Summary of Events and Information Refce Map MONTAUBAN 1/20.000 AMIENS 17 LENS 11 1/100000 JULY 1916	Remarks and references to Appendices
	July 10th		The night passed quietly no indications of counterattack being shewn. The relief by 110th Bde was accordingly carried out and was eventually	
	July 11th		complete at 4 am — a difficult relief The battalion moved to its former trenches ? left on the night of the 9th and rested till 9 a.m when moved off independently for transport lines at MEAULTE with orders to be ready to entrain at 12 noon. A hot meal was obtained there, and the battalion entrained at 2 p.m. for ~~[illegible]~~ AILLY-SUR-SOMME. The train moved off at 3 p.m. and the battalion detrained at SALEUX at 6 p.m. Marching off at 6.20 p.m. battalion arrived in billets at	
	12th		ST. PIERRE-À-GOUY at 1.30 am. after a fourteen mile march. The troops arrived in these billets in an exhausted condition. The Casualties during the second period of the battle were as under. <u>July 7th</u> MAJOR J. HALL BROWN Killed; CAPT. J.W. FISHER D.S.O., CAPT. N.H. PRATT, LIEUT. W.H.V. NELSON wounded 7th, died of wounds 8th; 2/Lt R.J.C. LONGSTAFFE wounded; 2/Lt R.R. JOYCE wounded rejoined 11th; CAPT. J.F.S. CROGGON wounded slightly at duty; 2/Lt D.F. PARR missing. <u>July 6th</u> MAJOR G.D. WALKER wounded; LIEUT R.B. MILWARD wounded 6th rejoined 17th O.R. Killed 19 Missing 41 Wounded 182 of whom 4 died of wounds and 7 slightly at duty.	GJP

1875 Wt. W593/826 1,000,000 4/15 J.B.C. & A. A.D.S.S./Forms/C. 2118.

Instructions regarding War Diaries and Intelligence Summaries are contained in F. S. Regs., Part II. and the Staff Manual respectively. Title Pages will be prepared in manuscript.

WAR DIARY
or
~~INTELLIGENCE~~ SUMMARY
(Erase heading not required.)

Army Form C. 2118

10th SHERWOOD FORESTERS

Place	Date	Hour	Summary of Events and Information	Remarks and references to Appendices
			Refce Map AMIENS 1/100,000 LENS 1/100,000 — JULY 1916	
			Total casualties during the operations 1–11 July	
			15 Officers 366 Other Ranks or roughly 40% of total strength.	
	12th to 13th.		Remained in billets at ST PIERRE à GOUY	
	14th		Marched off at 10 a.m. for billets in vicinity of BOSSUS with 51st M.G. Coy well ahead of remainder of brigade, via PICQUIGNY, LA CHAUSSEE – AILLY-LE-HAUT-CLOCHER where our billeting area was. 1½ hours halt for dinners near FLIXECOURT	
			Arrived billets 4.45 p.m.	
			During stay at AILLY LE HAUT CLOCHER following reinforcements arrived	
	16th		29 O.R. N. STAFFS Regt: MAJOR W.A. McCLELLAND, CAPT C. St.G. WHEELEY, 2/Lt C.F.S. COX, 2/Lt A. BRADBURY	
	17th		CAPT C.J.A. LEFROY, LIEUT R.G. MILWARD (rejoined)	
	18th		20 O.R joined battalion	
			Also 2/Lt. H.N. GREENWOOD, 2/Lt. R.S. GUSTARD	
	19th		99 O.R. joined battalion	
	20th		140 O.R. joined battalion.	
	21st		23 O.R. from S. STAFFS. REGT joined battalion	

1875 Wt. W593/826 1,000,000 4/15 J.B.C. & A. A.D.S.S./Forms/C. 2118.

Instructions regarding War Diaries and Intelligence Summaries are contained in F. S. Regs., Part II. and the Staff Manual respectively. Title Pages will be prepared in manuscript.

WAR DIARY
or
~~INTELLIGENCE SUMMARY~~

(Erase heading not required.)

Army Form C. 2118

10th SHERWOOD FORESTERS

Place	Date	Hour	Summary of Events and Information — Refce Map. AMIENS + LENS 1/100,000, 62D 1/40,000. — JULY 1916	Remarks and references to Appendices
	22nd		All 1st Line Transport less baggage wagons and field cookers marched off at 5.30 a.m. for CARDONNETTE. orders for this move were received at 1 a.m.	
	23rd		Battalion marched to HANGEST station to entrain for MERICOURT. First order was to arrive at station at 1.30 p.m. during march order received to delay 1½ hours. Arrived HANGEST 2 p.m. where tea was obtained. Entrained 8.15 p.m. departed 8.40 p.m.	
			Baggage wagons left by road at 7 a.m.	
	24th		Arrived MERICOURT at midnight and marched to bivouacs at D18.c.	
	24th –31st		Remained in bivouacs a few tents being received on 30th + 29th. During this stay following reinforcements joined battalion.	
	27th		2/Lts. A.W. NEWHOUSE, T. ROSE and R.W. JAMES.	
	28th		2/Lt G.R.Y. THORLOW and 2 O.R. rejoined battalion. Also on 27th 1 O.R. was accidentally wounded detonating bombs.	
	26th		Lt Col. W.E. Banbury C.M.G. having been appointed Brig. General Comdg 61st Inf. Bde. proceeded to take up his duties.	
			Casualties during the month	
			Officers Killed 2 Died of Wounds 3 Missing 1 Wounded 9	x
			O.R. Killed 32 Died of Wounds 4 Missing 49 Wounded 282	+
			x includes 1 slightly at duty + includes 18 slightly at duty, 1 accidentally.	

(GP)

1875 Wt. W593/826 1,000,000 4/15 J.B.C. & A. A.D.S.S./Forms/C. 2118.

51st Brigade

17th Division.

1/10th BATTALION

SHERWOOD FORESTERS

AUGUST 1 9 1 6.:

Confidential

17/51

Vol 12

WAR DIARY

10th SHERWOOD FORESTERS

AUGUST 1916

L 13

Instructions regarding War Diaries and Intelligence Summaries are contained in F. S. Regs., Part II. and the Staff Manual respectively. Title Pages will be prepared in manuscript.

WAR DIARY
or
~~INTELLIGENCE SUMMARY~~
(Erase heading not required.)

Army Form C. 2118

10th SHERWOOD FORESTERS

Place	Date	Hour	Summary of Events and Information Refce Map. MONTAUBAN 1/20.000. 62D. 1/40.000. LENS 1/100.000. AUGUST 1916	Remarks and references to Appendices
	1st.		Orders were received that Bde was to move to bivouac near POMMIERS REDOUBT. Guides were sent on in the morning to take over and meet the battalion which moved off at 6.30 p.m. Only 20 officers were taken forward remainder staying at Bde Depot near ALBERT.	
			Battn arrived in POMMIERS TRENCH completing relief at 10.50 p.m.	
	2nd.		The night of the 1st and morning of the 2nd were spent in picking up stores from Divisional and Brigade Dumps to complete carrying parties with their loads.	
			CAPT. L.D. SAUNDERS, RAMC. having been appointed to an Ambulance Train left the battalion and was replaced by CAPT. T.D. CUMBERLAND RAMC.	
			Some slight shelling in the evening caused 4 O.R. to be wounded none of them seriously.	
	3rd		B Coy were detailed as working party on a forward C.T. CAPT C.St.G. WHEELEY was wounded slightly "at duty."	
			At 10.30 p.m. orders were received to relieve 22nd Royal Fusiliers near MINE TRENCH on the 4th by daylight.	
	4th.		Battalion moved by companies to vicinity of Mine Trench the relief being complete at 5.45 p.m.	
	5th.		Orders were received that the battalion was to relieve the 9th Duke of Wellington's Regt at LONGUEVAL	GJP

1875 Wt. W593/826 1,000,000 4/15 J.B.C. & A. A.D.S.S./Forms/C. 2118.

Instructions regarding War Diaries and Intelligence Summaries are contained in F. S. Regs., Part II. and the Staff Manual respectively. Title Pages will be prepared in manuscript.

WAR DIARY
or
~~INTELLIGENCE SUMMARY~~
(Erase heading not required.)

10th SHERWOOD FORESTERS

Army Form C. 2118

Place	Date	Hour	Summary of Events and Information	Remarks and references to Appendices
			Refce Maps Montauban 1/20 000 Lens 1/100000, 62D. 1/40 000. AUGUST 1916	
	5th.		This relief was a difficult matter but working on an elaborate scheme by O.C Duke of Wellingtons Regt very few casualties were suffered. The relief commenced at 3 p.m and was complete at midnight. two platoons of the relieved regiment were held up in the support line by enemy barrage until nearly 5 a.m.	
	6th.		The line taken over was chiefly a series of shell holes roughly joined up with no connection between front line and supports. Every endeavour was made to improve the line but heavy shelling and the fact that the ground was so broken up made work extremely difficult.	
			Patrols also reported the enemy in posts inside the edge of DELVILLE WOOD to the right front of the right company.	
	7th.		At 1 a.m a message was received informing us that the 7th BORDER REGT on the right were clearing the N.W. edge of the wood & establishing observation posts in the edge of the wood. In conjunction with this the battalion was ordered to push forward an outpost line beyond the edge of the wood by night and observation posts by day.	
			The BORDER REGT were however unsuccessful in their attempt to clear the wood,	

1875 Wt. W593/826 1,000,000 4/15 J.B.C. & A. A.D.S.S./Forms/C. 2118.

Instructions regarding War Diaries and Intelligence Summaries are contained in F. S. Regs., Part II. and the Staff Manual respectively. Title Pages will be prepared in manuscript.

WAR DIARY
or
~~INTELLIGENCE~~ SUMMARY

(Erase heading not required.)

10th SHERWOOD FORESTERS

Army Form C. 2118

Place	Date	Hour	Summary of Events and Information — Refce Maps: Montauban 1/20.000, Sheet 62D 1/40.000, Lens 1/100.000 — AUGUST. 1916	Remarks and references to Appendices
	7th		Orders were received to make an attack on the enemy positions in Delville Wood and establish a line of posts outside the wood. A Coy were detailed to establish 1 post in conjunction with the Border Regt., & 1 post independently — D Coy 2 posts and C Coy 1 post. The attack was launched at 4.30 p.m. but was held up by M.G. and rapid rifle fire. On the left however D & C Coys were able to establish and maintain their posts. Later, orders were received to repeat the attack at midnight. This attack was again unsuccessful nor was the attack by the Border Regt launched at all.	
	8th.		Orders received that Border Regt were again attacking at 3.30 p.m. Coys were ordered to push forward if this attack was successful. This attack was not carried out owing to artillery barrage not being laid down nearer than N.W. edge of wood and not at all on the right. On the 7th 1 Coy of Lincolnshires was brought up into reserve near Church at LONGUEVAL and was used for carrying purposes.	

GJP

1875 Wt. W593/826 1,000,000 4/15 J.B.C. & A. A.D.S.S./Forms/C. 2118.

Army Form C. 2118

WAR DIARY
or
~~INTELLIGENCE SUMMARY~~
(Erase heading not required.)

Instructions regarding War Diaries and Intelligence Summaries are contained in F. S. Regs., Part II. and the Staff Manual respectively. Title Pages will be prepared in manuscript.

10th SHERWOOD FORESTERS

Refce Maps. Montauban 1/20.000 Sheet 62D 1/40.000 Lens 1/100.000

AUGUST 1916

Place	Date	Hour	Summary of Events and Information	Remarks and references to Appendices
	8th		Orders for relief by 7th Lincolnshires were received at 6.35 p.m and guides were immediately sent down to guide up the relieving platoons. Owing to shelling and resulting confusion in the dark the relief was not complete until 7.30 a.m. on the 9th.	
	9th		The battalion took over trenches vacated by 7th Lincolnshires — three Companies in MONTAUBAN ALLEY and one company in a new trench half way between LONGUEVAL and MONTAUBAN	
	10th		MAJOR R.J. MILNE took over command of the battalion (from the 9th DEVONS)	
			The battalion was relieved in the evening by the 12th MANCHESTER REGT. and took over dispositions near Mine Trench vacated on the 5th.	
			Relief by MANCHESTERS was complete at 8.30 p.m. and new dispositions were taken up by 9.25 p.m.	
	11th		Remained near MINE TRENCH.	
	12th		Orders were received at 1.40 a.m that battalion was being relieved at about 9 a.m. and was to move to bivouac at E13c near BOIRE.	
			Relief was complete at 12.30 p.m. and battalion arrived in bivouacs at 5 p.m	GLP

1875 Wt. W593/826 1,000,000 4/15 J.B.C. & A. A.D.S.S./Forms/C. 2118.

Instructions regarding War Diaries and Intelligence Summaries are contained in F. S. Regs., Part II. and the Staff Manual respectively. Title Pages will be prepared in manuscript.

Army Form C. 2118

WAR DIARY
or
~~INTELLIGENCE~~ SUMMARY
(Erase heading not required.)

10th SHERWOOD FORESTERS

Place	Date	Hour	Refer Maps. 62D 1/40 000 Lens 1/100 000 — Summary of Events and Information — AUGUST 1916	Remarks and references to Appendices
			Casualties during the period 4th – 9th August were as follows.	
			Officers: MAJOR W.A. McCLELLAND, 2/Lt W. BRADBURY wounded Shell Shock 7th.	
			2/Lt A.G. DENT wou 6th. 2/Lt. R.A. BARKER, R. GUSTARD, A.W. JAMES wou 7th.	
			Lt. R.G. MILWARD wou slightly at duty 7th.	
			O.R. Killed 38 Died of Wounds 5 Wounded 148 includes 6 slightly at duty Missing 23, five since reported wounded.	
	13th		At 9.15 p.m orders were received that all transport including bicycles but not Lewis Gun handcarts was to be ready to move off at 6.30 a.m on 14th.	
	14th		Transport moved off to vicinity of MOULLIENS AU BOIS	
			Orders received at 8.45 p.m. the battalion was to entrain at MERICOURT at 2.30 p.m to detrain at CANDAS and march to billets at LONGUEVILLETTE on 15th	
	15th		Transport moved by road to LONGUEVILLETTE	
			Battalion left ~~[illegible]~~ bivouac at 12.30 p.m arriving at MERICOURT STATION at 1.45 p.m Train however did not leave until 5.30 p.m and arrived at CANDAS at 12.45 a.m. 16th.	
	16th		Batt. marched to billets at LONGUEVILLETTE arriving at 2 a.m	

GJP

1875 Wt. W593/826 1,000,000 4/15 J.B.C. & A. A.D.S.S./Forms/C. 2118

Instructions regarding War Diaries and Intelligence Summaries are contained in F. S. Regs., Part II. and the Staff Manual respectively. Title Pages will be prepared in manuscript.

WAR DIARY
or
~~INTELLIGENCE SUMMARY~~
(Erase heading not required.)

10th SHERWOOD FORESTERS

Army Form C. 2118

Place	Date	Hour	Summary of Events and Information Refce Maps Lens 1/100.000 57D. 1/40000 AUGUST 1916	Remarks and references to Appendices
	16th.		At 2.20 a.m. a warning order was received that battalion was probably moving to NEUVILLETTE in the afternoon & to send on billeting party	
			Orders confirming these were received at 10 a.m. Head of battalion to be at cross roads S. of HAUTE VISEE at 4 p.m.	
			Battn arrived in billets all correct at 5 p.m.	
	17th -20th		Remained in billets at NEUVILLETTE	
			At 9.30 pm on Aug 18th orders were received to march to St AMAND on the 21st into Divisional Reserve - the head of the column not to arrive before 1 p.m.	
	20th		Billeting officer and party with two cookers moved off at 5 pm and billeted at HUMBERCOURT, moving on early on 21st the cookers taking up a position on high ground SE. of HUMBERCOURT and the billeting party moving on to St AMAND.	
	21st		Battalion moved off at 6.30 a.m. arriving at HUMBERCOURT for breakfast at 9.30 a.m. After 1½ hours halt battalion moved off again arriving at St AMAND at 1.30 p.m. settling down in billets by 2.30 p.m.	
			Reinforcement CAPT. A.A.P.R. STUART joined battalion	

1875 Wt. W593/826 1,000,000 4/15 J.B.C. & A. A.D.S.S./Forms/C. 2118.

Instructions regarding War Diaries and Intelligence Summaries are contained in F. S. Regs., Part II. and the Staff Manual respectively. Title Pages will be prepared in manuscript.

WAR DIARY
or
~~INTELLIGENCE~~ SUMMARY
(Erase heading not required.)

Army Form C. 2118

10th SHERWOOD FORESTERS

Place	Date	Hour	Summary of Events and Information	Remarks and references to Appendices
			Refce. 57D. 1/40.000 Trench Map — AUGUST 1916	
	21st–27th		Remained in Divisional Reserve at ST AMAND. Time was spent in continuing reorganisation of specialists re, reconnoitring the line to be taken up when relieving and the line held by other brigades of the Division.	
	26th		Reinforcements 6 O.R. joined the battalion	
	27th		Relieved 7th Lincolnshire Regt. relief complete at 12.45 pm.	
			Dispositions as follows: front line from right to left	
			D Coy Z54 and Z55 finding own supports	
			B Coy Z56, Z57, Z58 —	
			A Coy Z59, Z60, Z61 —	
			C Coy & Bn Bombers at Snipers Square	
			Bn HQ at FONQUEVILLERS N. of BREWERY	
	28th		News received that ITALY has declared war on GERMANY and ROUMANIA on AUSTRIA.	
	29th		Lieut T.W. DANIEL rejoined battalion and 2/Lt J.F. WORRALL.	
	31st		C & D Coys relieved mutually.	
			Except for a little spasmodic shelling there has been no enemy activity. Wet has interfered with work.	
			Further the gas cylinders in right company's front line trenches	

1875 Wt. W593/826 1,000,000 4/15 J.B.C. & A. A.D.S.S./Forms/C. 2118.

Instructions regarding War Diaries and Intelligence Summaries are contained in F. S. Regs., Part II. and the Staff Manual respectively. Title Pages will be prepared in manuscript.

WAR DIARY
or
~~INTELLIGENCE~~ SUMMARY

(Erase heading not required.) 10th SHERWOOD FORESTERS

Army Form C. 2118

Place	Date	Hour	Refer Map 57D. 1/40.000 Summary of Events and Information AUGUST 1916	Remarks and references to Appendices
			prevent any work being done in the line. Casualties during the month of AUGUST 1 Major 1 Capt. and 6 Subalterns wou. includes CAPT. + 1 Subaltern slightly at duty O.R Killed 38 Died of Wounds 5 Wounded 157 includes 6 slightly at duty Missing 18.	

GP

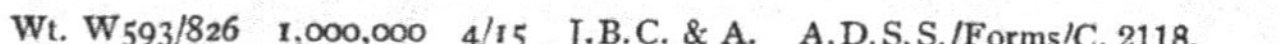

Army Form C. 2118

Instructions regarding War Diaries and Intelligence Summaries are contained in F. S. Regs., Part II. and the Staff Manual respectively. Title Pages will be prepared in manuscript.

~~WAR DIARY~~
or
INTELLIGENCE SUMMARY
(Erase heading not required.)

10th SHERWOOD FORESTERS

Place	Date	Hour	Summary of Events and Information	Remarks and references to Appendices
			Refce Maps 57D 1/40,000. Trench Map Lens 11 1/100.000 — SEPTEMBER 1916	
	1st – 4th		Remained in trenches E. of FONQUEVILLERS. Everything quiet except a little shelling of BASTION, ROBERTS AVENUE and Z 56. on the 3rd	
	3rd		3 O.R. wounded	
	4th.		2/Lt GREENWOOD H.N. detached for duty with 51 T.M. Batty.	
			Battalion was relieved in the afternoon by 7th Lincolnshire Regt. Relief commenced at 3pm. and was complete by 4.30 pm. Three companies moved into Brigade Reserve at BIENVILLERS, one company to dugouts W. of FONQUEVILLERS.	
			A quiet relief with no casualties.	
	4–9th		Remained at BIENVILLERS.	
			The whole battalion was used either by day or night for working parties for 181st Tunnelling Coy R.E. and 77th Fld Coy. R.E.	
	6th.		Relieved company at FONQUE VILLERS	
	7th.		Reinforcement 2/Lt W.R.L. DAVIS joined battalion. This officer was wounded at the BLUFF on Feb. 14th.	
			1 O.R wounded.	

1875 Wt. W593/826 1,000,000 4/15 J.B.C. & A. A.D.S.S./Forms/C. 2118.

Army Form C. 2118

Instructions regarding War Diaries and Intelligence Summaries are contained in F. S. Regs., Part II. and the Staff Manual respectively. Title Pages will be prepared in manuscript.

WAR DIARY
or
~~INTELLIGENCE SUMMARY~~
(Erase heading not required.)

10th SHERWOOD FORESTERS.

Place	Date	Hour	Refce Maps. 57D 1/40.000, Trench Map. Lens 11. 1/100.000. Summary of Events and Information SEPTEMBER 1916	Remarks and references to Appendices
	8th		Relieved company in FONQUEVILLERS.	
	9th		Reinforcements. 2/Lts. T. HUYTON, W.A. EDWARDS joined battalion.	
			Orders received for relief by a battalion of 19th Infy. Bde.	
	10th		Relieved at BIENVILLERS by a battalion of 19th Infy Bde at 4pm. and marched to MONDICOURT. Marched by platoons until clear of SOUASTRE where battalion joined up and resumed march.	
			A Coy were relieved at 6pm. at FONQUEVILLERS and moved independently to MONDICOURT.	
			D Coy and 35 men C Coy remained at BIENVILLERS to carry on working parties until 19th Bde had completed relief.	
	11th		Battalion marched at 2pm. to hutments at HALLOY.	
			D Coy and 35 men C Coy rejoined battalion at HALLOY at 9pm	
	11–17		Remained at HALLOY training over course near HURTEBISE Fm for attack.	
	13th		2/Lt C.C. BAKER and 137 O.R. reinforcements joined battalion.	
			2/Lt J.F. WORRALL left battalion to join 19th Bn., CHESHIRE REGT.	
	15th		Orders received for move to BAYENCOURT on 17th	GP

1875 Wt. W593/826 1,000,000 4/15 J.B.C. & A. A.D.S.S./Forms/C. 2118.

Army Form C. 2118

Instructions regarding War Diaries and Intelligence Summaries are contained in F. S. Regs., Part II. and the Staff Manual respectively. Title Pages will be prepared in manuscript.

WAR DIARY
or
~~INTELLIGENCE SUMMARY~~

(Erase heading not required.) 10th SHERWOOD FORESTERS

Place	Date	Hour	Refce Maps 57D/40000 Lens 11. 1/100.000 — Summary of Events and Information — SEPTEMBER 1916	Remarks and references to Appendices
	16th		Reinforcements 28 O.R. joined battalion. 1 O.R. died in Hospital.	
	17th		Moved from HALLOY at 1.30 p.m. to BAYENCOURT arriving in billets at 4.30 p.m.	
	18th		120 men working all day for 77th Fld Coy R.E. Party of officers and N.C.O.s visited trenches. Everyone wet through owing to heavy rain Evening of 18th 375 O.R. on night working parties 3 O.R. wounded including 2 slightly at duty. Warning order received of relief by battn of 98th Bde. on 19th.	
	19th		Battalion moved off at 4 p.m. for HUMBERCAMPS last party moving off at 4.20 p.m.	
	20th		Battalion moved to HUMBERCOURT moving off at 2 p.m. and arriving at about 4. p.m. Reinforcements 60 O.R. joined battalion	GJP

1875 Wt. W593/826 1,000,000 4/15 J.B.C. & A. A.D.S.S./Forms/C. 2118.

Army Form C. 2118

Instructions regarding War Diaries and Intelligence Summaries are contained in F. S. Regs., Part II. and the Staff Manual respectively. Title Pages will be prepared in manuscript.

~~WAR DIARY~~
or
INTELLIGENCE SUMMARY
(Erase heading not required.)

10th SHERWOOD FORESTERS

Place	Date	Hour	Summary of Events and Information — Refce Map. Lens 11. 1/100 000 — SEPTEMBER 1916	Remarks and references to Appendices
	21st		Remained at HUMBERCOURT.	
	22nd		Marched off at 9 a.m. into billets at DOULLENS arriving at 1 p.m.	
	23rd		Marched off at 9 a.m. into close billets at FROHEN-LE-PETIT arriving at 3.30 p.m. Owing to billets being allotted to two divisions at FROHEN the battalion halted for two hours near MEZEROLLES where dinners were eaten. 1 O.R. accidentally wounded.	
	24th		Marched into training area into billets at CONTEVILLE moving off at 8.45 am, and arriving in billets at 1 p.m. being held up by Cavalry moving North through CONTEVILLE.	
	25th		Battalion inspected by Brig Gen G.F. TROTTER, C.M.G., M.V.O., D.S.O., Comdg 51st Inf Bde.	
	26th - 30th		Remained at CONTEVILLE carrying out training. 2/Lts. EDWARDS, ROSE, CHARLESWORTH joined 2nd Battn on 27th. Casualties during month. Officers NIL O.R. Wounded 7 includes 2 at duty Also 1 O.R. accidentally wounded + 1 died	

1875 Wt. W593/826 1,000,000 4/15 J.B.C. & A. A.D.S.S./Forms/C. 2118.

Mr Thomas.

L 15

Confidential
Vol 14

WAR DIARY

10th

SHERWOOD FORESTERS

October 1916.

Instructions regarding War Diaries and Intelligence Summaries are contained in F. S. Regs., Part II. and the Staff Manual respectively. Title Pages will be prepared in manuscript.

Army Form C. 2118

WAR DIARY
or
~~INTELLIGENCE SUMMARY~~
(Erase heading not required.)

6th Sherwood Foresters

Place	Date	Hour	Summary of Events and Information	Remarks and references to Appendices
			Ref. Map. LENS 11. 1/100 000 OCTOBER 1916.	
CONTEVILLE	1st		Orders were received that battn. would march to billets in MEZEROLLES area.	
	2nd		Battn. marched to billets via AUXI-LE-CHATEAU – WAVANS. The 7th BORDERS were ahead of the battn. One lorry was allotted to the battn. and the 8/S. Staffs for heavy baggage.	
MEZEROLLES	2nd		Orders received for continuance of march on the 3rd.	
	3rd		Battn. marched to HALLOY to a hutment camp. via DOULLENS.	
HALLOY	~~4th~~ 3rd		Orders received for battn. to march to billets at BAYENCOURT on the 4th.	
	4th		Battn. marched to BAYENCOURT via THIEVRES – AUTHIE – St. LEGER – COIGNEUX. After COIGNEUX intervals of 100 yds between platoons and 400 yards between companies were kept.	
BAYENCOURT	~~4th~~ 5th		Bde. H.Q. moved to SAILLY-AU-BOIS. 7th Lincs. moved to SAILLY-AU-BOIS. S. STAFFS. moved to HALLOY. The battn. remained at BAYENCOURT. Orders received that battn. would relieve 7th BORDERS in trenches on the 6th + to be clear of BAYENCOURT by 1-15 p.m.	

1875 Wt. W593/826 1,000,000 4/15 J.B.C. & A. A.D.S.S./Forms/C. 2118.

Instructions regarding War Diaries and Intelligence Summaries are contained in F. S. Regs., Part II. and the Staff Manual respectively. Title Pages will be prepared in manuscript.

WAR DIARY
or
~~INTELLIGENCE SUMMARY~~
(Erase heading not required.)

Army Form C. 2118.

10/Sherwood Foresters

Place	Date	Hour	Summary of Events and Information	Remarks and references to Appendices
			Ref. Map 57D — OCTOBER	
BAYENCOURT	6th		Battn. relieved the 7th Borders and a bn. of the 6/Warwicks in trenches E. of HEBUTERNE. The battn. was disposed as follows – 1 Coy in front line trenches. 1 Coy in support trenches – 2 Coys. in HEBUTERNE – During this tour the bn. was occupied mainly on carrying parties & mining fatigues.	
HEBUTERNE	7th		Orders received that the bn. would be relieved on the 9th by the 8/S. Staffs.	
	9th		Battn. relieved by 8/S. Staffs. YANKEE ST. was reserved for up traffic. WOOD ST. for down traffic. On completion of relief the bn. less 1 coy marched to billets at BAYENCOURT – one coy to billets at SAILLY-AU-BOIS.	
~~BAE~~ BAYENCOURT	10th		Orders received that the BDE. would be relieved by the 19th BDE. 33rd Divn. on the 11th	
	11th		On completion of this relief the coy. of the bn. at SAILLY-AU-BOIS rejoined the bn. at BAYENCOURT. The battn. remained at BAYENCOURT until the 19th being occupied in training & working parties.	
	17th		Orders for march to HALLOY received	
	18th		Orders received on 17th cancelled.	

[initials]

2449 Wt. W14957/M90 750,000 1/16 J.B.C. & A. Forms/C.2118/12.

Instructions regarding War Diaries and Intelligence Summaries are contained in F. S. Regs., Part II. and the Staff Manual respectively. Title Pages will be prepared in manuscript.

WAR DIARY

~~or~~

~~INTELLIGENCE SUMMARY~~

(Erase heading not required.)

10/ Sherwood Foresters

Army Form C. 2118.

Place	Date	Hour	Summary of Events and Information	Remarks and references to Appendices
			Ref. LENS 1/100000 + 57.D 1/40000. OCTOBER –	
BAYENCOURT	18th		Orders received for march to LUCHEUX –	
	19th		Battn marched to huts & billets at LUCHEUX via SOUASTRE – HENU – PAS – MONDICOURT – The battn was behind the 77th Fd. Coy on the march – An officer preceded the bn. by half a mile to warn Traffic Control Posts.	
LUCHEUX	20th		Orders received for moving 1st Line transport to rendezvous at LE BON AIR S. of DOULLENS	
	21st		First line transport proceeded to join 57th Bde. Group transport at LE BON AIR. and moved thence to TALMAS & thence to MERICOURT on the 22nd.	
	22nd		1 Lorry carried the stores of the battn Bde. H.Q. & M.G. Coy to MERICOURT. A billeting party of 1 Officer & 5 OR. rode on this lorry –	
	22nd		Orders received for the transport of 57th Bde Group (less transport & No. 3 Coy Train) by bus & lorry to VILLE & MERICOURT.	
	~~23~~ 22nd		The battn embarked in buses. O.C. battn was in charge of convoy which consisted of 57th T.M. battery. 57th M.G. Coy. Bde H.Q. & the battn – 45 buses in all. The convoy left LUCHEUX at 1.30 p.m. & proceeded via DOULLENS – TALMAS – AMIENS – QUERRIEU – RIBEMONT to MERICOURT and arrived at 10 p.m.	

Instructions regarding War Diaries and Intelligence Summaries are contained in F. S. Regs., Part II. and the Staff Manual respectively. Title Pages will be prepared in manuscript.

WAR DIARY

or

~~INTELLIGENCE SUMMARY~~

(Erase heading not required.)

10/Sherwood Foresters

Army Form C. 2118.

Place	Date	Hour	Summary of Events and Information — Ref Map. ALBERT 1/40,000 — OCTOBER –	Remarks and references to Appendices
MERICOURT	22nd		The battn debussed & marched to billets in MERICOURT.	
"	26th		Orders were received that Bde Group would march to CITADEL CAMP	
"			(F.21.b.) Starting point was (E.26.c.6.2) and the route was	
"			MEAULTE – CARCAILLOT FARM – CEMETERY (F.9.A).	
"			East of VILLE 500 yds was maintained between battns & 200 between	
"			Coys. Tracks along the side of the road were used as much as possible.	
CITADEL CAMP			The battn went into huts at this camp.	
"	28th		Orders were received for the Battn to mend the road from CARNOY –	
"			MONTAUBAN the following day.	
"	28th	8.40pm	Orders were received cancelling this fatigue which was taken over by	
"			the 7th Lincolnshire Regt.	
"			At the same time a warning order was received that the battn would	
"			move up into reserve the following day.	
"	28th	10.45PM	Operation Orders were received that the 17th Divn would relieve the 8th Divn	
"			the relief to be complete by night 30/31st.	
"			This battn was to move to camp in TRONES WOOD and relieve a Battn of	
"			25th Bde in reserve. Route FRICOURT CEMETERY – Road Junction (F.4.c)	
"			– MAMETZ – MONTAUBAN. A reconnoitring party was to precede the Battn	
"			by bus to Cross roads S.W of BERNAFAY WOOD in (S.28.d). These buses	
"			however turned up 1½ hrs late owing to a breakdown, & the party found no guides.	YCN

2449 Wt. W14957/M90 750,000 1/16 J.B.C. & A. Forms/C.2118/12.

Instructions regarding War Diaries and Intelligence Summaries are contained in F. S. Regs., Part II. and the Staff Manual respectively. Title Pages will be prepared in manuscript.

WAR DIARY

or

~~INTELLIGENCE SUMMARY~~

(Erase heading not required.)

Army Form C. 2118.

10th Sherwood Foresters.

Place	Date	Hour	Summary of Events and Information	Remarks and references to Appendices
			Refce MAP ALBERT : 1/40000 — OCTOBER.	
F. CAMP	29th	8.30 AM	Message to the effect that the battn would move to F CAMP and not TRONES WOOD as previously ordered. The Battn started from CITADEL CAMP at 1 pm. and arrived in F CAMP (MONTAUBAN) about 4 pm. The battn were in tents, & came under the orders of G.O.C. 25th Bde on arrival.	
FRONT LINE	30th		Battn marched from F CAMP and took over from a battn of the Devons & a Bn of the R. I. Rifles. The march from F CAMP began about 3.15 pm and the first Coy to take up its position in the front line did so at 11 pm. This was due to the very bad condition of the ground.	
"	31st		The whole battn were in position by 7 AM (31-10-16). The guides of the battns being relieved did not know their way very thoroughly & went astray. When in position the battn was as follows:— from right to left — C Coy — B Coy — D Coy. — A Coy in Support line LARKHILL TRENCH.	
			Reinforcements during the month 1 officer. 2Lt W. E. TATE and 6. O Ranks joined 19th. 8 other ranks joined 3rd.	
			Officers struck off 2Lt A.W. BRITTAN to R.F.C. (20-10-16) Capt G. J. PARTRIDGE to England, to take up Staff apptmt.	
			Casualties during the month. 3 other ranks wounded. 1 other rank accidentally wounded.	YCN

2449 Wt. W14957/M90 750,000 1/16 J.B.C. & A. Forms/C.2118/12.

Vol 15

WAR DIARY

10th Sherwood Foresters

November 1916.

Instructions regarding War Diaries and Intelligence Summaries are contained in F. S. Regs., Part II. and the Staff Manual respectively. Title Pages will be prepared in manuscript.

WAR DIARY
or
~~INTELLIGENCE SUMMARY~~
(Erase heading not required.)

Army Form C. 2118.

10th SHERWOOD FORESTERS.

Place	Date	Hour	Summary of Events and Information — Refce MAP. ALBERT 1/40 000 — NOVEMBER.	Remarks and references to Appendices
Front Trenches	1st		While going into the trenches there was intermittent shelling which caused several casualties. It was soon found that it was impossible to use the communication trenches, & all runners had to go over the top. Telephonic communication was very bad owing to the continuous shelling of the ~~S~~ SUNKEN ROADS & LARKHILL TRENCH. Orders were received ~~at~~ midday that the battn would be relieved at night by the 7th Borders. An advanced party from each Coy consisting of 1 officer & 4 N.C.O's ~~per coy~~ reconnoitred the trenches in the afternoon & returned to guide up the battn. The companies started relieving at dusk. The relief being complete about 10.45 PM. The march back took a long time, on account of the track being very slippery & muddy, & the men's feet being very bad.	
MANSEL CAMP	2nd		The majority of the battn were in camp by 6.0 AM. On relief the battn went to MANSEL CAMP.	
	3rd		Orders were received that Bn would move up to F ~~ ~~ Camp in the evening. These orders were cancelled.	

2449 Wt. W14957/M90 750,000 1/16 J.B.C. & A. Forms/C.2118/12.

WAR DIARY
or
~~INTELLIGENCE SUMMARY~~
(Erase heading not required.)

10th Sherwood Foresters

Army Form C. 2118

Instructions regarding War Diaries and Intelligence Summaries are contained in F. S. Regs., Part II. and the Staff Manual respectively. Title Pages will be prepared in manuscript.

Place	Date	Hour	Summary of Events and Information	Remarks and references to Appendices
			57 D. Refce MAP. NOVEMBER.	
MANSEL CAMP	4th		Orders were received that Bn would move up to D CAMP in the evening. This move was complete by 6pm. Orders were received that the Bn would relieve the 7th LINCOLNS in the support trenches on the evening of the 5th.	
SUPPORT TRENCHES	5th		The Bn moved up to the support trenches and relieved the 7th Lincolns. Intervals of 500 yds were maintained between coys. 40 Sandbags per man were carried up from D Camp to the support trenches. Two coys carried up R.E material & two coys. cleared a derelict bomb stop.	
	5th		Orders were received to relieve the 8th S. Staffs in the line on the 6th. Since the capture of ZENITH Trench a new trench had been dug connecting the left of the Brigade front with ZENITH. The situation was not clear as to the position of the trenches & of our bomb stop in ~~Zenith~~ ECLIPSE. We were ordered to clear up the situation & if necessary advance the bombing stop in ~~ZENITH~~ ECLIPSE TRENCH & dig a trench thence to the left of the brigade front.	
Front Trenches.	6th		Relief carried out satisfactorily; the passage from the reserve to the front line was facilitated by flash lights. During the night 6th/7th enemy posts about 80 yds in front of the	JCN

1875 Wt. W593/826 1,000,000 4/15 J.B.C. & A. A.D.S.S./Forms/C. 2118.

Army Form C. 2118.

Instructions regarding War Diaries and Intelligence Summaries are contained in F. S. Regs., Part II. and the Staff Manual respectively. Title Pages will be prepared in manuscript.

WAR DIARY
or
~~INTELLIGENCE SUMMARY~~
(Erase heading not required.)

10th Sherwood Foresters

~~[illegible]~~ 57D — NOVEMBER.

Place	Date	Hour	Summary of Events and Information	Remarks and references to Appendices
Trenches	6th		centre of the right Coy were occupied by us, & connected [illegible] front line by a C.T. dug by the Bn	
"	7th		After reconnaissance of the line & posts it was found necessary to advance the stop in ECLIPSE TRENCH [illegible]. Orders were issued to the Coy Commanders concerned that an R.E. officer was asked for to lay a tape for the new trench. Orders were received that the Battn would take over a portion of the front then held by the 52nd Bde. During the night the stop in ECLIPSE was with some difficulty advanced & a new trench [illegible] long was dug to a depth of two ft. joining it with the [illegible] end of MISTY. Two platoons from the support Coy took over the abovementioned portion of the 52nd Bde front. Our dispositions now were front line 3½ Coys Support ½ company.	
"	7th/8th		Orders were received for a relief by the 7th Borders on the 8th. During the night the C.T. joining posts to front line on the right was deepened to 5 ft. The Bn was relieved by 7th Borders, a difficult relief owing to [illegible] a [illegible] whilst relief was in progress. Battn proceeding to reserve trenches, the Coy Rose, ~~two~~ NEEDLE and MALL	
H CAMP	9th		In accordance with orders issued on 7th Bn was relieved by 7th Lincolns as the afternoon was quiet two Coys were sent out at 3 pm with instructions [illegible] bridge in (T.8.) in artillery formation of sections. Remaining two Coys were relieved about 7 pm. Battn on relief proceeding to H CAMP, W of MONTAUBAN–[illegible] road where it remained until 11th inst.	

2449 Wt. W14957/M90 750,000 1/16 J.B.C. & A. Forms/C.2118/12.

Instructions regarding War Diaries and Intelligence Summaries are contained in F. S. Regs., Part II. and the Staff Manual respectively. Title Pages will be prepared in manuscript.

WAR DIARY
or
~~INTELLIGENCE SUMMARY~~
(Erase heading not required.)

Army Form C. 2118.

10th Sherwood Foresters.

Place	Date	Hour	Refce MAP. ALBERT 1/40000. Summary of Events and Information NOVEMBER.	Remarks and references to Appendices
H CAMP.	10th	–	Orders were received that the Battn would march to camp at the SANDPITS the following day.	
" "	11th	–	The Battn began the march at 10 AM. The route was CARNOY – CROSS ROADS (F.18.C) – FRICOURT CEMETRY – CARCAILLOT Fm – SANDPITS CAMP. An interval of 200 yds was maintained between coys + the transport followed at an interval of 300 yds. The Battn arrived in the camp about 1.30 pm.	
" "	14th	–	Orders received that the Bn. would entrain at EDGEHILL Stn + would proceed by train, the following day, to HANGEST from where it would march to LE QUESNOY into billets.	
EDGEHILL STATION.	15th	–	The Bn marched to EDGEHILL Stn starting from the SANDPITS CAMP about 6.30 AM. The Transport left the camp on the 13th + went by road under Brigade arrangements.	
	"		The Bn. were entrained by 10 AM ~~+ the train~~ + the train started about 10.15 AM.	
HANGEST	"		It arrived at HANGEST STATION about 1.30 pm. After detraining there was a message from Divn to say that ~~it~~ only ½ the Bn would be able to be billeted in LE QUESNOY that day, the remainder would billet in HANGEST for the night.	
	"		A+B Coys – Bombers – + all Lewis Gunners marched off to LE QUESNOY	
	"		The remainder C Coy – D Coy – HQ details – + Signallers were billeted	

2149 Wt. W14957/M90 750,000 1/16 J.B.C.& A. Forms/C.2118/12.

Instructions regarding War Diaries and Intelligence Summaries are contained in F. S. Regs., Part II. and the Staff Manual respectively. Title Pages will be prepared in manuscript.

WAR DIARY
or
~~INTELLIGENCE~~ SUMMARY

(Erase heading not required.)

Army Form C. 2118

10th Sherwood Foresters

Place	Date	Hour	Summary of Events and Information MAP AMIENS 17. 1/100000 NOVEMBER.	Remarks and references to Appendices
HANGEST	15th	–	in HANGEST for the night.	
"	"	10pm	About 10 pm a message came from Divn to say that the Bn would not be billeted in LE QUESNOY but would proceed the following day & take over billets in PICQUIGNY.	
PICQUIGNY	16	10AM	The Bn (less 2 Coys - Bombers + transport). marched to PICQUIGNY & took over billets there.	
"	"	1.0pm	The two companies marched from LE QUESNOY to PICQUIGNY. The whole Bn were in their new billets by 5pm. The transport arrived about 5.30pm, who had come by road. These billets were very bad, being very cold & draughty. It was decided to move in the morning into billets that the West Riding Regt were moving out of. This was completed by 12 noon on the 17th.	
"	17th	–		
"	18th	–	This day was spent cleaning up the billets, which were taken over very dirty.	
"	19th 20th 21st		Battn training commenced – Consisting of Drill, route marches, Schemes, night work & Specialist training. This was carried on during the remainder of the month. During this period of rest, a Guards Drill Instructor visited the Battn twice a week, to give Officers and N.C.O's a course of Drill Instruction. A bayonet fighting Instr also was sent round to Battns to supervise this training.	
"	23rd	–	Reinforcements joined 18. other ranks.	

JCN

1875 Wt. W593/826 1,000,000 4/15 J.B.C. & A. A.D.S.S./Forms/C. 2118.

Instructions regarding War Diaries and Intelligence Summaries are contained in F. S. Regs., Part II. and the Staff Manual respectively. Title Pages will be prepared in manuscript.

WAR DIARY
or
~~INTELLIGENCE SUMMARY~~
(Erase heading not required.)

Army Form C. 2118.

10th Sherwood Foresters.

Place	Date	Hour	Summary of Events and Information	Remarks and references to Appendices
			AMIENS 17 1/100000 NOVEMBER.	
PICQUIGNY.	25th		46 other ranks joined this day.	
	30th		Casualities during the month. 16 other ranks killed	
			52. other ranks wounded includes 8 at duty.	
			2 accidentally wounded & 10 reported missing.	
			Officers struck off. Capt. S. St G. Wheeley. Lt. R. A. C. Ruttle	
			2/Lt W. E TATE transferred to England sick.	
			2/Lt H. N. GREENWOOD transferred to 57th T. M. B.	
				JCN
				for O.C. 10 Sherwood Foresters

Instructions regarding War Diaries and Intelligence Summaries are contained in F. S. Regs., Part II. and the Staff Manual respectively. Title Pages will be prepared in manuscript.

WAR DIARY

or

~~INTELLIGENCE SUMMARY~~

(Erase heading not required.)

Army Form C. 2118.

Vol 16

10th Sherwood Foresters.

Place	Date	Hour	Summary of Events and Information — AMIENS. 17 1/100000 — DECEMBER.	Remarks and references to Appendices
PICQUIGNY.	1st	—	The Battn were still at PICQUIGNY doing training.	
"			A great part of this time was devoted to musketry. An Instructor	
"			from a Bn of the Scots Guards was attached to the Bde for discipline	
			who took the N.C.O's of the Battns in the Bde in drill.	
"	8th		Warning Order received that the Divn were under orders to	
			move into Corps Reserve.	
"	11th		A lorry was provided to take the billeting party by road to	
			CORBIE. It reported at Bn HQ. at 11 AM.	
"	11th		Orders received that the Bn (less wheeled transport) would move	
			to CORBIE the following day.	
"			A lorry would be provided to take the baggage to entraining station	
"			and two lorries would take stores straight through to CORBIE.	
"			This was because the G.S wagons of the Bn had been taken away	
			from the Bn.	
"	12th	7 AM.	The Battn marched to HANGEST to entrain for CORBIE at 9.10 AM.	
			Lorries previously promised reported to Battns.	
			The transport moved by road under the command of O.C. 17th Divnl Train	
			ROUTE. — AILLY — AMIENS. – VECQUEMONT.	

2449 Wt. W14957/M90 750,000 1/16 J.B.C. & A. Forms/C.2118/12.

Army Form C. 2118.

Instructions regarding War Diaries and Intelligence Summaries are contained in F. S. Regs., Part II. and the Staff Manual respectively. Title Pages will be prepared in manuscript.

WAR DIARY
or
~~INTELLIGENCE SUMMARY~~
(Erase heading not required.)

10th Sherwood Foresters.

Place	Date	Hour	AMIENS 17. 1/100000 Summary of Events and Information DECEMBER.	Remarks and references to Appendices
CORBIE	12th	—	The Battn arrived at CORBIE STN about 1.0 pm. & marched to billets & took over from the 1st BORDER Regt. 29th Divn. The Transport arrived about 8.0 pm the same night.	
"	13th		The period spent by the Battn at CORBIE like the previous one was spent in Musketry + Drill mainly. The Companies being on the range almost every day.	
"	18th		Warning Order received that the Brigade Group would move up on the 23rd & that the Bn would march to MERICOURT on that date.	
"	20th		Operation Orders received that Bn would march to MERICOURT on 23rd Dec + would move on to a camp at CARNOY on 24th.	
MERICOURT	23rd		~~The~~ Bn marched to MERICOURT arriving there about 1.0 pm. Lorries were provided to take the heavy baggage & blankets. All surplus baggage was dumped at CORBIE. It was notified in the O.O. for the 20th that the 17th Divn (less Artillery) would relieve the 20th Divn in the line. Relief to be complete by 10 AM Dec 25th. The line would be held on the group system one Brigade HQ resting, the Bn's of that Brigade would be attached equally to the other two. This Battn would come under the orders of the 52nd Bde on arrival in the forward area.	

2449 Wt. W14957/M90 750,000 1/16 J.B.C. & A. Forms/C.2118/12.

Instructions regarding War Diaries and Intelligence Summaries are contained in F. S. Regs., Part II. and the Staff Manual respectively. Title Pages will be prepared in manuscript.

WAR DIARY
or
~~INTELLIGENCE SUMMARY~~
(Erase heading not required.)

Army Form C. 2118.

10th Sherwood Foresters

Place	Date	Hour	Summary of Events and Information (Refce Map. ALBERT Combined Sheet 1/20000) DECEMBER	Remarks and references to Appendices
HERICOURT	23rd		The same orders detailed the Bn to move up to the forward Camps on 24th	
CARNOY (17 Camp)	24th		The Bn moved from HERICOURT to Camp No 17, accompanied by the transport whose lines were in CARNOY under the supervision of the Bde.	
"	"		The Battn were in Camp by about 2.30 pm & came under the orders of the 52nd Bde.	
"	25th		Some working parties were detailed from the Bn to lay water pipes & assist cleaning the camps in the forward area.	
(19 Camp)	"		It was then found that owing to a mistake the Bn. were in the wrong camp & had to move to 19 Camp to make way for the 7th Lincolns.	
"	"		This was carried out by about 3.30 pm on the 25th Dec.	
GUILLEMONT	26th		The Bn moved up to a hutment Camp in GUILLEMONT arriving there about 4.0 pm, staying the night there preparatory to relieving in the line on the following day. All details such as police, pioneers ~~& QMS~~ remained at Camp 17 & were formed into a Brigade Depot for working parties.	
"	"		The QrMr Stores remained at Camp 19.	
Front line	27th		The Battn relieved the 12th Manchesters (52nd Bde) in the line on the night 27th/28th. Relief was complete by 10.30 pm. Only 400 men were to be taken into the line. The Sapping platoon under 2Lt Day left the Bn at GUILLEMONT Camp & were under the direct orders of the Bde.	
"	27th		The disposition on relief was as follows:– A Coy + 2 platoons D Coy were in the front line under Capt Lauder (A Coy) – C Coy + B Coy (less 2 platoons) were in the supports ANTELOPE TRENCH under Capt Daniel (C Coy) & D Coy were in the reserve trenches. OX TRENCH near to BN. HQ. Lewis Guns were posted as follows.– 3 Guns on the right (front line, which was held by posts)–	

2449 Wt. W14957/M90 750,000 1/16 J.B.C. & A. Forms/C.2118/12.

Army Form C. 2118.

Instructions regarding War Diaries and Intelligence Summaries are contained in F. S. Regs., Part II. and the Staff Manual respectively. Title Pages will be prepared in manuscript.

WAR DIARY
or
~~INTELLIGENCE SUMMARY~~
(Erase heading not required.)

10th Sherwood Foresters

Place	Date	Hour	Summary of Events and Information	Remarks and references to Appendices
			Refce Map. 57 C. S.W. 1/20000 — DECEMBER.	
Front Line.	27th		Two Guns on the left (front line) — 3 Guns in Support (ANTELOPE TR) and 1 in reserve at Bn HQ. (T. 10. A 8. 6). The relief was complete by about 10.30 pm. The trenches in this part of the line were in very bad condition, the drainage having been neglected. The front line could not be approached in daylight, except in cases of great emergency. There was very little material in the front line & it was very difficult to do any digging owing to the rain. The front line consisted in a line of T head posts.	
"	28th	–	Work was commenced on the Support Line ANTELOPE & a certain part of the trench was deepened about 1ft. The T head posts were improved & drained. A considerable amount of material was carried up from OX TRENCH to ANTELOPE, this ~~was~~ became possible in the afternoon, as a thick mist fell. Practically no shelling or M.G. fire was directed onto the front line during the 48 hours. A patrol was sent out at about 10.0 pm to reconnoitre the enemy's advanced trench. This trench was estimated to be about 12O × from our front line. The patrol tried to work round & get in rear of this trench but owing to the mist bearing was lost & the patrol returned about 11.15 pm.	
"	29th		Enemy's artillery much more active during the afternoon, on the Support & Reserve trenches, caused probably by a working party who were carrying duckboards up to the support trenches. ANTELOPE trench is in full view of the enemy from the left in clear weather.	FCN

2449 Wt. W14957/M90 750,000 1/16 J.B.C. & A. Forms/C.2118/12.

Instructions regarding War Diaries and Intelligence Summarie are contained in F. S. Regs., Part II. and the Staff Manual respectively. Title Pages will be prepared in manuscript.

WAR DIARY
or
~~INTELLIGENCE~~ SUMMARY
(Erase heading not required.)

Army Form C. 2118.

10th Sherwood Foresters.

Place	Date	Hour	Summary of Events and Information — Rogue Map. 57 C. S.W. 1/20000 — December. 1916	Remarks and references to Appendices
Front Line	29th	—	Most of the day was spent in carrying material to ANTELOPE TRENCH preparatory to carrying it to the front line at dusk. OX TRENCH was drained & a considerable amount of improvement in this respect was effected.	
		3.30 pm	ANTELOPE was fairly heavily shelled, & it was evident that the enemy has this trench well registered as he obtained several direct hits with 5.9". The Battn was relieved by the 9th Duke of Wellington's relief commencing about 4.30 pm. There was practically no shelling during the night & the relief was complete by about 9.0 pm. On relief the Bn marched to No. 19 Camp CARNOY. Tea was obtainable at GUILLEMONT CAMP, where Gum boots were changed.	
Camp 19. CARNOY.	30th 31st		The day was spent in kit inspections & generally cleaning up equipment etc. Some working parties were detailed to work under R.E. on camp improvements.	
			Officers joined during the month. 2Lt T.A.S. NICHOLS. – Lt J.N. KNIGHT (both rej.) 2Lt W.P. FOWLER – 2Lt R.B. SILVERWOOD – 2Lt S.S. MOSLEY – 2Lt F. MARCHANT.	
			Officers struck off. Capt. C.J.A. LEFROY. (sick). 2Lt R.H.P. BLAKLEY (sick) both to England.	
			Reinforcements during month. 94.	
			Casualties. 1. O.R. Killed. – 8 O.R.s wounded – 4 other ranks wounded at duty.	JCN

2449 Wt. W14957/M90 750,000 1/16 J.B.C. & A. Forms/C.2118/12.

Instructions regarding War Diaries and Intelligence Summaries are contained in F. S. Regs., Part II. and the Staff Manual respectively. Title Pages will be prepared in manuscript.

WAR DIARY
or
~~INTELLIGENCE SUMMARY~~
(Erase heading not required.)

Army Form C. 2118

Vol 17

10th Sherwood Foresters

Place	Date	Hour	Refce Map 57 C SW — Summary of Events and Information — JANUARY 1917	Remarks and references to Appendices
CAMP 19. CARNOY	1st	-	Orders were received that Bn would relieve a Bn of 2nd Guards Brigade on night of 2/3rd January & that Bn would move to GUILLEMONT CAMP on night 1/2nd. The Bn were in camp by 4.30 pm.	
Front Line	2		The Relief started from Camp about 4 pm & marched via COMBLES Coys were marched off at 10 minutes interval On reaching COMBLES a duckboard track was taken which led past Battn HQ at (T6 A 7.5) & then to the support trench Mules came up with each Coy carrying water ammunition & Bombs & were unloaded at Battn HQ & the Coys carried on from there The Relief was complete by 7.30 pm The dispositions were A Coy on right - B Coy (Right Centre). C Coy (left Centre) & D Coy on left. Gum boots were taken over in the line but were only used for patrols, as the trenches for the most part had duckboards. The time was spent in wiring and improving the trenches as much as possible. Patrols also were sent out each night, who reported the Enemy trenches to be very scantily wired and not continuously. No Enemy Patrols were encountered, Snipers were not very active & Machine Gun was directed against the trenches only after dusk.	R.W.

1875 Wt. W593/826 1,000,000 4/15 J.B.C. & A. A.D.S.S./Forms/C. 2118.

Army Form C. 2118.

Instructions regarding War Diaries and Intelligence Summaries are contained in F. S. Regs., Part II. and the Staff Manual respectively. Title Pages will be prepared in manuscript.

WAR DIARY
or
~~INTELLIGENCE SUMMARY~~
(Erase heading not required.)

10th Sherwood Foresters.

Place	Date	Hour	Summary of Events and Information	Remarks and references to Appendices
			Refce Map. 57 C. S.W. JANUARY 1917.	
Front Line	4th		Orders were received that the Bn would be relieved in the line on the night 5th/6th by the 9th Duke of Wellingtons.	
	5th		The relief was complete by about 8 pm & Bn marched back to camp 19 Carnoy.	
Camp 19. CARNOY.	6th		Orders were received that the Bn would relieve the same sector in the line on the night 8th/9th. Bn HQ however would not be in the same sector but would be situated in SUNKEN Rd. (T.10.A.8.6) also that the Bn would be on a shorter front from (U.1.D.4.6) to (T.6.B.7.6). On the afternoon of the 6th the Bn moved into camp at GUILLEMONT.	
	7th		The morning of the next day was spent in sandbagging the huts in order to make them splinter-proof. This camp being occasionally shelled. The relief started from GUILLEMONT at 4.0 pm & were to take over from the 12th Bn. Manchesters. During the tour the right became (U.1.D.1.7.) This relief however was to proceed via duckboard track at GINCHY which runs N. of MORVAL & thence to the line as before. Gum boots were taken up for patrolling purposes only. Bombs Ammunition etc were drawn at O.X Dump (T.15.B).	
Front Line	8th		The relief was complete by 9.30 pm.	JCN

2449 Wt. W14957/M90 750,000 1/16 J.B.C. & A. Forms/C.2118/12.

Army Form C. 2118.

WAR DIARY
or
~~INTELLIGENCE SUMMARY~~
(Erase heading not required.)

Instructions regarding War Diaries and Intelligence Summaries are contained in F. S. Regs., Part II. and the Staff Manual respectively. Title Pages will be prepared in manuscript.

10th Sherwood Foresters.

Place	Date	Hour	Summary of Events and Information — Refce Map. 57. C. S.W. — JANUARY.	Remarks and references to Appendices
Front Line	8th	–	Bn HQ were at (T.10.b.8.8.) This tour lasted 3 days, & work was concentrated on wiring the front line. 40 coils of barbed wire being put out during the tour.	
	10th		Battn were relieved on night of 10/12th & proceeded to Camp 19 CARNOY	
CARNOY.	11th		The Battn marched into billets at MEAULTE.	
MEAULTE	13th		The first few days were spent in rest, cleaning, reequipping & organisation. 200 of the last draft went to the Army Musketry Camp at Pont Remy for 5 days. Training was commenced on the lines of the training manual	
MALTZHORN + BOIS DORÉE	26th		On the 26th the Battn marched 2 Coys + HQ to MALTZHORN, two Coys to Bois Dorée. The Battn was in Divnl reserve under orders of G.O.C. 20th Divn.	
BOULEAUX WOOD.	27th		Bn moved into the BOULEAUX Wood Area & became Bde Support & was disposed as under. – One Coy intermediate line (T.18.A). One Coy at MORVAL Rd dugouts T.17.D, One Coy MUTTON TRENCH. (T.23.A). One Coy BOULEAUX WOOD HQ were in dugouts (T.21.d.8.1).	
Line.	28th		On the night 28/29th Bn relieved 7th Borders in the line. Left Bn of left Group. (North Copse Sector), & was disposed as under – Front line 11 platoons. 8 L.Guns. – Support. 2 platoons +1 L.Gun. and Reserve 5 platoons + 3 L.Guns. Bn HQ were at (T.7.c.5.9) An uneventful tour. Attempt was made to extend the island posts but little progress was made owing to the hard + frosty ground.	

2449 Wt. W14957/M90 750,000 1/16 J.B.C. & A. Forms/C.2118/12.

Army Form C. 2118.

WAR DIARY
or
~~INTELLIGENCE SUMMARY~~
(Erase heading not required.)

Instructions regarding War Diaries and Intelligence Summaries are contained in F. S. Regs., Part II. and the Staff Manual respectively. Title Pages will be prepared in manuscript.

10th Sherwood Foresters

JANUARY 1917

Place	Date	Hour	Summary of Events and Information 57.C, S.W.	Remarks and references to Appendices
MALTZHORN + Bois Dorée	30th		On the night 30/31st the Bn were relieved by 9th West Ridings & proceeded ~~to~~ ~~Bo~~ Coys to MALTZHORN (less 2 Coys who went to BOIS DOREE.	
BRONFAY CAMP. 108.	31st		At midday the Bn marched into Divnl reserve at BRONFAY CAMP. 108	
			Officers joined during month :- Capt. L.R. HALFORD - 2Lt- W.J.P McCOOMBE - 2Lt. E.C. MARSHALL - 2Lt R.S. GUSTARD. joined 13th inst. Lt and QrMr S.J. Pearsall joined 20th inst. 2Lt. F.C. GEZZ joined 24th. 2Lt. FOWLER to England sick 23th. 228 O. Ranks joined 4th. 13 O. Ranks joined 24th inst.	
			Casualties during month. 1 Officer 2Lt L.1 McCandless wounded 2/1/17. One other rank killed & 14 other ranks wounded.	

FCN

2449 Wt. W14957/M90 750,000 1/16 J.B.C. & A. Forms/C.2118/12.

Army Form C. 2118.

Vol 18

WAR DIARY
or
~~INTELLIGENCE SUMMARY~~
(Erase heading not required.)

Instructions regarding War Diaries and Intelligence Summaries are contained in F. S. Regs., Part II. and the Staff Manual respectively. Title Pages will be prepared in manuscript.

10th Sherwood Foresters — February. 1917.

Place	Date	Hour	Summary of Events and Information	Remarks and references to Appendices
BRONFAY.	1st	—	Battn were resting in Bronfay Camp.	
BOULEAUX Area.	2nd	—	Battn moved to the BOULEAUX WOOD area. - One Coy intermediate line - One Coy MORVAL Rd. dugouts - MUTTON TRENCH - BOULEAUX WOOD.	
Line.	3rd	—	The Bn relieved the 7th Bn BORDERS. in the line. This was a very uneventful tour. A very heavy frost preventing much work being done in the line. The line was wired with knife rests as it was impossible to put screw pickets in, it being too hard.	
~~MALTZHORN CAMP~~	5th	5.30 am	~~On the night 5th/6th Bn moved to MALTZHORN CAMP, two companies going to BOIS DORE dugouts.~~ The Bn was raided by the enemy	9c
	~~6th~~		~~Bn moved to BRONFAY CAMP~~	10
	~~8th~~		~~Bn moved~~ whilst in the line. A party of the enemy came in to our line at the gap on the right of the right post. The raiding party consisted of about 20 men. Some of the party were dressed in white overalls & so were very inconspicuous in the snow. One of the party was wounded & remained in the trench, but died about 1.0 pm ~~in~~ the afternoon. The remainder after throwing bombs went back to their lines. 5 or 6 of the party however were killed on their return. The prisoner who remained in our hands belonged to the 120.th Regt.	JCN

2449 Wt. W14957/M90 750,000 1/16 J.B.C. & A. Forms/C.2118/12.

Army Form C. 2118.

WAR DIARY
or
~~INTELLIGENCE SUMMARY~~
(Erase heading not required.)

Instructions regarding War Diaries and Intelligence Summaries are contained in F. S. Regs., Part II. and the Staff Manual respectively. Title Pages will be prepared in manuscript.

10th Sherwood Foresters. February 1917.

Place	Date	Hour	Summary of Events and Information	Remarks and references to Appendices
Line	5th	–	On the night 5th/6th Bn were relieved by 9th Duke of Wellingtons & returned, two Coys to BOIS DORE & two Coys & HQ to MALTZHORN CAMP.	
MALTZHORN.	6th		Bn marched back to BRONFAY Camp.	
BOULEAUX WOOD.	8th		Bn moved up to the BOULEAUX WOOD area.	
Line.	9th		On the night 9th/10th the Bn relieved the 7th Borders in the line, relief was complete by about 9.0 pm. The frost still hindered work in the line very much & on that account the Bn remained in the trenches an extra 48 hours & the Bn in the BOULEAUX WOOD area sent working parties up to assist work in the line. This was a very uneventful tour, patrols were sent out to examine the bodies lying in no-man's land. One of these bodies had the identification of a man in the 99th Regt. At the end of this tour the thaw began to set in, & a great deal more work was possible.	
MALTZHORN.	13th		The Bn were relieved in the line & marched to MALTZHORN CAMP.	
BRONFAY. CAMP.	14th		Bn marched to BRONFAY CAMP.	
BOULEAUX WOOD	16th		The Battn again moved up to the BOULEAUX WOOD area.	
Line.	17th		On the night 17th Bn relieved the 7th Borders in the line. Dispositions were as follows – A Coy left front line – B Coy Right front line – C Coy CHARLES Strong Point – D Coy CHEESE TRENCH & COPSE RESERVE.	JCN

2449 Wt. W14957/M90 750,000 1/16 J.B.C. & A. Forms/C.2118/12.

Army Form C. 2118.

Instructions regarding War Diaries and Intelligence Summaries are contained in F. S. Regs., Part II. and the Staff Manual respectively. Title Pages will be prepared in manuscript.

WAR DIARY

or

~~INTELLIGENCE SUMMARY~~

(Erase heading not required.)

February 1917.

Place	Date	Hour	10th Sherwood Foresters. Summary of Events and Information	Remarks and references to Appendices
Line.	18th		As the thaw had now set in a great deal of work could be done, but by this time the trenches were in a very bad condition.	
"	"		A great deal of revetting however was accomplished & the trench was made much more continuous, several blocks between posts being removed.	
BRONFAY CAMP.	19th.		The Bn were relieved & orders received that the Bn would go straight to BRONFAY CAMP. A train however was waiting at TRONES WOOD Sidings to convey the Bn to the PLATEAU. This train arrived at the PLATEAU about 1.30 AM. Orders were received that the ~~Brin~~ would be relieved & that Bn would go ~~[illegible]~~ into Corps reserve to BONNAY.	
BONNAY.	20th		The Bn marched to the PLATEAU Station & entrained for HEILLY. Arriving there about 10.0 pm they marched on to BONNAY, arriving there about 12.0 midnight.	
BONNAY	21st – March 1st		Bn in training in the neighbourhood	
			Reinforcements.	
BRONFAY CAMP	19th		4 officers. 61. O.R. Officers: Lieut. F. H. M. COLLIER, 2nd Lt. J. W. BOWMER, 2nd Lt C. K. HANSON, 2nd Lt C. K. HOPE	JCN

2449 Wt. W14957/M90 750,000 1/16 J.B.C. & A. Forms/C.2118/12.

Instructions regarding War Diaries and Intelligence Summaries are contained in F. S. Regs., Part II. and the Staff Manual respectively. Title Pages will be prepared in manuscript.

WAR DIARY
or
INTELLIGENCE SUMMARY

(Erase heading not required.)

Army Form C. 2118.

February 1917.

Place	Date	Hour	10th Sherwood Foresters. Summary of Events and Information	Remarks and references to Appendices
BONNAY	21st		1. Sgt. 1. Cpl + 5 men join.	
			Casualties	
	27th		Lieut DAY S.C. struck off the strength. (ordered medical board while on leave).	
			Other ranks.	
			Killed. 8.	
			Wounded. 9. (1. at duty)	
			Missing. 3.	

2449 Wt. W14957/M90 750,000 1/16 J.B.C. & A. Forms/C.2118/12.

Army Form C. 2118.

WAR DIARY
or
~~INTELLIGENCE SUMMARY~~
(Erase heading not required.)

Instructions regarding War Diaries and Intelligence Summaries are contained in F. S. Regs., Part II. and the Staff Manual respectively. Title Pages will be prepared in manuscript.

10th Sherwood Foresters.

Refer. LENS. 11. MARCH. Vol

Place	Date	Hour	Summary of Events and Information	Remarks and references to Appendices
BONNAY	1st	–	The Bn were in BONNAY the time being spent in training.	
"			Orders were received that the Battn would move to HERISSART.	
"	2nd		The Bn ~~moved~~ marched into billets at HERISSART. Here the Bn trained for open warfare. The Bn while in this area was G.H.Q. reserve.	
"	13th		The Bn ~~moved~~ marched to LONGUEVILLETTE.	
"	14th		The Bn marched into billets at CONTEVILLE, & came under the orders of III army. The route taken was – FIENVILLERS – BERNAVILLE – BEAUMETZ – AGENVILLE – CONTEVILLE.	
"	15th		The march was continued on the 15th & the Bn marched to LE QUESNOY-en-ARTOIS. – Route AUXI-le-CHATEAU – LE PONCHEL – GENNE-IVERGNY – LA BROYE – REGNAUVILLE – EREMBEAUCOURT – LE QUESNOY. Lorries were provided to assist in the carting of the heavy stores.	
			The Battn while in this area continued its training – ranges bayonet-fighting gallows etc being constructed.	
	21st		Orders were received that the Battn would move on the 22nd to the Auxi-le-CHATEAU area.	
	22nd		The Bn marched to ROUGEFAY, arriving there about 3.0 pm.	

Instructions regarding War Diaries and Intelligence Summaries are contained in F. S. Regs., Part II. and the Staff Manual respectively. Title Pages will be prepared in manuscript.

WAR DIARY
or
~~INTELLIGENCE SUMMARY~~
(Erase heading not required.)

Army Form C. 2118.

10th Sherwood Foresters.

Place	Date	Hour	Summary of Events and Information LENS. 11. 1/100,000 MARCH.	Remarks and references to Appendices
ROUGEFAY	23rd	–	The Bn marched to LE SOUICH. Route ROUGEFAY – WAVANS – FROHEN-LE-GRAND – REMAISNIL – BARLY – NEUVILLETTE – BOUQUEMAISON – LE SOUICH.	
			While the Bn were in this area, the time was spent in training. A fatigue party was found on alternate days of 500 men besides officers + NCO's to work on the road between DOULLENS and BOUQUEMAISON on the main road from ARRAS to DOULLENS.	
			Great trouble was experienced in getting boot repairs done while in this area. The boots were in a very bad condition + news pairs were only obtainable in very limited numbers.	
	28th.		The Battn started a band which arrived out from England on this date. Several professional musicians were found in the Bn to form this.	
			Orders were received that when the Bn went into action a Corps depot would be formed at St POL for men + officers left out of the trenches for instructional purposes. Only 4 officers per Coy were to be taken into the trenches.	[illegible]

2449 Wt. W14957/M90 750,000 1/16 J.B.C. & A. Forms/C.2118/12.

Army Form C. 2118.

WAR DIARY
or
INTELLIGENCE SUMMARY

(Erase heading not required.)

Instructions regarding War Diaries and Intelligence Summaries are contained in F. S. Regs., Part II. and the Staff Manual respectively. Title Pages will be prepared in manuscript.

10th Sherwood Foresters.

Place	Date	Hour	LENS. 11 1/100,000 Summary of Events and Information MARCH.	Remarks and references to Appendices
LE SOUICH.	31st	–	Draft of 65 other ranks joined the Bn. ~~2nd~~ Lieut S.C Day was struck off ~~[illegible]~~ on 1st inst. 2nd Lieut. J. HUYTON was struck off on the 6th inst. 1 Sergeant and 11 men joined the Bn on the 3rd inst. 2nd Lieut. E. J. H. Brooksbank, 1 Sergeant + 8 men joined on 8th inst. 46 other ranks joined the Bn on the 21st inst. Casualties during the month . Nil.	FCN.

Vol 20

Army Form C. 2118.

WAR DIARY
or
~~INTELLIGENCE SUMMARY~~
(Erase heading not required.)

Instructions regarding War Diaries and Intelligence Summaries are contained in F. S. Regs., Part II. and the Staff Manual respectively. Title Pages will be prepared in manuscript.

10th Sherwood Foresters.

Place	Date	Hour	Summary of Events and Information LENS. 11. 1/100,000 April 1917.	Remarks and references to Appendices
LE SOUICH	1st	-	The Bn were at LE SOUICH and the time here was spent in Training & Road mending on alternate days.	
" "	5th	-	Orders were received that the Brigade group would move to the ST POL area.	
MAISNIL ST POL.	6th	-	The Bn moved to MAISNIL ST POL. Route. HOUVIN – MONCHEAUX – MAISNIL ST POL.	
AMBRINES	7th	-	The Bn moved to AMBRINES.	
HABARCQ.	8th	-	The Bn marched to HABARCQ, the whole Brigade being billeted in the HABARCQ area for the night.	
ARRAS AREA	9th	-	The Division went up to be in readiness to follow the cavalry when they broke through the trench system.	
"			The 3 brigades marched on different roads towards ARRAS. the 57th Bde moving on the centre route.	
"			On marching from HABARCQ Echelon B & C remained behind waiting for orders. Echelon A under the Bn Transport Officer accompanied the	
"			Bn by road. The 57th Bde were the reserve Brigade, & on nearing ARRAS the 52nd Bde moved first the 50th Bde second and the 57th Bde last.	
ARRAS	10th		The Bn bivouaced for the night in a field 2½ miles W. of ARRAS at 6.0 AM ~~in the~~ the Bn marched into ARRAS into billets in the cellars and were at 50 minutes notice. Three days were spent there ~~at~~ with the same orders to be ready to move at 50 minutes notice.	

Army Form C. 2118.

WAR DIARY
or
~~INTELLIGENCE SUMMARY~~
(Erase heading not required.)

Instructions regarding War Diaries and Intelligence Summaries are contained in F. S. Regs., Part II. and the Staff Manual respectively. Title Pages will be prepared in manuscript.

SCARPE VALLEY 1/40 000 — 10th Sherwood Foresters — April 1917.

Place	Date	Hour	Summary of Events and Information	Remarks and references to Appendices
ARRAS RAILWAY TRIANGLE.	12th	–	The Bn moved from the cellars in ARRAS to the RAILWAY TRIANGLE in (H.19. central), became Brigade reserve and were bivouaced on the Railway embankment. While here working parties were found, to work on the railway.	
BATTERY VALLEY.	13th		3 Coys moved to BATTERY VALLEY approx (H.26.B) and were bivouaced there. Orders were received that the Bn would relieve a Bn of the 29th Divn N.E of MONCHY on the night 13th/14th. The Bn marched to the S. end of Battery Valley ready to cross the 'BROWN LINE directly after dusk.	
"	13th	7.30pm	Orders were received that the Bn would relieve ~~the~~ a Bn of the 52nd Bde in the BROWN LINE + ~~that~~ not a Bn of the 29th Divn.	
BROWN LINE.	14th	2.0 AM	The Bn arrived in the BROWN LINE, the Bn HQ being at about (H.34.A.9.9). Working parties were sent from here to dig assembly trenches N.E of MONCHY	
" "	17th	–	The Bn moved to the left in the BROWN LINE and took over from the 9th WEST RIDINGS ~~Northumberland Fusiliers~~ and became ~~the~~ supporting Bn. The Bn HQ was in (H.28.A. central) and the companies were in a Support Line in (H.28.B). The relief was complete about 9.30 pm.	
RAILWAY TRIANGLE.	18th		The Bn were relieved in the Support Line by the 6th Dorsets + moved into reserve in the RAILWAY TRIANGLE.	
	20th		An Operation order was received that an advance of the whole Line would take place, date to be notified later. The attack for the 51st Bde was – The BORDERS on right + STAFFORDS on left would attack the front line system + push on to the BLUE LINE and consolidate, this Bn on the right + the LINCOLNS on left would then pass through + take KEELING COPSE and PELVES respectively.	

2449 Wt. W14957/M90 750,000 1/16 J.B.C. & A. Forms/C.2118/12.

Army Form C. 2118.

Instructions regarding War Diaries and Intelligence Summaries are contained in F. S. Regs., Part II. and the Staff Manual respectively. Title Pages will be prepared in manuscript.

WAR DIARY
or
~~INTELLIGENCE SUMMARY~~
(Erase heading not required.)

10th Sherwood Foresters

Place	Date	Hour	SCARPE VALLEY. 40,000 Summary of Events and Information April. 1917.	Remarks and references to Appendices
RAILWAY TRIANGLE.	20th	-	The 10th Sherwood Foresters were to be in the front line from (H. 36. A) to X roads in (H. 29. d. 8. 7)	
BROWN LINE	21st	-	The Bn moved again into the Brown Line, Bn HQ this time being at (H. 28. C. central).	
	22nd		The Bn moved into SUNKEN Road in (H. 36. A). Bn HQ being in (H. 35. B).	
Front Line.	23rd	4:50AM	The ~~moved~~ Bn moved from SUNKEN Road across the open towards BAYONET TRENCH. Very heavy M. Gun fire was opened from the direction of ROEUX and only the right of the line got into the trench. The remainder took shelter in shell-holes + short pieces of trench which were available. It was then ascertained that only the right portion of BAYONET TRENCH was in our hands, the remainder being occupied by the enemy. The left of the line therefore had to stay in shell holes which they commenced to make into one continuous line as far as possible. A bombing attack was planned on the right to drive the enemy from BAYONET TRENCH. This however was cancelled by the Division. The first attack on BAYONET TRENCH by the Borders + Staffords was not successful owing to M. Guns.	
" "	24th	4.0AM.	The Bn were relieved in the line by the 10th West Yorkshire Regt. On relief the Bn moved back by Coys independently to the RAILWAY TRIANGLE. Here the Brigade Depot details came to the Bn as reinforcements.	
RAILWAY TRIANGLE	25th	-	The Bn moved into ARRAS starting from the triangle at 6.0 AM. Breakfasts were had in a field near the Gasworks. At 10.0 AM the Bn fell in + marched to the Station ARRAS and entrained for SAULTY Station arriving there 12.30 pm the Bn marched to GRAND RULLECOURT, were ~~they~~ it was billeted. The Bn was relieved in the Triangle by a Bn of 35th Division. The time here was spent in reorganising as far as possible.	
GRAND RULLECOURT.	29th		Orders were received that Bn would move by buss to AGNES + would be billeted there in a hutment camp.	JCN

2449 Wt. W14957/M90 750,000 1/16 J.B.C. & A. Forms/C.2118/12.

Army Form C. 2118.

Instructions regarding War Diaries and Intelligence Summaries are contained in F. S. Regs., Part II. and the Staff Manual respectively. Title Pages will be prepared in manuscript.

WAR DIARY
or
~~INTELLIGENCE SUMMARY~~
(Erase heading not required.)

10th Sherwood Foresters.

April. 1917.

Place	Date	Hour	~~SHEET~~ LENS. 11. 1/100 000 Summary of Events and Information	Remarks and references to Appendices
GRAND RULLECOURT.	30	–	Casualties during the month. a/Lieut Col. L. Gilbert – wounded & prisoner of war. a/Capt. J. P. Tucker. } Lieut. F.H.M. Collier. } " W.R.L. Davis. } killed in action. 2Lt W.J.P. McCombe. } " G.R.Y. Thurlow } " C.C. Baker. wounded. All these officer casualties were on 23/4/17. Casualties Other ranks. Killed. 16. Wounded. 80. Missing. 9. Strength decrease. 2Lt Williamson. T.B, to England sick. 69 other ranks to hospital. Strength Increase. Capt. Meads J.A. – Capt. L. ROE. – Lieut. W. E. BRANDT these officers joined April 4th. 2Lt. J. E. LEWIS – 2Lt H. TUGWELL – joined 29/4/17. Strength Increase during month. 65 other ranks joined 1st April. 143 " " " 29th ". 81 " " " 30th ".	JCN

2449 Wt. W14957/M90 750,000 1/16 J.B.C. & A. Forms/C.2118/12.

Vol 21

Instructions regarding War Diaries and Intelligence Summaries are contained in F. S. Regs., Part II. and the Staff Manual respectively. Title pages will be prepared in manuscript.

WAR DIARY
or
~~INTELLIGENCE SUMMARY.~~
(Erase heading not required.)

Army Form C. 2118.

17/51

MAY. 1917.

Place	Date	Hour	Summary of Events and Information	Remarks and references to Appendices
			Refce. BIACHE 1/20000	
			" 51B.N.W. "	
			10th Sherwood Foresters.	
GRAND RULLECOURT.	1st		The Bn moved by motor bus to Y Camp situated at the junction of the HABARCQ with the main ARRAS - ST POL Road (Refce. LENS. 11).	
Y HUTS. ST NICHOLAS CAMP.	3rd		The Bn marched from Y Hut Camp to a bivouac camp East of ST NICHOLAS (G.17. central). While at this camp the Battalion was used for digging a Cable trench under the supervision of the Corps Signals. The men worked very well indeed in spite of the fact that some parties, working in day light were heavily shelled.	
RAILWAY CUTTING.	10th		The Bn moved at about 10'30 AM into the RAILWAY CUTTING. (H.7.B.). The Cable Burying parties still continued daily.	
LEMON TRENCH.	12th		The Bn moved up into the Green Line into LEMON TRENCH and started from RAILWAY CUTTING about 8.30 pm, with about 300 yards between Coys. On reaching LEMON TRENCH (H.10.D) the Bn came under the orders of the 50th Brigade. We Bn were sent up to be in Reserve to the 50th Brigade in case of an enemy counter-attack. From the moment the Bn arrived in the 50th Brigade area it ~~they~~ was used to do most of the carrying parties for 50th Brigade. Carrying rations & Bombs, SAA & other stores both day & night. On several occasions the whole Bn was out at one time on various parties leaving only HQ details in the trench. In this way the whole Bn both Officers and men became worn out before ever they went in to hold the line.	96 / 22
FRONT LINE.	14th		The Bn received orders to relieve ~~[illegible]~~ the 10th West Yorks in CUBA TRENCH.	

A5834 Wt. W4973 M687 750,000 8/16 D. D. & L. Ltd. Forms/C.2118/13.

Army Form C. 2118.

Instructions regarding War Diaries and Intelligence Summaries are contained in F. S. Regs., Part II. and the Staff Manual respectively. Title pages will be prepared in manuscript.

WAR DIARY
or
~~INTELLIGENCE SUMMARY.~~
(Erase heading not required.)

10th Sherwood Foresters.

Place	Date	Hour	Summary of Events and Information	Remarks and references to Appendices
			Refce. 51B.N.W. 1/20000. MAY. 1917.	
Front Line	14th	–	Two Coys only namely "A" on the right and "C" on the left relieved the West Yorks. The Bn was responsible from CUT trench on the right exclusive to (I.7.B.0.6). The Support Coy, "B" Coy was in CHILI situated in the habitable parts of the trench between (H.12.B.7.6) to junction of CHILI and HALCYON. No other trenches nearer the front line could be found that had not been destroyed by shell-fire. "D" Coy remained in reserve in LEMON TRENCH.	
" "	16th	–	The enemy attacked on our right at dawn but there was no change on our front. A counter attack however on our right drove him back to his original line. Everything was normal on our front during the whole attack. On a report that the enemy were in CLYDE being received, our "B" Coy proceeded to bomb down CHILI and the trenches round. However only one wounded prisoner was found in CLYDE. No more being seen anywhere near. "B" + D Coys were used every night for carrying up the front Coys rations, + also for carrying up S.A.A, Bombs, Sandbags etc. Parties were also sent up from these two Coys to assist in repairing the front line trench. Work on CHILI TRENCH was very difficult. The trench was cleared for some distance one day but was blown in almost immediately. CHILI seemed to be a favourite trench, + was fired on regularly, the range appeared to be known exactly. Bn HQ were situated in HUSSAR TRENCH about (H.11.B.6.9).	

A5834 Wt. W4973 M687 750,000 8/16 D. D. & L. Ltd. Forms/C.2118/13.

Instructions regarding War Diaries and Intelligence Summaries are contained in F. S. Regs., Part II. and the Staff Manual respectively. Title pages will be prepared in manuscript.

WAR DIARY
or
~~INTELLIGENCE SUMMARY.~~
(Erase heading not required.)

Army Form C. 2118.

10th Sherwood Foresters.

Place	Date	Hour	Summary of Events and Information — Refce. 51 B. N.W. 1/20000. MAY. 1917.	Remarks and references to Appendices
Front Line	18th		Early in the morning an enemy aeroplane flying low over our trenches was fired at by our Lewis Guns & rifle fire & was brought down and fell just over the parapet about (I. 7. B. 2. 4). The Pilot and observer were taken prisoner. The pilot could talk a little English & both could speak French very well. On the night 18th/19th "C" Coy were relieved on the left in the line by our "B" Coy, on relief "C" Coy took over Support in CHILI TRENCH.	
" "	19th		On the night 19th/20th the front line was reorganised into a Two Bn front. The Bn on our left extending to their right. The 7th Border Regt on our right with a Company of the ~~8th~~ S. Staffords took over from our two Coys in the line. The junction between the two Bns on the 51st Brigade front became the Grid line running E in (I. 7.). Our left Coy relief was delayed until almost daylight, owing to the Company of 8th S. Staffs not turning up. The 7th Borders eventually took over that portion of the line & relieved them. On ~~this~~ relief A Coy went into the SUNKEN Rd in (H. 11. A) & B Coy went into HUDSON and HUSSAR. Bn HQ moved into the Sunken road to about (H. 11. A. 6. 2.).	
Reserve Line.	20th		The Bn were relieved in reserve by the 10th West Yorkes & on relief marched by Coys to camp E of ST NICHOLAS. (G. 17. C. 6. 7). The relief was very late in arriving & the Coys were not all in until daylight about 3.15 AM. The next day was a day of rest.	
ST NICHOLAS CAMP.	21st		The day was spent in kit inspections also a thorough medical inspection,	

A5834 Wt W4973 M687 750,000 8/16 D. D. & L. Ltd. Forms/C.2118/13.

Instructions regarding War Diaries and Intelligence Summaries are contained in F. S. Regs., Part II. and the Staff Manual respectively. Title pages will be prepared in manuscript.

WAR DIARY
or
~~INTELLIGENCE SUMMARY.~~
(Erase heading not required.)

10th Sherwood Foresters

Army Form C. 2118.

Place	Date	Hour	Summary of Events and Information — Refce. 51 B. N.W. 1/20,000 — MAY, 1917.	Remarks and references to Appendices
ST NICHOLAS CAMP to BLACK LINE	22nd		The Bn were ordered to move up to the BLACK LINE as soon after dinner as possible. The orders were not received ~~at~~ until nearly 1·0 pm. An advance party was immediately sent to erect bivouacs which were drawn from a dump near the Black Line. The Bn arrived in the Black Line about 5·0 pm. In the meantime orders were received that the whole Bn would be required as strong as possible for Cable Burying.	
BLACK LINE	26th		The Bn received orders that they would relieve the 7th Yorks in the GREEN Line on night 27th/28th. Also that the 9th Northumberland Fus. would relieve the Bn at the cable Burying the same night. During the whole time the Bn have been cable burying the men have worked with a wonderful spirit, this was borne out by the Corps Signals Officer. The bivouacs were heavily shelled in the Sunken road on the 26th + the bivouacs were all moved into the trench. During the time that the Bn were in the Black Line the Bn were out every night as strong as possible Cable Burying.	
GREEN LINE.	27th		The Bn relieved the 7th Yorks in the Green line, in HERON TRENCH. While in this line the Bn was used for carrying parties.	
	29th		Orders were received that the Bn would relieve the 7th Lincolns in the Left Sector the same night. This order was cancelled, + the Bn remained where it was with the exception of "A" Coy who formed a new Strong point at the junction of HUDSON + HUSSAR TRENCHES.	

A5834 Wt. W4973 M687 750,000 8/16 D. D. & L. Ltd. Forms/C.2118/13.

Instructions regarding War Diaries and Intelligence Summaries are contained in F. S. Regs., Part II. and the Staff Manual respectively. Title pages will be prepared in manuscript.

WAR DIARY
or
~~INTELLIGENCE SUMMARY.~~
(Erase heading not required.)

Army Form C. 2118.

10th Sherwood Foresters.

Refce. LENS 11 — MAY. 1917.

Place	Date	Hour	Summary of Events and Information	Remarks and references to Appendices
Green Line	30th		The Bn were relieved by a Bn of the 101st Brigade (15th Royal Scots). On relief the Bn marched to ST. NICHOLAS CAMP	
ST. NICHOLAS CAMP	31st	9.0 AM	Bn marched to ARRAS Station & entrained at 10 AM for MONDICOURT. Bn arrived at MONDICOURT about 1.30 pm & went into billets there.	
			Casualties during the month: - 2/Lt. MARSHALL - 2/Lt BOWMER wounded. 2/Lt LEWIS. Shell-shock.	
			Other ranks. 19 Killed - 72 Wounded - 8 wounded at duty.	
			Officers struck off during month. 2/Lt. L. JACQUES to Eng. Sick - CAPT. T.P.C. WILSON. To 51st Bde as Staff Captain.	
			Other ranks struck off. 90.	
			Strength Increase. Lieut. S.C. DAY (rejoined) 31st 2/Lieut R.A. PAGE (") " P. DORRINGTON. (joined) " C.R. REYNARD. " " F.J. EMSON. " " J.C. BALLANTYNE "	
			Other ranks joined. 76.	

PCN

A5834 Wt. W4973 M687 750,000 8/16 D. D. & L. Ltd. Forms/C.2118/13.

Army Form C. 2118.

Vol 22

Instructions regarding War Diaries and Intelligence Summaries are contained in F. S. Regs., Part II. and the Staff Manual respectively. Title Pages will be prepared in manuscript.

WAR DIARY
or
~~INTELLIGENCE SUMMARY~~
(Erase heading not required.)

10th Sherwood Foresters.

Place	Date	Hour	Summary of Events and Information — LENS 11. & 57 D. — JUNE. 1917.	Remarks and references to Appendices
MONDICOURT	1st	–	The Bn had a day of rest & prepared for training.	
~	2nd		Baths were allotted to the Bn & thorough kit inspections were held & indents for deficiencies were sent in. ~~Some~~ All available men were inocculated.	
~	3rd		This was a day of rest after the inocculation.	
	4th		The Bn were inspected by the Commanding Officer.	
	5th		Bn trained as per programme – Bayonet fighting – Musketry etc on training ground (U.25.c.).	
	6th		Training as for yesterday.	
	7th		Training continued in the morning. In the afternoon the Divisional Horse Show was held in a field near MONDICOURT STATION.	
	8th		Brigade route march – The route was POMMERA – GRENAS – Pas – MONDICOURT. Training continued up to the 19th in the usual way.	L 23
	19th		On ~~the~~ the 19th there was a Brigade Field day this was carried out on ground near HURTEBISE FARM (C.19). These Brigade days were ordered with a view to showing what a quantity of detail is forgotten when a position is captured in real warfare. Walking parties are not detailed straight away nor are Lewis Guns sent forward, as should be the case.	
	20th		There was another Bde day on the same ground as before, tins & drums were used to represent our barrage fire.	YCN

Instructions regarding War Diaries and Intelligence Summaries are contained in F. S. Regs., Part II. and the Staff Manual respectively. Title Pages will be prepared in manuscript.

WAR DIARY
or
~~INTELLIGENCE SUMMARY~~
(Erase heading not required.)

Army Form C. 2118

10th Sherwood Foresters

Place	Date	Hour	Summary of Events and Information — LENS 11. & 57B. — JUNE 1917.	Remarks and references to Appendices
MONDICOURT	21st		The Battalion embussed for ARRAS at approx. (U.27.B.3.5) the Brigade marched there at intervals of 5 minutes between Battalions. The time of embussing was 8.30 AM. The Battalion passed the starting point (X roads N.W of MONDICOURT (near MONDICOURT Stn) at 7.50 AM. The Transports moved independently starting from the Xroads near BELLEVUE (U.23.B.0.8) at 6.15 AM. Everyone was embussed by 9.45 AM & the Buses moved off arriving in ARRAS & at the debussing point (ROND POINT) at about 1.0 pm. The Bn then marched into camp at ST NICHOLAS arriving in camp about 2.15 pm. The Transport arrived in camp about 4.0 pm.	
ST NICHOLAS CAMP	22nd		Orders were received from Bde who were in the next camp that the Training would continue & ground suitable for the purpose was reconnoitred near MAISON ROUGE NW of ST CATHERINE. The Bn then had orders that it would be required for digging a Cable Trench on the South side of the river SCARPE, the Bn were employed on this for three nights – about 350 other ranks being found each night. The last night 150 other ranks from the 3/4 W. Kents were attached for digging.	YCN

1875 Wt. W593/826 1,000,000 4/15 J.B.C. & A. A.D.S.S./Forms/C. 2118.

Army Form C. 2118.

WAR DIARY
or
~~INTELLIGENCE SUMMARY~~
(Erase heading not required.)

Instructions regarding War Diaries and Intelligence Summaries are contained in F. S. Regs., Part II. and the Staff Manual respectively. Title Pages will be prepared in manuscript.

10th Sherwood Foresters

Place	Date	Hour	51. B. N. W. Summary of Events and Information JUNE 1917.	Remarks and references to Appendices
ST NICHOLAS CAMP.	27th	–	Orders were received that the Bn would relieve in the left Sector of the Divisional front on the night 29/30th. Relief was to be complete by 4.0 AM 30th.	
			All Company commanders were sent up to reconnoitre the line, & also on the 28th all available officers reconnoitred the Bn front.	
Front Line	29th		One officer per Coy was sent as the Bn front had been changed.	
			For this tour one Coy of 3/4 W. Kents were attached to the Bn for training in Trench warfare. These were split up by platoons & occupied the front line alternately with our "A" Coy.	
			The Bn left ST NICHOLAS CAMP about 9.0 pm, as the orders stated they were not to pass the bridge over the RAILWAY CUTTING until 10.15 pm.	
			They moved off in order A – B – C – D.	
			The communication trenches to be used by the Bn were CALEDONIAN and CIVIL.	
			Dispositions in the line were A Coy + 1 Coy. 3/4 W. Kents in Front Line. B Coy in Close Support. C " in Support. D " " Reserve.	
	30th		Relief was complete by 3.30 AM.	HCN

2449 Wt. W14957/M90 750,000 1/16 J.B.C. & A. Forms/C.2118/12.

Instructions regarding War Diaries and Intelligence Summaries are contained in F. S. Regs., Part II. and the Staff Manual respectively. Title Pages will be prepared in manuscript.

WAR DIARY
or
~~INTELLIGENCE SUMMARY~~
(Erase heading not required.)

Army Form C. 2118.

10th Sherwood Foresters.

JUNE 1917.

Place	Date	Hour	Summary of Events and Information	Remarks and references to Appendices
Front Line.	30th		Officers joined. – Nil	
			Officers struck off – 2Lt. C. K. HOPE. to England sick 26th.	
			Other Ranks joined. – 83 other ranks.	
			Wastage during the month. 103 other ranks.	
			Casualties during the month. Officers – Wounded – Capt. A. J. M. Lawder wounded 30th.	
			Other ranks. Nil.	

2449 Wt. W14957/M90 750,000 1/16 J.B.C. & A. Forms/C.2118/12.

Army Form C. 2118.

Vol 23

WAR DIARY
or
~~INTELLIGENCE SUMMARY~~
(Erase heading not required.)

Instructions regarding War Diaries and Intelligence Summaries are contained in F. S. Regs., Part II. and the Staff Manual respectively. Title Pages will be prepared in manuscript.

JULY. 1917.

Place	Date	Hour	Summary of Events and Information — 51. B. N. W. 1/10000 — 10th Sherwood Foresters.	Remarks and references to Appendices
Front Line.	1st	–	Nothing of importance happened, ordinary trench warfare.	
" "	2nd		Enemy started Trench mortaring at night about 1.0 AM + also again at "Stand To" with medium Trench mortars.	
" "	3rd		Nothing to record except the Trench mortaring as for yesterday at the same times.	
" "	4th		Battalion were relieved by 7th Borders in the line on the left Sector, + took over the shelters vacated by the Borders in the Black Line. Relief was complete by 2.15 AM on the 5th. at 10.30 pm on the night 4th the artillery carried out a Creeping barrage on WHALE TRENCH.	
Black Line	5th		The day was spent in cleaning up + upitching shelters.	
"	6th		Nothing to record.	
"	7th		Training was carried on as usual.	96
"	8th		The Battalion relieved the 7th Borders in the front line left Sector also 1 Coy 3/4 R. West. Kents in HELFORD TRENCH. Bn HQ were situated in HELFORD. Dispositions were as follows:– D Coy left Front Line – C Coy Right Front Line – A Coy left Support – B Coy Right Support. A + B Coys were both situated in CORK TRENCH. Coys moved from Black line at 200 yds interval in order D.C.A.B. D Coy moved at 8.45 pm. Relief was complete at 2.0 AM on 9th.	2 4
Front Line	9th		Two Coys of Borders ~~remained~~ to HURRUN TR. + did not leave the area. These came under the orders of O.C. 10th Sherwood Foresters.	JCR

2449 Wt. W14957/M90 750,000 1/16 J.B.C. & A. Forms/C.2118/12.

Instructions regarding War Diaries and Intelligence Summaries are contained in F. S. Regs., Part II. and the Staff Manual respectively. Title Pages will be prepared in manuscript.

WAR DIARY
or
~~INTELLIGENCE SUMMARY~~
(Erase heading not required.)

Army Form C. 2118.

JULY 1917.

Refce 57 B. N.W. 1/20000

10th Sherwood Foresters.

Place	Date	Hour	Summary of Events and Information	Remarks and references to Appendices
Front Line	9th		These 2 Coys of Borders were used for various carrying parties. Patrols were sent out by the Bn to try & ascertain (1) whether the shell-holes were occupied in front of CONRAD & (2) the condition of the enemy's wire. The shell holes were empty & the wire was found to be quite good.	
" "	10th		Hurricane one minute bombardments were carried out on various enemy positions on night 10th/11th. A great deal of work was done in revetting the front line trenches & deepening them. The two support Coys were used for carrying rations every night & also for work on CORK TRENCH. Patrols were sent out & saw a large enemy wiring party, so returned & opened L. Gun fire on them.	
" "	11th		A gas bombardment was carried out on night 11th/12th on enemy trenches some rounds in front of COLIN fell short. Orders were received that the 7th Borders would make a raid on enemy trenches on night 14/15. B.G.C of 51st Inf Bde held conference on above raid at Sherwood HQ on morning of 11th.	
" "	12th		Divisional artillery bombardment as under:- At 4.0 pm for a one minute bombardment all 18 Pdrs barraged WIT TRENCH and 4.5 Hows bombarded WOBBLE. Special precautions were taken to avoid casualties from short rounds, of which there were a few.	FCM
" "	13th		Preparations for Raid were made, trench bridges were carried up &	

2449 Wt. W14957/M90 750,000 1/16 J.B.C. & A. Forms/C.2118/12.

Army Form C. 2118.

Instructions regarding War Diaries and Intelligence Summaries are contained in F. S. Regs., Part II. and the Staff Manual respectively. Title Pages will be prepared in manuscript.

WAR DIARY
or
~~INTELLIGENCE SUMMARY~~
(Erase heading not required.)

JULY. 1917.

Place	Date	Hour	Refce 51. B. N.W. 1/20000 — Summary of Events and Information — 10th Sherwood Foresters.	Remarks and references to Appendices
Front Line	13th	—	The ~~party~~ numbering 4 officers + 100 OR's came into the trenches on the night 13/14 + were accomodated by 10th Sher. Fors. All necessary Stokes + heavy trench mortar ammunition was carried up on this night. The idea was to carry out a raid from CONRAD TR. the object being to kill Germans ~~+~~ destroy dugouts + secure identifications. The party was divided into 2 the objective of (1st) was WIT TRENCH 50 yds on each side of C.T. at (I.1.B.7.7) (2nd) was C.T. from (I.1.B.7.7) to trench junction at (I.1.B.8.8) inclusive.	
	14th		All the party for above raid were in CONRAD TRENCH in position by 8.30 pm. Zero hour was 10.0 pm. By 9.45 pm all raiding party were out of the trench + lying in front of the parapet. At 10.0 pm the artillery barrage dropped on WIT. The party got into the trench + saw Germans running away as far as was known no Germans were killed. The party returned + the casualties were very slight, being 1 missing + about 5 slightly wounded. A patrol was sent out from the b.atta about 2.0 AM + this patrol found a body, which was afterwards found to be the body of the missing man of the Borders.	FCN

2449 Wt. W14957/M90 750,000 1/16 J.B.C. & A. Forms/C.2118/12.

Army Form C. 2118.

Instructions regarding War Diaries and Intelligence Summaries are contained in F. S. Regs., Part II. and the Staff Manual respectively. Title pages will be prepared in manuscript.

WAR DIARY
or
INTELLIGENCE SUMMARY.
(Erase heading not required.)

JULY, 1917.

10th Sherwood Foresters.

Place	Date	Hour	Summary of Events and Information (57. B. N.W. 1/20000)	Remarks and references to Appendices
Front Line	14th	–	Rockets were sent up from the New Bn HQ in CIVIL to let the party know which way to return. This was found to be of great assistance in knowing the way back.	
" "	15th		A special artillery test was carried out at 10.0 p.m. night 15/16th. Golden rain rockets were sent up & the artillery answered with one round per battery. Machine guns with one short burst per gun. The first shot from the 18 Pdrs arrived in 30 seconds. Machine guns opened instantaneously. The Bn were relieved by the 9th West Ridings & proceeded on relief to ST NICOLAS CAMP. Owing to the relieving Bn being very late in starting the relief was not complete till 3.0 AM.	
ST NICHOLAS	16th		The day spent in cleaning up & kit inspections.	
" "	17th		Baths were allotted to the Bn & A+B Coys were detailed, the remainder carried on training.	
" "	18th		C+D Coys had baths & A+B carried on as yesterday.	
" "	19th		Route March. The route taken was ST NICHOLAS – MAISON ROUGE – ST. CATHERINE – ANZIN – G.1.D.6.0 – MADAGASCAR – MON. ROUGE – ST. NICHOLAS. In the afternoon there was a lecture to all Officers by the G.S.O. I on the Battle of MESSINES.	
" "	20th		Training as usual. While Bn were out for this tour 1 Officer + 25 O.R's were working on Tunnelling under R.E + lived at Railway Bridge on ATHIES Road.	JCN

A5834 Wt. W4973 M687 750,000 8/16 D. D. & L. Ltd. Forms/C.2118/13.

Instructions regarding War Diaries and Intelligence Summaries are contained in F. S. Regs., Part II. and the Staff Manual respectively. Title pages will be prepared in manuscript.

WAR DIARY
or
~~INTELLIGENCE SUMMARY.~~
(Erase heading not required.)

Army Form C. 2118.

JULY. 1917

Place	Date	Hour	57. B. N.W. 20000 — Summary of Events and Information — 10th Sherwood Foresters.	Remarks and references to Appendices
ST. NICHOLAS,	21st.	–	Route march with small Coy schemes at intervals such as artillery formations etc. Route taken was – ST NICHOLAS – ST. CATHERINE – ANZIN – MADAGASCAR – MAISON ROUGE – ST. NICHOLAS. Lecture in afternoon by Brigadier on "Trench Warfare".	
" "	22nd		The Bn were shelled in their camp by a naval gun, only one slight casualty. This cancelled church parade & the Bn moved into a vacant camp ~~at~~ on the BAILLEUL – ST NICHOLAS road about 200 yds N.E of the old one.	
Green Line now called "GAVRELLE SWITCH"	23rd		The Bn moved up to the Green Line or GAVRELLE Switch as it is now called & took over from the 10th West Yorks. They were ordered not to pass the railway Bridge at (H.14.C.1.3) before 10.55 pm. Battn HQ were in the TANK dump Sunken Road. at about 11.0 pm the enemy started shelling on the right of the river SCARPE. One Officer per Coy was sent on ahead to take over.	
"	24th		Working parties were found. for carrying rations & trench mortar ammunition	
"	25th		Trench work as usual & repairing trenches. At night working & carrying parties were found amounting to 4 Officers + 140 other ranks.	
"	26th		Carrying parties as usual numbers found were 9 Officers + 220 O.R's.	
"	27th		The same as for yesterday carrying parties of 8 Officers + 242 O.R's.	
"	~~28th~~		~~Working + carrying parties as usual~~ The following bombardments were carried out of the 27th.	

A5834 Wt. W4973/M687 750,000 8/16 D. D. & L. Ltd. Forms/C.2118/13.

Army Form C. 2118.

Instructions regarding War Diaries and Intelligence Summaries are contained in F. S. Regs., Part II. and the Staff Manual respectively. Title pages will be prepared in manuscript.

WAR DIARY
or
~~INTELLIGENCE SUMMARY.~~
(Erase heading not required.)

JULY. 1917.

Place	Date	Hour	Summary of Events and Information	Remarks and references to Appendices
			51. B. N.W. 1/20000. 10th Sherwood Foresters.	
GREEN LINE	27th	–	Zero hour was 3.0 pm. The bombardment lasted 3 minutes one Brigade R.F.A searched as follows:- (I. 20. c. 80.15) to (I. 21. C. 20.15) Road (I. 20. C. 75.37) to (I. 21. C. 20. 15). Road (I. 20. C. 70. 65) to (I. 20. D. 70. 70). 4.5 Hows (I. 27. a. 40. 40) Road Junction (I. 21. C. 38. 10) and point (I. 21. C. 35. 20), Cross Roads at (I. 20. d. 70. 70). Orders received that the following would take place. Barrage to be put down on WIT TRENCH at 5.0 pm and on WART TRENCH at 3.0 pm on 28th inst. On the 27th the 4.5 Hows fired on WOOL TRENCH + WIBBLE TRENCH.	
" "	28th		On the 28th 4.5 Hows fired on T.M. emplacement at (I. 2. C. 38. 57) + S. end of WHIP at (I. 2. C. 55. 10). New work at (I. 8. A. 70. 10) work at (I. 8. B. 20. 55) + work at (I. 8. B. 60. 35). Rate of fire was 18 Pdrs. 3 rounds per gun per minute and 4.5 Hows was 2 rounds per gun per minute. Time was checked at 3.30 pm on 27th + 1.0 pm on 28th. A gas bombardment was ordered for 12 midnight on night 27/28 but was cancelled. Working + carrying parties as usual were asked from the Battalion.	
	29th		Bn were called upon to find working + carrying parties.	
	30th		Ordinary trench work. Carrying parties were found for 7th Borders on this night for their rations, as the enemy's shelling during the day seemed to point to an attack. It was therefore thought advisable not to weaken the Bn in the front line more than was absolutely necessary.	FCN

A5834 Wt. W4973/M687 750,000 8/16 D. D. & L. Ltd. Forms/C.2118/13.

Army Form C. 2118.

Instructions regarding War Diaries and Intelligence Summaries are contained in F. S. Regs., Part II. and the Staff Manual respectively. Title pages will be prepared in manuscript.

WAR DIARY
or
~~INTELLIGENCE SUMMARY.~~
(Erase heading not required.)

JULY. 1917.

Place	Date	Hour	Summary of Events and Information	Remarks and references to Appendices
			Map. 57. B. N.W. 1/20000. 10th Sherwood Foresters.	
Front Line	31st		The Battn relieved the 7th Borders in the line on the night 31st/1st Aug. Dispositions were as follows:– A B + C Coys were in the Front Line with two platoons of each Coy respectively in support to them. D Coy were in reserve + found the carrying parties for rations etc to the Bn dump from the canal. all rations etc coming up by barge on the canal The right of the Battn rested on (I. 20. A. 45. 95) The left " " " " " (I. 14. A. 50. 50). Battn HQ were in CRETE (H. 24. 3. 80. 90). Reserve Coy were in the railway embankment in (H. 18. D). Casualties during the month. Capt T. M. WILLCOX wounded 6-7-17. Lieut. E. J. de Groot. (shell shock) 4-7-17 other ranks killed 18 :– wounded 27 :– wounded at duty 3 Wastage Officers Nil :– other ranks 35 (evac. hospital) Reinforcements 16th July 2Lieut T. J. Couch. 18th " 2Lieuts R. W. ELGAR – F. G. Ferguson and G. R. BARTEN. 26th July 2Lieut – W. C. WICKS. other Ranks reinforcements. 16th July 23. 18th " 21 26th " 14	

A5834 Wt. W4973/M687 750,000 8/16 D. D. & L. Ltd. Forms/C.2118/13.

Instructions regarding War Diaries and Intelligence Summaries are contained in F. S. Regs., Part II. and the Staff Manual respectively. Title pages will be prepared in manuscript.

WAR DIARY
or
~~INTELLIGENCE SUMMARY.~~
(Erase heading not required.)

Army Form C. 2118.

Vol 24

10th Sherwood Foresters.

PLOUVAIN 1/10000

August. 1917.

Place	Date	Hour	Summary of Events and Information	Remarks and references to Appendices
Front Line	1st		The first day in the Right Sector of the Divisional Front. The left front line were trench mortared during the night. Patrols were sent out from all Companies and Lieut R. S. Gustard was wounded. The reserve Company (D Coy) were used each night for carrying up stores of R E material & water & rations to the Front line Companies. Artillery barraged WIT TRENCH and HART TRENCH.	
" "	2nd		Trench Warfare as usual. Artillery programmes of harassing fire were carried out as usual. Patrols were sent out as usual to try & get a specimen of the enemy's wire in front of shell holes in (I. 14 c) which were reported to be held. This however was not obtained.	
" "	3rd		Trench Warfare as usual. Artillery programmes on enemy's trenches were carried out. Patrols were sent out & a dead German was found quite freshly killed with nearly new clothes on. His shoulder straps were cut off & brought in, but owing to the proximity of the enemy's patrols his body could not be brought back.	
" "	4th		Orders were received that on the night 5th/6th a barrage would be put down on enemy's occupied shell holes in I. 14. c & that the Battn would send out patrols afterwards to secure identifications. Gaps were cut in the wire on this night.	
" "	5th		Trench Warfare as usual. Operation orders were received re action of patrols on night 5/6th. Zero hour was ordered for 10.30 pm. (See. Operation Orders attached).	

A5834 Wt. W4973 M687 750,000 8/16 D. D. & L. Ltd. Forms/C.2118/13.

Army Form C. 2118.

Instructions regarding War Diaries and Intelligence Summaries are contained in F. S. Regs., Part II. and the Staff Manual respectively. Title pages will be prepared in manuscript.

WAR DIARY
or
~~INTELLIGENCE SUMMARY~~.
(Erase heading not required.)

10th Sherwood Foresters

Place	Date	Hour	Summary of Events and Information — PLOUVAIN 1/10,000. August 1917.	Remarks and references to Appendices
Front Line	5th	–	A Patrol of 3 officers - 3 NCO's + 30 men was sent out in 3 parties under Lieut. C.F.B. Cox - Lieut S.C. DAY - and 2Lt F. MARCHANT to secure identifications from wounded or dead of the enemy (see operation orders attached). The Artillery were not successful in silencing the enemy's machine guns which will be seen from the reports of the officers engaged in this patrol (attached). No identifications were secured but the casualties on the whole were slight.	
" "	6th		Trench warfare as usual. Patrols were sent out at night but no definite information was gained.	
" "	7th		Trench warfare as usual. Patrols sent out at night ran into large enemy working + wiring parties.	
" "	8th	3.45 AM	At 3.45 AM the enemy dropped a heavy barrage on our front + support lines also on the Lincolns on our left. He entered the Lincolns lines with a large raiding party. This party was afterwards found out to be 3 officers + 150 other ranks strong. Casualties were heavy from the bombardment. One wounded German was captured + taken to the Battn Aid Post. The men of the Battn showed excellent pluck + determination during this raid + several men distinguished themselves. Dead were seen lying in No Man's Land in the daylight + efforts were made to secure further identification. At about noon a sentry reported that he could see some of the enemy near one of the Sap-heads in our lines. He at once notified 2Lt. W.C. Weeks. This officer with	JCM

A5834 Wt. W4973 M687 750,000 8/16 D. D. & L. Ltd. Forms/C.2118/13.

Instructions regarding War Diaries and Intelligence Summaries are contained in F. S. Regs., Part II. and the Staff Manual respectively. Title pages will be prepared in manuscript.

WAR DIARY
or
~~INTELLIGENCE SUMMARY.~~
(Erase heading not required.)

Army Form C. 2118.

10th Sherwood Foresters

Place	Date	Hour	Summary of Events and Information — PLOUVAIN 1/10000. — August 1917	Remarks and references to Appendices
Front Line	8th		great presence of mind at once got a party of 4 other ranks & went to the Sap-head named. They got out in the grass into No man's land & almost immediately were received with Bombs which wounded all the 4 other ranks. 2Lt. W. C Wicks at once with one of his men who was already hit in the arm charged straight for them. The enemy of which there were nine turned round to run away. 2Lt Wicks shot 3 with his revolver & his bomber with him shot another with his rifle, who was just levelling his rifle at 2Lt Wicks thereby saving his life. They brought one of these bodies in. The remainder of the enemy party running away. During the day the body of a German Officer was found in No man's land with explosives on him for blowing in dugouts etc. The raiding party were hereby found out to be STORM troops Specially picked men from the 6th German Army. These men were kept & fed up solely for raiding. Letters of appreciation on the above were received from Both the Divisional & Bde Commanders copies of which are attached.	
– –	8th		The Battn was relieved by the 12th Manchesters & on relief moved back to ST. NICHOLAS CAMP, arriving there about 3.30 AM.	JGW

Instructions regarding War Diaries and Intelligence Summaries are contained in F. S. Regs., Part II. and the Staff Manual respectively. Title pages will be prepared in manuscript.

WAR DIARY
or
~~INTELLIGENCE SUMMARY.~~
(Erase heading not required.)

Army Form C. 2118.

10th Sherwood Foresters

August 1917.

Place	Date	Hour	57. B. N. W. 1/20000 + PLOUVAIN, MAP. Summary of Events and Information	Remarks and references to Appendices
ST NICHOLAS CAMP.	8th	—	Lieut Col. H. J. King took over Command of the Battalion from Lieut Col R. J. Milne.	
" "	9th	—	The day was spent cleaning up.	
" "	10th	—	Parades as usual.	
" "	11th		Lt Col. R. J. Milne left the Battalion + proceeded to join the 7th Somerset Light Infantry as 2nd in Command.	
" "	12th		Training as usual was carried on with small route marches ~~to the training~~ Ground. Range practice was got on the ARRAS MOAT Range + also the Butte de TIR range ARRAS.	
~~Frontline~~ GAVRELLE SWITCH.	16th		The Bn moved up to the GAVRELLE SWITCH Line + became the left Support Battalion.	
	17th		While in this area the Battalion was called upon for large working parties both by day + by night working on the communication trenches + assisting the R.E in laying the pipe line. Parties for night work averaged about 300 men per night.	
	20th		There was a special working party ordered this night to dig a new reserve line called CHICKEN RESERVE. The line runs behind CORK SUPPORT. The party ordered was 4 officers + 150 other ranks. The Battn were allotted the piece to dig between CIVIL + CALEDONIAN C.T's, approx from H.6.B.50.45 to H.6.D.60.60	

Army Form C. 2118.

Instructions regarding War Diaries and Intelligence Summaries are contained in F. S. Regs., Part II. and the Staff Manual respectively. Title pages will be prepared in manuscript.

WAR DIARY
or
~~INTELLIGENCE SUMMARY.~~
(Erase heading not required.)

10th Sherwood Foresters.

Place	Date	Hour	Summary of Events and Information — PLOUVAIN, 1/10000. August. 1917.	Remarks and references to Appendices
GAVRELLE SWITCH.	21st		Working parties as usual.	
	22nd		A further working party was ordered to continue the digging on CHICKEN RESERVE on night 22/23.	
"	23rd		Working parties as usual.	
Front Line	24th		The Battalion relieved the 7th Borders in the line on the left of the Brigade Sector. This relief was carried out in daylight, starting from the GAVRELLE SWITCH at 5.0 pm. Relief was complete by 8.30 pm.	
"			The dispositions in the line were C Coy right front line — B Coy centre — D Coy left, + A Coy in Battn Support in CORK trench. A Coy were used during this tour, while in support to carry rations + water for the 3 front line Coys.	
"	25th		Enemy trench mortars were active at "Stand to" on the right + left front line Coys also on CORK TRENCH. They were also active during the night.	
"	26th		Trench warfare as usual with patrols at night.	
"	28th		Trench warfare as usual. Capt. D.H. COHEN. joined the Battalion.	
"	29th		Enemy very quiet all day. ~~Nothing of note to report.~~ 2Lieut C.R. BARTEN accidentally wounded, while inspecting rifles in front line about 7.0 pm.	
B	30th		2Lieut. H. Tugwell wounded on patrol about 1.0 AM. It appeared in D.R.O. that the following officers had been awarded the M.C for gallantry Lieut. C.F.S. Cox. — 2Lt. W.C. Wickes	
	31st		Nothing of note happened.	JCN

A5834 Wt. W4973 M687 750,000 8/16 D. D. & L. Ltd. Forms/C.2118/13.

Army Form C. 2118.

Instructions regarding War Diaries and Intelligence Summaries are contained in F. S. Regs., Part II. and the Staff Manual respectively. Title pages will be prepared in manuscript.

WAR DIARY
or
~~INTELLIGENCE SUMMARY.~~
(Erase heading not required.)

10th Sherwood Foresters.

August 1917.

Place	Date	Hour	Summary of Events and Information	Remarks and references to Appendices
			PLOUVAIN. 1/0000	
Front Line.	31st.		Officers joined during the month. 2/Lieut. N.D. Brown 2-8-17.	
			2/Lieut. O. Scott " " (still at the 17th Divl Batn),	
			2/Lieut. H.L.L. Cooper " "	
			Lieut Col. H.J. King 8-8-17 (assumed Command on that date).	
			2/Lieut. H.E. MERRETT. 15-8-17.	
			Capt. H.D. COHEN. 23-8-17.	
			2/Lieut. P. GARTON. 14-8-17.	
			Officers Struck off during month.	
			Lieut R.S. GUSTARD. Wounded. 2-8-17.	
			Lieut Col. R.J. Milne. 9-8-17 (To 7th Somerset L.I).	
			Major. A.A. Stuart. To England Sick 20-8-17.	
			2/Lieut E.J.H. Brooksbank " " 16-8-17.	
			2/Lieut. H. Tugwell. Wounded. 30-8-17.	
			2/Lieut. C.R. Barlen Accidentally wounded. 29-8-17.	
			STRENGTH Increase. 66 other ranks joined from hospital & 17th Divl Depot Bn.	
			Decrease during month in O.R's. Killed & died of wounds. 12	
			Wounded. 43.	
			Sick Wastage. 48.	

HCN

Operation Order No. 65 — Secret.

by

Lieut. Col. R.J. Milne

Commanding ROSE.

Ref. Map 1/10 Sin. T.B.
FAMPOUX 1/10000
PLOUVAIN 1/10000

4/August 1917.

1. On the night of the 5th/6th August the artillery will put down a barrage as per programme attached.

2. Three Patrols each consisting of 1 Officer 1 NCO and 10 men will move out keeping as close to the barrage as possible and will visit the CRUST COAL and CUB line of shell holes (which are partially joined up) on the line approximately
I.14.C.90.62 to I.14.C.70.94.

3. Objective. To get an identification and any prisoners and M.G's which the Patrols may find.

4. North boundary of action of Patrols.
A line running East & West through
I.14.A.0.0 — I.14 Central.

II

RUTH boundary of action of patrol.
I.14.C.5.8 – I.14.D.0.5.

5. In front of main objectives there are two enemy listening posts and a machine gun which will be dealt with by the patrols.

6. The O.C. RUBY will send with the rifle grenadiers to a point about 100 yards west of WART to fire on WART, from Zero to Zero + 14 minutes. They will be in position at Zero hour.

7. The O.C. RIME will arrange for one Bangalore Torpedo to be carried by R E personnel to follow in rear of the centre patrol. This torpedo will on no account be used unless absolutely necessary.

8. RHODES will co-operate between Zero and Zero plus 14 minutes with 2 in T.M.s and M.G.s, Rifle Grenades and Lewis Guns.

9. Watches will be synchronised at 2.30 pm and 5.30 pm on August [illegible]th.

10. Zero hour will be at 10.30 pm.

Special instructions.

1. Objective. To secure identification, [illegible] and Machine Guns.

2. Patrols. (a) The right patrol will consist of 1 N.C.O. and 10 men of A Coy under the command of Lieut. S.C. Day, M.C.

(b) The centre patrol will consist of 1 N.C.O. & 10 men of B Coy under the command of Lieut. F.S. Cox. The R.E. personnel will be attached to this party.

(c) The left patrol will consist of 1 N.C.O. & 10 men of C Company under the command of Lieut. F. MARCHANT.

3. Exit. The right patrol will leave CROFT at I.14.c.60.50(?) & will move direct on to I.14 C 81.60.
The centre patrol will leave CROFT at I.14.c.58.73 and will move direct on to I.14.c.87.73(?).

The left patrol will leave CROFT at [illegible] and will move direct on [illegible].

ACTION of PATROLS

The patrols will leave CROFT at Zero hour and will move out in single file until through our wire when they will advance ([illegible]) in line (102 [illegible])

pairs of men at 5 paces interval.
The patrol leader in front of and the N.C.O. in rear of the centre pair.
If no wire is encountered they will push on until the line of shell holes C[illegible] - [illegible] - [illegible] is met with which will be searched.
If wire is met with -
The right and left patrols will endeavour to find an entrance and if necessary cut one.
The centre patrol will make use of the R.E. personnel with the Bangalore Torpedo. Care being taken that all the patrol are lying down 20 yards in [illegible].
The fuse will be [illegible] seconds - immediately it has exploded they will rush through the gap thus made.
It is absolutely essential that [illegible]

[illegible] impressed on all ranks taking part that they must keep as close to our own barrage as possible. They should be within 70 yards of the barrage before Zero + 3 ready to dash in.
If any unwounded prisoners are taken or any wounded ones found the patrol will at once return them.
The artillery barrage will remain on until Zero plus 12 minutes as per sub para (ii) of artillery action, which will allow of plenty of time to make a thorough search and return.
The N.C.O with the patrol will carry a sandbag and will search all new enemy dead encountered & bring in all identification marks. If no live prisoners or wounded enemy are taken any fresh corpses must be brought in to be thoroughly examined.

__Equipment.__ Bayonets fixed – 1 round in chamber 5 in magazine – one charger in pocket. Box respirators will be left in CROFT & OC B Coy will station a guard of 2 men over each pile ready to hand them to the patrols on their return

On return of patrols if all is quiet they will at once alert the CRAFT TROOPS but should an enemy barrage be put down they will remain in CRAFT until all is quiet.

The patrols will be [illegible] by [illegible]. [illegible] each pair of men will be one hand [illegible] & one pair wiring gloves.

The [illegible] of [illegible] in [illegible] will be [illegible] by every man taking part in the patrol. These will all be handed to the Adjutant at 7 o'c pm.

Each patrol will take a length of D III Cable. If it is impossible to carry to [illegible] [illegible] the end of the cable will be [illegible] attached [illegible] and brought back to CRAFT & the [illegible] [illegible]. Patrols will withdraw [illegible] [illegible] by [illegible] in any case before the artillery barrage ceases.

Rifle Grenadiers. The [illegible] [illegible] [illegible] will [illegible] rifle grenade batteries in [illegible] of [illegible].

At zero hour fire batteries will [illegible] on to the shell holes in I.14.c 80.30.
At Zero + 1 fire will be directed into I.14.c 80.30, & will continue until Zero + 14.

Lewis Guns.

O.C. A Coy will push forward 1 Lewis Gun to I.14.c 60.50 to watch the right flank & engage any M.G. having fire. To return at Zero + 12.

O.C. D Coy will push forward 1 Lewis Gun to I.14.c.70.90 to watch the left flank.

These guns will [illegible] at the top of the ridge at Zero hour & will not fire unless a target is seen.

To return at Zero + 12.

Support. O.C. B Coy will send forward a party consisting of 1 N.C.O. & 10 men to support the centre patrol & assist in bringing in prisoners. This party will follow immediately behind the centre patrol & will halt 50 yds in front of our wire.

This party will return with the patrol.
O.C. "B" Coy. will also detail men to go forward & lie down in the gaps so as to guide the patrols back & return with them.

GAPS. Gaps in our wire will be cut tonight under the supervision of the Batt. Int. Officer.
Boards will be placed in CROFT opposite these gaps & a tape will be laid from the gap to the boards care being taken to render it as inconspicuous as possible to aircraft. Gaps will be 9 feet across.
Gap for right patrol. I.14.c.60.60.
Gap " centre " . I.14.c.52.73.
Gap " left " . I.14.c.58.90.

Advanced Aid Post. An advanced aid post will be established in CEYLON TRENCH about I.20.c.90.55.
Any stretcher cases will be brought down CROFT to CEYLON.

Watches. Representatives of each Company will attend at Batt HQ at 2.30 pm & 5.30 pm to synchronise watches.

Reports. All reports etc will be at once sent to the Commanding Officer at "A" Coy's Headquarters in COLOMBO.

Telephone No reference to these operations will be made on the telephone.

4-8-17

R[illegible] Lieut Col.
ROSE

Copies No 1 RAM.
2 RISE. Acknowledge.
3 14 CA.
4 B.
5 C.
6 D.

Issued at 9.15 pm.

SECRET

Artillery Programme

Artillery action will be as follows.

1 Barrages on front of patrols.

ZERO to ZERO plus 3 minutes

(a) Standing 18 pdr Shrapnel barrage on the line

I 14 d 2.3 – I 14 b 2.2

(b) 18 pdr Shrapnel barrage on the line of Shell holes

I 14 c 85.30 – I 14 c. 95. 55 –
I 14 c 85. 85 – I 14 central –
I 14. b. 0. 2

At Zero plus 3 minutes barrage (b) will lift and join barrage (a). Both barrages will continue until ZERO plus 12 minutes.

Barrage (b) will be as dense as possible

II. Supplementary barrage to cover the action of the patrols ZERO to ZERO plus 12 minutes.

(c) Barrage with searching fire the area

I 14 b 2.2 – I 8 c. 9.0 – I 8 d 8.4 – I 14 b 75.20. Fire to be more intense South than North of Railway particular attention being paid to WIG and CANDY and tracks.

(d) Barrage CRUST Trench between I 14 c 85.30 and I 14 c 8.0 and the area I 14 c. 85.30 – I 15. c. 0.5. I 15 c. 0.0. – I 14 c. 8.0. paying particular attention to tracks and Strong point I 14 d 1.1.

(e) Barrage enemy Trench Mortar Emplacements at S. W. Corner of HAUSA WOOD and also CHALK PIT in I 20. a * (see 2 pages on)

Machine Guns

O.C. 51st M. G. Coy will arrange to fire as follows.

Zero to Zero + 14 minutes.

(a) 4 guns to search on HAUSA WOOD. DELBAR WOOD. CHALK PIT Road and Tracks leading from PLOUVAIN to strong point I 14 d 1.1.

(b) 4 guns to fire on Trench System of CYRIL. CLIFF. CHIN + CRIB.

(c) 4 guns to search the Tracks leading from WORM to WART in I 8.d

Trench Mortars

O.C. 51st Trench Mortar Battery will arrange to fire as follows –

2 guns in CARBUNCLE to fire on Machine Gun at I 14 c. 80.30 with hurricane fire from Zero to Zero plus 3, then to lengthen range on to I 14 d 1.1. with steady rate of fire from Zero plus 3 minutes to Zero plus 14 minutes.

2 guns in CUPID to fire on Southern edge of Cutting between WIG and COST from point I 14 b. 0.5. to I 14. b. 40. 70. with steady rate of fire from Zero to Zero plus 14.

O.C 2" Medium T.M. Battery will arrange to fire 1 gun in CUPID on WIG Trench from ZERO to Zero + 14 minutes.

— " —

Trench Mortars in CEYLON will fire from Zero to Zero + 14 minutes

on I 20 a.

— " —

Rifle Grenadiers from CEYLON will also fire from I 20 a from Zero to Zero plus 14 minutes

— " —

* Artillery Action. At Zero + 30 minutes an 18 Pdr Shrapnel + H.E barrage will be placed for one minute on the line

I 14 c 85.30 – I 14 c 95.55. – I 14 c 85. 85 – I 14 d central – I 14 b. 9. 2.

— . —

C O P Y.
Z

51st. Inf. Brigade No.G.1895

7th. Lincolnshire Regt.
10th. Sherwood Foresters.

The G.O.C. Brigade is very pleased with the behaviour and offensive spirit of the 7th Lincoln Regt and 10th Sherwood Foresters during the raid last night, also for the way in which the work of repair to the trenches has been undertaken without any loss of time.

The G.O.C. wishes his hearty congratulations to be conveyed to all ranks.

(signed) C. Fisher-Rowe Captain,

8/8/17.

Bde. Major, 51st. Infy. Bde.

COPY.

51st. Inf. Brigade No. G. 1900

7th. Lincolnshire Regt.
10th. Sherwood Foresters.
51st. M.G.Coy.

The following wire received from 17th. Division:-

"GOC Division wishes his appreciation conveyed to all ranks RUBY and "ROSE for the spirited manner in which the determined raid of the enemy "early this morning was thwarted and to all ranks of the artillery and "M.G.Coys concerned for the excellent support they gave the Infantry. "As far as can be judged the artillery and machine gun fire caused the "enemy appreciable losses"

(sugned) E. R. Stanley 2/Lt. for
Captain,
Brigade Major, 51st. Infy. Bde.

8/8/17.

C O P Y.

7th. Lincolnshire Regt.
7th. Border Regt.
8th. South Staffordshire Regt.
10th. Sherwood Foresters.
51st. M.G. Coy.
51st. T.M. Battery.

51st. Infantry Brigade No G 1914

With reference to the enemy raid on the night of the 7/8th instant on the front held by the 7th Lincolnshire Regt. and the 10th. Sherwood Foresters.

There is no doubt that the raiding party was broken up by the strong wire put out by the Brigade in front of COAL. The G.O.C. wishes the attention of all ranks to be called to this fact, so that the men may realize that the hard work put in by the Brigade during the last tour in the trenches has produced very effective results.

(signed) C. Fisher-Rowe Captain,

9/8/17. Brigade Major, 51st. Infy. Brigade.

Instructions regarding War Diaries and Intelligence Summaries are contained in F. S. Regs., Part II. and the Staff Manual respectively. Title pages will be prepared in manuscript.

WAR DIARY
or
~~INTELLIGENCE SUMMARY.~~
(Erase heading not required.)

Army Form C. 2118.

Vol 25

10th Sherwood Foresters.

Place	Date	Hour	51. B. N.W. 1/20000. Summary of Events and Information September 1917.	Remarks and references to Appendices
Front Line	1st	–	The Battalion were relieved by the 12th Manchester regt in the front line on the night 1st/2nd On relief Companies marched independently to ST Nicholas Camp.	
ST NICHOLAS CAMP.	2nd	–	Training was carried on as usual – with Route marches + Battalion Schemes, during the period at HULL CAMP ST NICHOLAS which ended on	
Support line.	9th	–	Battalion relieved the 7th Yorkshire regt in the right support CHEMICAL WORKS subsector. Dispositions:– C and D Coy + Battn HQ were in PUDDING TRENCH B Coy HQ was in CRETE A Coy in CRASH + CORDITE. Relief was complete by 11.30 pm. While in support the Battalion found working parties every night	
" "	16th		Orders were issued that the Battalion would make a raid on the enemy's trenches on the night 16/17th to destroy dugouts – kill Germans – and secure identifications. Operation orders + reports of this raid are attached also congratulations from various authorities.	L 25
Front Line	17th		The Battalion relieved the 7th Borders in the line on the night 17th/18th with Battn HQ in CRETE TRENCH.	HCN

A5834 Wt. W4973 M687 750,000 8/16 D. D. & L. Ltd. Forms/C.2118/13.

Army Form C. 2118.

WAR DIARY
or
~~INTELLIGENCE SUMMARY.~~
(Erase heading not required.)

Instructions regarding War Diaries and Intelligence Summaries are contained in F. S. Regs., Part II. and the Staff Manual respectively. Title pages will be prepared in manuscript.

10th Sherwood Foresters.

Place	Date	Hour	Summary of Events and Information — 51.B. N.W. 1/20000. — September 1917.	Remarks and references to Appendices
Front Line	18th	–	While in the front line the enemy used trench mortars against our line every day. During this tour there was nothing happened of note. A great deal of trench repair work was completed during this tour & the trenches were handed over in good repair.	
Front Line	23rd	–	The Brigade were relieved in the front line by the 182nd Bde. This Battalion was relieved in the CHEMICAL Sector by the 2/6th Warwickshire regt on the night of 23rd. On relief Companies marched to billets in ARRAS & did not go to HULL CAMP.	
ARRAS	24th	–	The Battalion marched into a hutment camp at SIMENCOURT ROUTE. DAINVILLE – WARLUS – BERNEVILLE – SIMENCOURT. here the Battalion were reinforced by a large draft from the Derbyshire yeomanry.	
[...]COURT	26th		The Battalion marched to GRAND RULLECOURT into billets. ROUTE. GOUY-en-ARTOIS – FOSSEUX – BARLY – SOMBRIN – GRAND RULLECOURT. Here a large draft from the Balloon Section joined the Battalion	

A5834 Wt. W4973/M687 750,000 8/16 D. D. & L. Ltd. Forms/C.2118/13.

Instructions regarding War Diaries and Intelligence Summaries are contained in F. S. Regs., Part II. and the Staff Manual respectively. Title pages will be prepared in manuscript.

WAR DIARY
or
~~INTELLIGENCE SUMMARY.~~
(Erase heading not required.)

Army Form C. 2118.

10th Sherwood Foresters.

Place	Date	Hour	~~[illegible]~~ LENS 11. Summary of Events and Information Sept. 1917.	Remarks and references to Appendices
GRAND RULLECOURT.	27th		While in this area the Battalion trained, special attention being paid to the new drafts that had recently joined the Battalion.	
			Officers joined during month. - Nil.	
			Other ranks " " " - 168 on the 24th	
			" " " " - 105 on the 25th.	
			" " rejoined from hospital. 44.	
			Officers struck off during month. 2 Lieut. O. Scott to Eng. sick.	
			Lieut. P. Cuckow " P.T. + B.F. Aldershot.	
			2 Lieut F. J. Emson. to Eng. sick.	
			CASUALTIES. 2 Lieut W. C. Wickes killed during the raid.	
			Other ranks killed. 4.	
			" " D of W. 3.	
			" " wounded. 15.	
			" " " at duty. 6.	
			Wastage. Other ranks. 34.	

A5834 Wt. W4973 M687 750,000 8/16 D. D. & L. Ltd. Forms/C.2118/13.

7CN

Operation Orders
By Lieutenant Colonel H.J.King commanding
10th.,Batt.Sherwood Foresters.

War Diary

Ref. Maps PLOUVAIN 1/10,000
GREENLAND HILL TENCH MAP
17th.,DIV. MAP E.1. MAP 1/2500

The Battalion will carry outa minor operation on the night of Z day at the hour of Zero. (Both to be notified later).

OBJECT a. To kill Germans.
b. To secure identifications.
c. To blow up dugouts,Trench Mortars and trench mortar emplacements.

OBJECTIVES.
CRUST trench from I.14.C.35.40 to I.14.C.89.17 and the close support trench running 50 yards East of these points.

RAIDING PARTY
Will consist of 4 Officers 8 N.C.O.s and 42 other Ranks,2 Signallers and 4 Stretcher Bearers of this Battalion. In addition there will be 1 Officer and12 other Ranks attached from the 77th., Coy R.E.
This party will be as follows.
Captain Day in command
Lieuts JOYCE, WICKS, HANSEN.
2 N.C.O.s and 10 men each from A.B.C.D. Coys.
2 Stretcher Bearers from B Coy 2 Stretcher Bearers from C Coy.
2 Signallers from Hdqrs.
Lieut Stone (R.E.)
4 N.C.O.s 6 other ranks 77 coy. R.E.

Captain Meade of D Coy is also detailed with a party of 25 men to be repsonsible for the suppling of all material required by the raiders , to keep in touch with the raiders and to take overall wounded and prisoners on their arrival in our trench system. He will also be responsible for keeping Battle Battalon Hdqrs. informed of progress being made.

PLAN OF ATTACK.
a The assaulting troops will be divided into four parties 2 parties will attack the flanks,blocking the Front line trenches and clearing up the close support trench in the rear.
b. The centre party will attack and clear up the front line and the small C.T. connecting the front and close suport trench.
c. ~~[illegible]~~ The reserve party will take a position as near the point of entry as possible and will be responsible for the passing back of prisoners and wounded, they will also act as a covering party to protect the raiders on their return.
d. The entire party will be formed up in our trench system between SAPS 1 and 2 and will move forward at ZERO.
e. All troops will be withdrawn at ZERO plus 15 minutes. AT ZERO plus 10 minutes Captain Meade will be responsible for firing two Golden Rain Rockets from the bott bottom of SAPS 1 and 2. At ZERO plus 13 minutes this will be repeated as a warning to the raiders to return. A repitition of this will be carried out at intervals until all have returned.
f. Raiders will use their own judgement about returning immediately to our trenches. If there is heavy artillery or M.G. fire across NO MAS LAND it may be wise to remain out in shell holes.

g.

Capt. Meade will be resonsible for providing two Lewis guns to protect each flank of the raiding party, from attack in No Mans Land and to engage any M.G.s which may open fire from theflank.

f. Signallers attahed to raiders will oen communication between Capt.Day and Capt Meade as soon as possible.

I. R.E. parties will be attached to each party. They will be responsible for using Bangalor Tubes for blowing up wire, if necessary and for properly demolishing Emplacements and Dug outs. The Officer will atach himself to the Reserve party and be guided in his actons by circumstances arising.

ARTILLERY ACTION. A. ZERO to ZERO plus one minute 18 pounder shrapnel barrage on CRUST.

B. ZERO plus one minute to ZERO plus two minutes ditto ut yards in rear.

C. ZERO plus two minutes to plus fifteen minutes box barrage around trenches to be raidd.

D. 4.5 Howitzers on CRUST T.M. and M.G. Emplacements.

E. 6 inch Howitzers on HAUSA WOOD.

Stokes ACTION. 1. Zero to Zero plus two minutes barrage with four guns 10 ronds pr minute on Close Support trench.

2. In addition Medium Trench Mortars and Stokes Guns will fire on secially selected positions as instructed.

CO-OPERATION.

The Brigade on our right and the Battalon n our left will coNoperate with M.G. fire under Brigde arrangements.

EQUIPMENT.

Each man will carry his Box respirator at "alert". Rifle loaded and charged with Bayonet fixed. Knob kerry and four bombs. 20 rounds of S.A.A in pockets. [illegible]
R.E. will provide 7 Bangalor Tubes and neesary explosives.
Each party will be provided with Mats for crossing partly broken wire.

MEDICAL First aid post will be established in Corona Support trench and all Stretcher cases will be carried out along CEYLON Trench.

General.

On ZERO night at six P.PM. three motor lorries will convey party from training ground a s far forward as possible when they will proceed to their allotted positions. On returning to our trenches Capt. Meade will be responsible for checking all back. They will thn proceed in small parties and rejoin their lorries in FAMPOUX.
All faces will be blackened in th trenches previous to ZERO

IDENTIFICATIONS

1. All papers and identifications will be left behind at Camp under guard supplied by Transort Officer.

PRISONERS.

All prisoners and identifications will be taken to Battle Battalion Hdrs. No papers will be removed from prisoners and nothing that would lead to their identification will be taken by theraiders.

SIGNAL TIME

Watches will be synchronized at 5 P.M. and 7 P.M.

BATTALION BATTLE HDQRS. One hour beforeZero Battalion Hdqrs will move to CORONA SUPPORT trench now occupied by centre Coy hdqrs of Right Battalion.

NO MENTION OF THIS OPERATION WILL BE MADE ON ANY WIRE.

ACKNOWLEDGE.

COPY NO.

C O

REPORT ON RAID.

Refce Maps:- 17th. Div. E.I. Map No. 5.Part 2. Scale 1/2500

1. Raiders left our saps S1 & S2 at ZERO minus 3 minutes in four parties.

D party from	S1	(I.14.c.65.22)	on a bearing of			
C " "	S1	(")	"	"	"	
B " "	S2	(I.14.c.65.47)	"	"	"	
A " "	S2	(")	"	"	"	

Direction was given by tapes laid out beforehand for a distance of twenty yards. This was a great help.

All parties formed up at Sap Heads ready to move off as soon as barrage allowed.

2. Barrage started at ZERO on enemy front line and support. The shooting was excellent throughout. At ZERO plus one minute the lift of the 18 pdrs. was easily observed.

Stokes Guns, shooting on to Support Trench, were very accurate. There were no casualties from our own shelling or T.M.s

3. RIGHT SECTION. followed guide tape and laid their own beyond this. Enemy Wire was "NA POO" but on enemy parapet the section found NEW Concertina Barbed Wire apparently continuous to right and left. The Section got over this wire and into trench at I.14.c.83.16. Part moved right and part moved left.
(a) Right part of section found dugout at I.14.c.84.14 & threw Football and several Mills Bombs. Two men moved on twenty yards and passed several shelters, leaving bombs in each. Also saw two enemy approaching and claimed to have killed them.
(b) Left part of section went round support and found two deep dugouts at I.14.c.87.22, bombed them and proceeded along support: met two enemy ten yards further and claim to have killed them.
When golden rain rocket went up this party returned same way.

4. CENTRE SECTION. - followed guide tape and continued in same direction. Met no enemy wire. Found enemy trench at junction of C.T. (I.14.c.83;29.). Half moved right, half left.
(a) Right Half. - Found four shelters empty. About twenty yards along found prisoner and eventually handed him to right section. At I.14.c.83.25 found firestep with two full boxes PINEAPPLES. Mortar could not be found. Blew up pineapples with gun cotton. Established connection with right section.
(b) Left Half. - Found shelter four steps down. Killed one man inside and brought his equipment back. He was in marching order. Connected with Left Section, meeting no more enemy.
Section returned when golden rain went up.

5. LEFT SECTION. - Followed guide tape and straight on. Found new uncut concertina barbed wire on parapet. Used Bangalor Torpedo which made good gap. Entered trench at I.14.c.89.42. Two men to left established stop at 20" and claim to have killed one HUN. Remainder to right and down Support Line. Met opposition at I.14.c.89.38. and claim to have killed nine. Dug out two yards further. This was blown up by Football. Found one dugout at I.14.c.91.32 and used Football on this. Found one dugout at I.14.c.88.30 and used Guncotton and Stkes Shell. Saw four enemy running East and claim to have killed these. Returned by C.T. when Golden Rain was seen. Officer i/c was killed at I.14.c.88.30 He was carried to head of C.T. but enemy shelling rendered it impossible to bring him from there. He was searched and there were no identifications on him.

6. SUPPORT SECTION. - Followed guide tape and straight on. Met centre section fifteen yards from enemy trench. Crossed over Sap at I.14c.75.32. This was quite "WASHED OUT". Found no enemy wire. Halted behing centre section. Established telephone to Hdqrs for seven minutes. Wire then cut in our front line. Saw all parties returning and followed them in.

7. CASUALTIES.

	KILLED.	WOUNDED.
Right Section	-	1 Cpl. 1 Sapper
Centre Section	1 Pte.	1 Pte.
Left Section.	1 Officer: 1 Pte.	1L/Cpl. 1 Pte.

8. ENEMY MACHINE GUNS.

One firing high from RAILWAY. One firing high from HAUSA WOOD. No inconvenience caused.

9. ENEMY BARRAGE. - till 10.30 p.m. on front line & support.

SUMMARY.

(1) BARRAGE was excellent and well on time.
(2) ENEMY WIRE was destroyed everywhere except for the concertina barbed wire obviously newly put out.
(3) DIRECTION TAPES served their purpose well.
(4) ALL PARTIES completed their tasks without serious hitch.
(5) GOLDEN RAIN served its purpose well both as a signal and as a guide.
(6) TELEPHONE worked for seven minutes until instrument in our trench was knocked out.
(7) BANGALOR TORPEDOES and FOOTBALLS were very successful.
(8) CONNECTION TAPES were well used and achieved their object.
(9) BLACKENED FACES as a preliminary put everybody in a good humour and assisted in identification later.
(10) ENEMY TRENCHES. were originally good and revetted with sandbags The barrage knocked them in very badly everywhere.
(11) ENEMY MORALE. In two cases enemy showed fight but remainder "cut and ran".
(12) OBJECTIVES.
(a) To kill Germans. Result :- 19 claimed by raiders also large numbers reported found killed by barrage. It may be assumed that some enemy were in dugouts blown up.
(b) To secure identifications. Result:- One prisoner consisting of a MAIL CLERK with numerous papers and letters.
(c) To destroy enemy emplacements &c. Result:- 6 deep dugouts engaged, - three with "footballs", three with MILLS. Numerous shelters knocked out. Two boxes "pineapples" blown up. T.M. Emplacements evidently destroyed by barrage. Likewise sap at I.14.c.75.32. Wire destroyed everywhere except for new concertina as above.
(13) ENEMY RETALIATION. Two long range M.G.s firing high from RAILWAY and HAUSA WOOD. BARRAGE NOT KNOWN BY ME.

10.(14) CASUALTIES. - RAIDERS.

Killed:-	2/Lieut.		W. C. Wicks.		
	14626	Pte.	Doxey	W.	
	33486	"	Copson	J.W.	
Wounded:-	17833	Cpl.	Baker	E.	
	56486	L/C.	Waterhouse	T.	
	19830	Pte	Gleave	R.	
	70504	"	Paling	J.H.	
	43000	Spr.	Harris	W.	(77th Field Coy R.E)

OTHER CASUALTIES.

Killed:-	4525	Pte.	Stevenson	G.
Died of Wounds:-	13742	Cpl.	Shardlow	E.
Wounded:-	18099	Cpl.	Drabble	W.
	58847	Pte.	Cusworth	P.
	19877	"	Hardwick	M.

Also one Pte. of 7th. Border Regiment.

Secret   Headquarters RAM

I forward herewith reports of the 3 officers commanding the patrols.

There is not the least doubt both from their reports and from what Major Daniels MC (Officer superintending front line) that our barrage was well beyond the first objective. The enemy was not in the least disconcerted.

The patrols received orders to be outside our wire by Zero and everything in that way worked most satisfactorily.

From COLOMBO Trench it appears that the enemy's barrage did not come down until at least Zero + 6 and was then [illegible] mostly being to the west. The machine gun from the direction of HAMSA WOOD continued firing at the line and was not at all [illegible].

Telephone communication was in excellent order all the time.

The enemy's trenches were undoubtedly held strongly and he must have advanced posts as reported by patrols. Being' close up to our own wire. Undoubtedly it is an extraordinary hard place for artillery to range on.

I am of opinion that a "raid proper" with no artillery preparation or barrage, simply a strong bombing party supported by rifle grenadiers on both flanks and in rear would be much more likely to secure identification and to harass the enemy's advanced posts. The party could crawl out in twilight and wait the enemy come in and then deal with them. The howitzer might deal with the trench mortar at N.E. end HAUSA WOOD.

The patrols were full of keenness and were well led and I am certain that if the barrage had only been of use, good results might have been obtained. The barrage appears to be by no means dense enough, and was not on the objective by which I mean barrage (box).

The standing and box barrage was in my opinion satisfactory.

The Stick Hole are the cause of all the trouble and these must be dealt with by either howitzers or heavy trench mortars.

Line of CROFT was evacuated

I very much doubt if the artillery could do much good owing to the ridge.

It seems essential we should push forward our saps and establish ourselves on the ridge and so then command such approaches to the Stick Hole.

I much regret to state the following casualties occurred.

1 O.R. Killed. (died on being brought into CROFT)

8 O.R. Wounded

1 O.R. R.E. Wounded

All the wounded were brought in.

I have not yet received reports from the patrols sent out after the 11 pm barrage.

6/8/17 [illegible]

1.52 am Cmdg ROSE.

Left Patrol

"C" Company - 2 Lieut F. MARCHANT States.

I left CROFT 10.29 pm. and just on passing through our wire - rifle grenades commenced and a few seconds afterwards the barrage. I formed the men up and went straight forward and continued as the barrage seemed a long distance ahead. After proceeding 30 yds a machine gun opened from my direct front and a Very light went up from the same place. I went forward about 10 yards and ran into the enemy wire, a machine then opened from point flank and 5 men were wounded, one dangerously. I tried to work round the left flank and was held up by more wire but I only had one man with me then. Riflemen were firing rapid from what appeared to me to be a trench well wired, semi-circular in shape. As our barrage then ceased I withdrew to CROFT.

I am of opinion that the barrage was at least 50 yds beyond

the trench and the enemy were not at all disconcerted by it.

The gap in our wire was well cut and easily found.

F. Marchant 2/Lt

Right Patrol

A Company under Lieut S.C. DAY. M.C.

At 10.29 pm I left CROFT and went out through our wire. As we were extending in front of the wire the barrage commenced. I then proceeded straight forward. After 25 yds we came across the first shell holes, unoccupied. After about 50 yds a sniper was firing on my left and one man of the patrol threw a bomb at him but the sniper continued firing. After about another 50 yards we came across a line of men firing apparently from a trench. There was some concertina wire in front. We opened fire point blank at them. A man on the right of the patrol was badly hit and I took advantage of the scramble to look at my watch and found it was Zero + 10 minutes. I called up the F.C.O. and we decided that nothing could be done as far as the objective was concerned.

We then withdrew to CROFT. On the way back we came across shell holes again about 25 yards from our wire & examined them for identification and finding nothing returned to CROFT.

Our barrage was well over when the Enemy were firing too and appeared to have caused him no inconvenience. A machine gun to my left rear was firing all the time.

I did not notice what time the Enemy barrage commenced.

The L.C.O. stayed with the wounded man to bring him in and the machine gun continued firing.

The box barrage on the right appeared to have silenced machine guns on that flank.

[illegible signature] 2nd Lt.

Centre Patrol

— " —

"B" Company and 1 N.C.O + 3 men
93rd Coy R.E. under Lieut C.F.S. Cox.

At 10.26 pm we left CROFT. Every man was in his place as the barrage opened. As soon as the shells burst we went forward at a sharp walk chasing the barrage. At Zero + 2½ minutes the R.E. and myself spotted the enemy's wire 10 yds in front.

Our barrage appeared to be a good 50 yards behind the wire. Immediately on seeing the wire the Corporal led his three men forward at the double, and our men got down. The men were scattered on account of the explosion of the torpedo and it was Zero + 8 before I collected the men and got right up to the enemy's wire whereupon a machine gun behind the wire, about 15 yards direct to our left, opened fire and a Very light went up from the same place. Also on the right several riflemen were firing at us.

We lay down for 30 seconds and the NCO & myself examined the wire. The machine gun continued firing. At that time our barrage had slackened off. I passed the word down to crawl back. The R.E.'s torpedo proved efficient in the first lot of wire but one unexploded one was left behind.

From the very start the enemy Very lights were going up well our side of the barrage. The grass close to the enemy wire has been cut quite short. I only passed one shell hole but it does appear to be used regularly.

I considered the R.E. carried up their work with the greatest daring in action and keenness. Also the Corporal of the R.E. rendered me great assistance in collecting the men and taking them forward after the torpedo had been fired.

From what I could gather the enemy barrage opened at Zero + 9 minutes. The enemy trench mortar from the direction of the railway, about zero + 5 minutes, fired.

C.F.S. [illegible] Lt.

COPY

Third Army No. G.12/114.
XVII Corps No.G.48/10

The Army Commander has the gratest pleasure in communicating the following message received from the Commander-in-chief, and wishes to add his sincere congratulations to those who have prepared and carried out these successful enterprises.

"The Commander-in-chief congratulates you and your troops on the repeated successes gained in your local operations which show excellent spirit and skill. These successes help appreciably in the general plan."

(Sd) Louis Vaughan.
Major General.
General Staff, Third Army.

13/9/17

COPY

51st Infantry Bde No. G 695
XVII Corps No G. 5/11

The following remarks, made by the Army Commander on your raid of the night Sept. 16/17th., are forwarded for communication to the troops :-

"A most successful and enterprising operation. The loss to the enemy is great in casualty and greater in moral. The conduct of all who took part is most commendable."

(Sd) J.R.C.CHARLES
Brigadier General.
General Staff.

H.Q.,XVII Corps.
22nd September 1917.

COPY

51st Infantry Brigade G 711

17th Division.

On the accasion of the Division leaving the XVII Corps, I wish to express to all ranks my appreciation of the fine soldierly spirit which has been conspicuous in the Division during the last few months while serving on this Front.

Its activity in patrolling, its keenness in Raids have been both admirable. But most conspicuous of all has been the splendid spirit shown in the work done in consolidating the line. In spite of weakness in numbers and the absence of the Pioneer Bn., the work done has been remarkable: showing not only excellent organisation on the part of the Staff, but also energy and zeal on the part of Regimental Officers and men All ranks may be proud of their record in this respect, R.A. and R.E. as well as Infantry.

I wish goodbye, and good luck to all in the Division, with every confidence that they will fully maintain the reputation they have gained whereever their duty may call them.

(Sgd) CHARLES FERGUSON,
Lieutenant General,
Commanding XVII Corps

24/9/17

1

L27

War Diary

~~4th R. W. Kents~~

10 North'd Derbys

Vol 26

17/5

18

51/7

Army Form C. 2118.

Instructions regarding War Diaries and Intelligence Summaries are contained in F. S. Regs., Part II. and the Staff Manual respectively. Title Pages will be prepared in manuscript.

WAR DIARY
or
~~INTELLIGENCE SUMMARY~~

(Erase heading not required.)

10th Sherwoods — October 1917

Place	Date	Hour	Summary of Events and Information (Rifle map LENS 11 – HAZEBROUCK 5a)	Remarks and references to Appendices
GRAND RULLECOURT	1st		Warning order was received that Division would entrain for XIV Corps area on 3rd inst	
"	2nd		Billeting parties entrained for Corps staging area St SIXTE	
GRAND RULLECOURT to ST SIXTE	4th		Battalion less 1 Company entrained at SAULTY commencing 2pm D Company entrained at 5pm – Hot meal was served to troops before entraining – Battalion detrained at PESELHOEK 8pm and marched to SWINDON Camp St SIXTE D Company arriving 4 hours later – Orders were received that Brigade would move to HERZEELE on 5th inst	
ST SIXTE to HERZEELE	5th		Battalion marched to HERZEELE passing starting point at 9.30am 500 yds being kept between units and 200 yds between Coys.	
HERZEELE	6th		Battalion commenced training special attention being paid to mopping up etc	
"	7th		Training continued Orders received for Battalion to march back to St SIXTE	
HERZEELE to ST SIXTE	8th		Battalion marched from HERZEELE to SWINDON Camp commencing 1pm	

2449 Wt. W14957/M90 750,000 1/16 J.B.C. & A. Forms/C.2118/12.

Army Form C. 2118.

WAR DIARY
or
INTELLIGENCE SUMMARY.
(Erase heading not required.)

Instructions regarding War Diaries and Intelligence Summaries are contained in F. S. Regs., Part II. and the Staff Manual respectively. Title pages will be prepared in manuscript.

10th Sherwood Foresters — October 1917

Place	Date	Hour	Summary of Events and Information	Remarks and references to Appendices
			Reference map HAZEBROUCK 5A — Sheet 11 attached	
ST SIXTE to HARROW Camp to SUPPORT LINE	9th		The Battalion entrained at International Corner at 11am and detrained at ELVERDINGE from there marched to HARROW CAMP. Here the men rested for a few hours & had a hot meal. The Battalion then marched to the SUPPORT LINE relieving the LANCS FUS of 56th Bde. - CAPT MEADS was killed on the way in.	
SUPPORT LINE to FRONT LINE	10th		The Battalion moved into front line & relieved the MIDDLESEX & WORCESTER Regts. Disposition: B Coy on right D Coy on left A right support C left support. Line held was approx U12a 88 to V13a86	
FRONT LINE	11th		Orders received for an ~~attack~~ attack from Brigade (see attached) this meant Battn closing in to the right which was done at dark. The 7th Lincoln filling in the gap. New approx line then ran thus V13a86 to road inclusive V7c 35	
"	12th		The Zero hour for the attack was 5.25am - By 4.45am the Battn was formed up in front of the road [illegible] — CONTD	[illegible signature]

A5834 Wt. W4973/M687 750,000 8/16 D. D. & L. Ltd. Forms/C.2118/13.

Instructions regarding War Diaries and Intelligence Summaries are contained in F. S. Regs., Part II. and the Staff Manual respectively. Title pages will be prepared in manuscript.

WAR DIARY
or
~~INTELLIGENCE SUMMARY.~~
(Erase heading not required.)

10th Sherwood Foresters

OCTOBER 1917

Army Form C. 2118.

Place	Date	Hour	Summary of Events and Information	Remarks and references to Appendices
			Refce Map HAZEBROUCK 5a [illegible] Sheet 1	
FRONT LINE	12th		[illegible] in the following order B Coy on right D Coy on left A Coy right support C Coy left support The [illegible] Battn were on our right, the 7th [illegible] on our [illegible]	
			The Barrage according to attached table came down on our front line at ZERO Our first objective BERTHIER Fm to V 7 d 7 4 was reached at 6.40 am without having received any opposition a few prisoners were taken from SENEGAL FARM & a few from BERTHIER FARM	
			The Barrage halted in front of our first objective for [illegible] at 7.05 am the barrage lifted & ~~[illegible]~~ A & C Coys having passed thro' B & D Coy advance on to final objective V 7 b 7.6 to V 8 c 45 80 This was reached at 7.30 am	
			A little ~~[illegible]~~ opposition was [illegible] at GRAVEL FARM	
			The Number of prisoners who passed Batt HQ (CEMENT HOUSE) during the day numbered 9 officers 250 OR	[signature illegible]

A5834 Wt. W4973 M687 750,000 8/16 D. D. & L. Ltd. Forms/C.2118/13.

Army Form C. 2118.

WAR DIARY
or
INTELLIGENCE SUMMARY.
(Erase heading not required.)

Instructions regarding War Diaries and Intelligence Summaries are contained in F. S. Regs., Part II. and the Staff Manual respectively. Title pages will be prepared in manuscript.

10th Sherwood Foresters — Ref. map HAZEBROUCK 5A — Corps Sheet 28 — OCTOBER 1917

Place	Date	Hour	Summary of Events and Information	Remarks and references to Appendices
FRONT LINE	12th		The Enemy attempted three Counter attacks during the day all of which were dispersed by MG fire & artillery fire. Congratulated on the information sent back to Div & Brigade. Observation Posts were established at BIRDIE [illegible] & [illegible] HOUSES. Number of casualties during the day were Officers Killed 2 wounded 4 OR killed approx 15 wounded 150.	
Front Line	13th		Line consolidated & held. Relieved at night 13/14th by 7th Yorkshire Regt & marched back to PARROY Camp. Men were very done up having done 5 nights in the line. Relief complete 1 am.	
PARROY CAMP	14th		Were bombed by GOTHAS no casualties. Battalion marched to DUBLIN Camp arriving there 5 pm. Were bombed again at night.	
DUBLIN CAMP	15th		Orders received to move to PRATTLE CAMP [illegible] situated at INTERNATIONAL CORNER	[signature]

A5834 Wt. W4973 M687 750,000 8/16 D. D. & L. Ltd. Forms/C.2118/13.

Instructions regarding War Diaries and Intelligence Summaries are contained in F. S. Regs., Part II. and the Staff Manual respectively. Title pages will be prepared in manuscript.

WAR DIARY
or
INTELLIGENCE SUMMARY.
(Erase heading not required.)

10th Sherwood Foresters

Army Form C. 2118.

OCTOBER 1917

Place	Date	Hour	Summary of Events and Information — Ref. Map HAZEBROUCK 5A [illegible] 13	Remarks and references to Appendices
DUBLIN CAMP to PRATTLE CAMP	16		Battn Entrained at INTERNATIONAL Corner at 10 am & detrained at PROVEN from there Battn marched to PRATTLE Camp arriving midday	
PRATTLE CAMP	17th 18 19		Reorganising of Battn & training & Baths	
	20th		Orders received to move to [illegible] Transport moving by road Battn to move by bus – Transport left 6am, also billeting party sent in advance	
PRATTLE CAMP to SANGHEN	21st		Battn Embussed on POPERINGHE – PROVEN road at 8am & moved via PROVEN – WATOU – WATTEN – SANGHEN arriving SANGHEN about 8pm. Transport arriving same time	
SANGHEN	22nd 23rd		Training carried on as laid down, special attention be paid to mopping up & points brought forward by recent Operations.	[illegible]
SANGHEN	24th		Training as usual, warning order received to move back to	

A5834 Wt. W4973 M687 750,000 8/16 D. D. & L. Ltd. Forms/C.2118/13.

Instructions regarding War Diaries and Intelligence Summaries are contained in F. S. Regs., Part II. and the Staff Manual respectively. Title pages will be prepared in manuscript.

Army Form C. 2118.

WAR DIARY
or
INTELLIGENCE SUMMARY.
(Erase heading not required.)

10th Sherwood Foresters — OCTOBER 1917

Place	Date	Hour	Summary of Events and Information — CALAIS 13 - HAZEBROUCK 5A — Sheet 27 — BROEMBEEK	Remarks and references to Appendices
SANGHEN	24th		PROVEN AREA on 25th Billeting Parties sent on in advance	
SANGHEN to PROVEN	25th		The Battalion moved from SANGHEN marching via NORDAUSQUES, ZUTKERQUE to AUDRUICQ starting 7.30am arriving entraining point 3pm. Hot dinner were given to the men before entraining. – Battalion entrained 5pm detrained at PROVEN 11.30pm from where they marched to P5 area. B Coy were loading party & came on with transport 8am 26th inst.	
PROVEN to BOESINGHE to SUPPORT LINE	26th		Orders received to entrain to BOESINGHE – Bn entrained PROVEN 10.30am arriving BOESINGHE 12 midday & marched to Huts at B 5 d 5.0 – Orders received to proceed to support line after rations were to be received first – Rations received 7pm & Battn moved to support line ~~on~~ to relieve 17th West Yorks via CANAL – 15 WOOD – WIDDENDRIFT. Dispositions as follows: D Coy from U11c 90.20 to U11c 50.25 – A Coy U11c 55.25 to U11c 60.40 & 1 Platoon CRAONNE FARM 1 Plat MONTMIRAIL FARM 1 Platoon U11b 00.70. B Coy along breastwork U5d 50.00 to U5d 80.15. Battalion HQ at WIDDENDRIFT. Relief complete 11.30pm.	[illegible signature]
Support LINE	27th		Coys reconnoitred way to front line so as ~~[illegible]~~ to know where to go to in case of counter Attack.	

A5834 Wt. W4973 M687 750,000 8/16 D. D. & L. Ltd. Forms/C.2118/13.

Instructions regarding War Diaries and Intelligence Summaries are contained in F. S. Regs., Part II. and the Staff Manual respectively. Title pages will be prepared in manuscript.

WAR DIARY
or
INTELLIGENCE SUMMARY.
(Erase heading not required.)

Army Form C. 2118.

10th Sherwood Foresters — OCTOBER 1917

Place	Date	Hour	Summary of Events and Information	Remarks and references to Appendices
			SHEET: BROEMBEEK [illegible] 5th	
	27th		Battalion used for carrying rations - bottled water, S.A.A., Very lights, to each of front line Battalions	
Support Line	28th		One company used for building shelters under R.E. - 1 Company carrying - remaining two Companies improving accommodation. At night A & D Companies were used for carrying wiring material to right front Battalion - Enemy gas shelled very heavily causing a few casualties	
—	29		1 Company used for R.E. fatigue building shelters - Remaining three Coys improving accommodation - Relief orders received - C Coy headquarters very heavily shelled - Capt [illegible] killed, 2nd Lt Hanson wounded. Batt relieved by 15th Cheshires commencing 8pm - Relief complete 9.30pm - On relief Bn moved to BOESINGHE Hutments for the night arriving there 11pm. Hot tea was given to the men on arrival	
Boesinghe to PROVEN	30		The Battn entrained at BOESINGHE at 9.0 a.m. detrained PROVEN 10 a.m. marching to P3 area - same camp as before -	[illegible signature]

A5834 Wt. W4973 M687 750,000 8/16 D. D. & L. Ltd. Forms/C.2118/13.

Instructions regarding War Diaries and Intelligence Summaries are contained in F. S. Regs., Part II. and the Staff Manual respectively. Title pages will be prepared in manuscript.

Army Form C. 2118.

WAR DIARY
or
INTELLIGENCE SUMMARY.
(Erase heading not required.)

10th Sherwood Foresters

OCTOBER 1917

Place	Date	Hour	Summary of Events and Information	Remarks and references to Appendices
			Refce map HAZEBROUCK 5a	
PROVEN	31st	–	Battn employed in cleaning up – Orders received to move to WORMHOUDT area	
			Statement of Strength and Casualties attached	

[signature illegible] Lt Col
Cmdg

A5834 Wt. W4973 M687 750,000 8/16 D. D. & L. Ltd. Forms/C.2118/13.

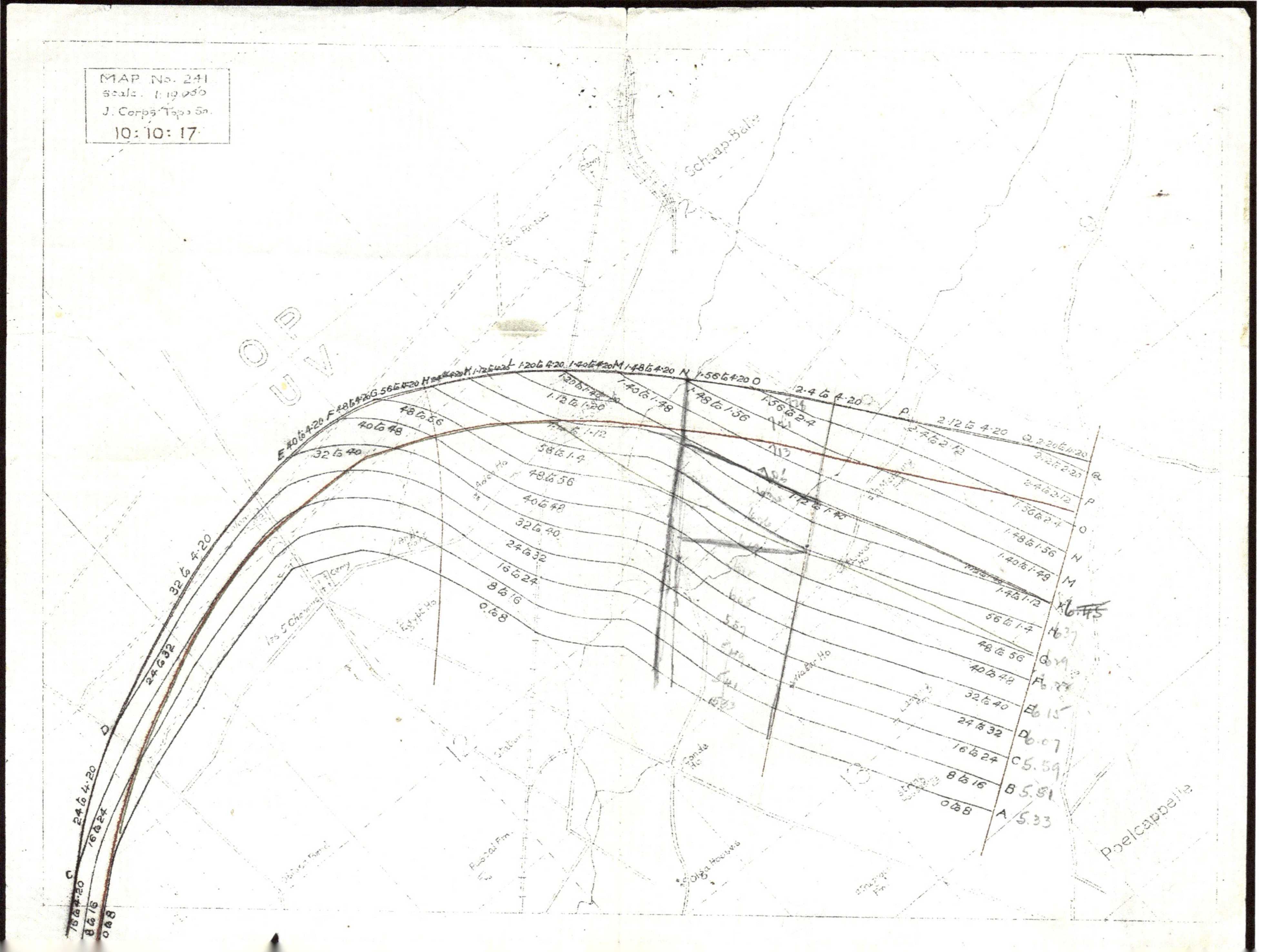
MAP No. 241
scale 1:10,000
J. Corps Topo Sn.
10:10:17
Schaap-Balie
Poelcappelle
A
B
C
D
E
F
G
H
M
N
O
P
Q
0 to 8
8 to 16
16 to 24
24 to 32
32 to 40
40 to 48
48 to 56
56 to 1.4
2.12 to 4.20
2.4 to 4.20
32 to 4.20
24 to 4.20

Copy of message pad used by Coys during action Oct 12/17

[illegible] Lt Col

Cmdg 10th [illegible]

Message Pad.

Your Message must be such as will enable the Addressee to know what the Situation is with You and your Neighbours.

NEGATIVE INFORMATION IS ALSO VALUABLE.

Strike out and alter sentences as necessary.

TO..

1. Am advancing to..
2. Am putting out (Have put out) protective parties.
3. Am sending out. Have sent out and am keeping out patrols to keep touch with the enemy.
4. Am (Have) consolidating (ed).
5. Our line now runs... ....
6. I require (give article or articles and number required) :—

   Send the above to...
7. Troops on my right are (give situation)
8. Troops on my left are (give situation)
9. My strength now is.....................................
10. Am being shelled from...
11. Am held up by M.G., T.M., rifle, artillery fire from............................
12. Am now ready to...
13. Enemy line runs...
14. Enemy (strength)....................................at.................................
    doing.. ....
15. Have captured...
16. Enemy prisoners belong to...
17. Enemy counter-attack forming up at...
18. Other remarks—

Time a.m. (p.m.).
Date...
Place...
(Map Ref. or mark on back of map.)

Name...
Rank...
Platoon.................... Company...................
Battalion...

10th Sherwood Foresters (attached to War Diary October 1917)

1:10 000 J.1.

5th FIELD SURVEY COY. R.E. (1489)

26-8-17

No 2 Advanced Section, A.P & S.S.

Scale. 1:10,000.

YARDS 500 400 300 200 100 0 500 1,000 YARDS

attached to War Diary for October 1917 of 10th Sherwood Foresters

SECRET

Copy No.________

51ST INFANTRY BRIGADE ORDER NO 204.

Octr 11th 1917.

1. The 17th Division will attack on the 12th Octr in conjunction with the 4th Divn on the right and Guards Divn. on the left.
Zero hour will be notified later.

2 The 51st Infantry Brigade will attack, the 50th Infy Brigad will be in Support, the 52nd Infy Brigade will be in Divisional Reserve.

3. OBJECTIVES.

The GREEN and RED Lines as shewn on the map attached.

4. METHOD OF ATTACK.

10th Sherwood Foresters will attack on the right.
7th Lincoln Regt will attack in the centre.
8th South Stafford Regt will attack on the left.

Each Bn. on a two company front.

Bn. Boundaries (a) Between 10th Sherwood Foresters and 7th Lincoln. Regt line from road junction V.7.c. 80.15 through V.7.c.5.5. - V.7.b.8.7.
(b) Between 7th Lincoln Regt and 8th South Stafford regt - the Railway (latter inclusive to South Staffords)

4.a. The following lines will be consolidated - the RED line - the dotted GREEN Line.

5. TASKS for ATTACKING BNS.

(a) 10th Sherwood Foresters will capture and consolidate SENEGAL FARM - HUTS V.7.d.3.2. - BERTHIER FARM - GRAVEL FARM - RED LINE
(b) 7th Lincoln Regt will capture and consolidate TAUBE FARM - STRONG POINT V.7.c.60.65. - V.7.b.10.20. COLIBRI FARM - TURENNE CROSSING - GREEN LINE and RED LINE.

(c) 8th South Stafford Regt. will capture and consolidate ADEN HOUSE - STRONG POINT V.1.d.05.25. GREEN and RED Line.

In addition the 7th Lincoln Regt will establish a strong point at V.7.a.85.60.
The 8th South Stafford Regt a strong point at V.1.c.5.0.

6. FORMING UP.

Each battalion will form up in depth in front of the road running from U.12.b.3.6. through TRANQUILLE HOUSE CONDE HOUSE - to U.13.a.30.35.
They will form-up on taped lines under battalion arrangements

All troops East of this ~~line~~ road will be withdrawn to the forming up position one hour before ZERO. to conform with the barrage.

11.a. **Machine Guns.**

2 guns to the 10th Sherwood Foresters.

4 guns to the 7th Lincoln Regt

2 guns to the 8th South Stafford Regt.

8 guns in reserve.

Particular attention being paid to road leading from VIJFWEGEN to TURENNE CROSSING and the RAILWAY.

11.b. **3" Stokes Mortars.** At ZERO 1 gun will barrage (a) SENEGAL FARM (b) HUTS.

1 gun will barrage (a) TAUBE FARm (b) STRONG POINT V.7.a.60.65.

1 gun will barrage ADEN HOUSE.

13. Tanks may operate in the area of attack, attacking troops will be warned to act entirely independantly from the Tanks and not to base their actions on the movement of the Tanks. Details as to action of Tanks will be issued later.

A contact aeroplane will fly over the Corps front at Zero plus one hour and 15 mins, Zero plus ~~one hour and 22 x~~ 3 hours and 30 mins, 12 Noon and subsequently as ordered.

Leading troops will show their positions to the contact aeroplane only when demanded (a) by Klaxon Horn (b) by series of white lights. No flares will be lit untill called for.

As far as possible flares should be lit in threes Red Flares will be used.

Each Bde and Bn H.Qrs. will be marked by ground sheets of authorised shape, with the code letters of the Unit laid out with white strips ~~laid~~ along side.

A protective aeroplane will be up continuously during daylight whose mission it will be to detect the approach of enemy counter attacks; whenever this patrol observes hostile parties of 100 or more moving to counter attack it will drop a smoke bomb over that portion of the front to which the enemy is moving.

The smoke bomb will burst about 100 feet below the machine into a white parachute flare which decends slowly leaving a long trail of brown smoke about 1 foot broad behind it.

14. S.O.S. The S.O.S. Signal will be a succession of S.O.S. Rifle Rockets, each bursting simultaneously into 4 Red ~~Flares.~~ Stars

A Brigade Orderly Officer will give correct Corps time to all concerned. He will leave Bde. H.Q. at 12.30.p.m. to day 11th inst and 6.30.p.m.

15. Brigade H.Q. will be situated at AU BON GITE forward report centre for runners U.23.b.6.4.

16. MEDICAL.

Stretcher cases will be taken to PASCAL FARM and OLGA HOUSES where they will be taken over by the 52nd Field Amb.

~~18~~.17 Prisoners will be sent to ~~Bde. H.Q.~~ Div Cage IRON CROSS C 3a.

C. Fisher Rowe

Captain,

Issued at Brigade Major. 51st Inf. Bde.

Copy No.			
1.	7th Lincoln Regt	9.	12th Inf. Bde.
2	7th Border Regt	10.	Staff Captain.
3	8th South Staffords.	11	B.T.O.
4th	10th Sherwood Foresters.	12.	77th R.E.
5.	51st M.G. Coy.	13	Bde. Sigs.
6th	51 T.M. Battery.	14	War Diary.
7.	52nd Fld. Amb.	15	Office
8.	3rd Guards Bde.	16.	6th Dorset Regt.
		17.	17th Div.

War Diary

H.Q. 51st Inf. Brigade.
No. Q.3673.

HEADQUARTERS 2/1004 10th SHERWOOD FORESTERS

7th Lincolnshire Regt.
7th Border Regt.
8th South Staffordshire Regt.
10th Sherwood Foresters.
51st M.G. Coy.
51st T.M. Btty.

The following message from Brigadier-General C.E. BOND, C.M.G., D.S.O., to the Officers and men of the 51st Infantry Brigade is forwarded for communication to all ranks.

Captain,

16.10.1917. Staff Captain, 51st Inf. Bde.

"I wish to congratulate all ranks on their fine achievement during the recent operations. I had hoped to do so on parade but have had, unfortunately, to go to hospital.

I wish especially to congratulate the drafts recently received in the Brigade, who previously had a very short training. All Commanding Officers agree that their behaviour was excellent. The conditions as regards weather and shell fire were very trying and the spirit and endurance shown by all was of the very highest quality. All Battalions have added fresh laurels to the records of their Regiments"

(Sd). C.E. BOND, Brigadier-General,
Commanding, 51st Infantry Bde.

15.10.1917.

Attached to War Diary (October 1917)

HEADQUARTERS,
51st
INFANTRY BRIGADE.
No. G 858
Date.........

10th Sherwood Foresters

7thbLincolnshire Regt.
7th Border Regt.
8th South Staffordshire Regt.
10th Sherwood Foresters.
51st M.G.Company.
51st T.M.Battery.
51st Field Amb.
77th Field Coy.R.E.
No.3.Coy. Train.

15/10/17. Following Message received from Corps Commander begins :-

"Well done everybody AAA Wonderful performance in awful conditions AAA Hearty congratulations and thanks to you and all your great troops".

15/10/17. Following message received from 17th Div.

"The Divisional Commander heartily congratulates HOBBY and all others who took part in the attack of yesterday on their splendid performance".

for Captain,
Brigade Major, 51st Infy. Brigade.

15/10/17.

War Diary October 1917 — 10th Sherwoods.

Strength

Increase Officers

2nd Lt.	A.R. Bucklow	18/10/17	
"	J.W. Eastwood	"	
"	H.T. Attfield	Joined Corps Depot 26/10/17	

Other Ranks 74.

Decrease Officers

Capt.	D.H. Cohen	Wounded	12. 10 17
"	J.A. Meads	Killed	10. 10 17
"	F.C. Nodder	To England	10 10 17
"	R.C. Wilmot	Killed	29. 10 17
Lt. A/Capt.	S.C. Day	Killed	12. 10 17
Lieut.	C.F.S. Cox	Killed	29 10 17
2nd Lieut.	H.E. Hodding	To England Sick	25. 10 17
"	P. Dorrington	Killed	12 10 17
"	R.B. Silverwood	Wounded	29 10 17. (Gas)
"	T.J. Couche	Wounded	13. 10 17
"	R.W. Elgar	Wounded	12. 10 17
"	N.D. Brown	Wounded	12. 10 17
"	P. Garton	Wounded	12 10 17
"	C.K. Hanson	Wounded	29 10 17
"	F. Marchant	Wounded	12. 10 17

Other Ranks

	Killed	Wounded	(Wounded Gas.)	Missing
Battle Casualties	34 (4. Died of wounds)	181	10	9

Wastage. 74.

[signature]

Instructions regarding War Diaries and Intelligence Summaries are contained in F. S. Regs., Part II. and the Staff Manual respectively. Title pages will be prepared in manuscript.

WAR DIARY
or
INTELLIGENCE SUMMARY.
(*Erase heading not required.*)

Army Form C. 2118.

Vol 27

10th Sherwood Foresters

Place	Date	Hour	Summary of Events and Information — Reference Map HAZEBROUCK 5a SHEET 27. November 1917	Remarks and references to Appendices
PROVEN to ZERMEZEELE	1st		The Battalion move to WORMHOULT 'B' Area passing Starting Point 10.40 am. Route Starting point (Cross Roads by INN 5 of M in MONNERBEEK) HOUTKERQUE - HERZEELE - WORMHOULT - 'B' Area. The Battalion halted outside WORMHOULT & received dinners & waited for guides. Battn arrived in billets 4.30 pm	
ZERMEZEELE	2nd to 7th		Training was carried out by Platoons & Companies. Special attention being paid to Gas Drill	
ZERMEZEELE to PROVEN	8th		Battalion moved from ZERMEZEELE to PROVEN - marching off at 9.0 am. Route - Starting Point (Road 22) LEDRINGHEM - WORMHOULT. Cross roads C12 d 9 1 - HERZEELE - HOUTKERQUE - PROVEN along the PROVEN - POPERINGHE road. [illegible] was maintained between companies. Battalion arrived PRATTLE Camp 2.30 pm	
PRATTLE CAMP	9th		Battalion cleaned up camp & built sandbag walls round tents	
do	10th		Companies went a route march during the morning & were paid in the afternoon	

Army Form C. 2118.

Instructions regarding War Diaries and Intelligence Summaries are contained in F. S. Regs., Part II. and the Staff Manual respectively. Title pages will be prepared in manuscript.

WAR DIARY
or
INTELLIGENCE SUMMARY.
(Erase heading not required.)

10th Sherwood Foresters

Place	Date	Hour	Summary of Events and Information	Remarks and references to Appendices
			[illegible] MAP BELGIUM [illegible] 28 NW 1/20000 [illegible] 1917	
PROVEN	11 12		Battn. [illegible]	
ELVERDINGHE	13		Battn. [illegible] LANGEMARCK [illegible] HUTS	O.O. No. 87
			Battn. [illegible] FORWARD [illegible]	
	14/15		Battn. [illegible] E.A.	
	16		[illegible] TRENCH [illegible] Battn. [illegible]	
	17/18		Wire Parties for Support line daily.	
	19		Battn. [illegible] of BRIDGE CAMP [illegible] the 7 Yorks. [illegible] the front line V. 7 a – V. 14 b. at 9.15 am. Relief of the front line was complete by 12 midnight. The Battn. was somewhat heavily shelled en route to the front line, and lost killed 4 O. Ranks, Wounded: 14. During the 3 days in the front line the situation was normal.	O.O. No. 88.
	22/23		On the night of Nov. 22/23 the Battn. was relieved in the front line by the 7' BORDER Regt. and reoccupied the Close Support line A+B Coys. EAGLE TRENCH. Battn. HQ. DOUBLE COTS, C+D Coys. CANDLE TRENCH. Relief complete, without casualties by 9 pm.	O.O. No. 89

A5834 Wt. W4973 M687 750,000 8/16 D. D. & L. Ltd. Forms/C.2118/13.

Instructions regarding War Diaries and Intelligence Summaries are contained in F. S. Regs., Part II. and the Staff Manual respectively. Title pages will be prepared in manuscript.

WAR DIARY
or
INTELLIGENCE SUMMARY.
(Erase heading not required.)

Army Form C. 2118.

10th Sherwood Foresters

Refce. Map. Belgium. Sheet 28. N.W. 1/20 000 — November 1917

Place	Date	Hour	Summary of Events and Information	Remarks and references to Appendices
ROUSSEL CAMP B.13.a	25/26		On Night 25/26. The Batn. was relieved by the 10 Bn Lanc. Fusiliers and went into Bde. Reserve at ROUSSELL CAMP. Relief complete by 11 pm. Casualties nil: Weather Raining:	
	27:		Kit Inspection and cleaning up: Weather. wet,	
	28 } 29 }		Time occupied in erecting Huts, Cookhouses and a Bayonet Course: Two Companies A & B. bathed on morning of the 28th. Companies were thoroughly inspected and a certain amount of drill done every day: Foot Drill each morning:	
	30		Batn. as strong as possible proceeded to 'G' Camp to be put through Gas HUT: Work on Bayonet Assault Course continued during afternoon:	
Nov:	12		Officers joined during month: Capt. C. H. PAGE; Lt. G. F. MARCH. M.C.; 2Lt. H. R. DODDS; " A. E. GREENSLADE; " E. B. GREENWOOD; " G. A. KITCHING; " G. M. SMITH; " W. J. WILLIAMS	
"	6		Lt. T. B. WILSON	
	21		2Lt. R. A. BARKER; A. PETERKIN; R. G. BARNES; L. JACQUES	
			Officer Casualties during Month: 2'Lt. F. G. FERGUSON.	
			Officers left the Batn.: Lt. H. E. HODDING Sick to England. 20/10/17; 2Lt. R. A. PAGE Absorbed 3rd ARMY MUSK. Sch.; 2Lt. F. W. HEWITT " 4 " Sniping Sch.	
			Casualties — Off / OR: Killed: – / 4; Wounded: 1 / 16; Missing: – / 1	

F. W. Daniel Major
Comdg: 10 Bn Sherwood Foresters

A5834 Wt. W4973/M687 750,000 8/16 D. D. & L. Ltd. Forms/C.2118/13.

Army Form C. 2118.

10th Sherwood Foresters

WAR DIARY
or
~~INTELLIGENCE SUMMARY.~~

Instructions regarding War Diaries and Intelligence Summaries are contained in F. S. Regs., Part II. and the Staff Manual respectively. Title pages will be prepared in manuscript. MAP Rfc: BELGIUM Sht 28. N.W. 1/20000

(Erase heading not required.) December. 1917

Vol 28

Place	Date	Hour	Summary of Events and Information	Remarks and references to Appendices
SOULT CAMP LANGEMARCK II. AREA	1st		51st Inf. Bde: moved up into Support. Battn: moved out of ROUSSEL CAMP at 2.45 pm and proceeded to SOULT CAMP, arriving there at 4pm. Rain: Men in Tents: This day a Work Party of 6 officers and 300 O.R. were working on CADDIE TRENCHES. (Bde O.O. 221, for Move)	O.O. No. 91.
	2nd		Work Parties at SOLFORINO CAMP + PARROY CAMP. Weather v. cold. little aircraft activity	
	3rd		6 off. 300 OR. Work parties on CADDIE TRENCHES: Weather fine. Cold.	
PROVEN	4th		51st Bde. moved by road to CANADA AREA. Battn: arrived in PHEASANT CAMP at 3 p.m. by march route. Weather. Dry + v. cold. Frost:	O.O. 92
	5th		Day spent in Cleaning up:	
	6th		C/O: Inspected the Battn: by Companies, and training was carried out during the morning. Weather v. cold. Frost	
	7th		Route March in morning: Battn: bathed at COUTHOVE in afternoon. Fine.	
	8		Training carried on as usual. Rain at night. Operation Order for move to LICQUES AREA issued to all concerned.	O.O. 93
	9		Battn: (less some Transport moving by March Route) moved by Rail to SANGHEN AREA, Bde. HQ LICQUES. (HAZEBROUCK 5A and CALAIS 13 MAPS) Rain. Detrained at AUDRUICQ and marched to SANGHEN. arrived 2 AM. 10/12/17.	
SANGHEN.	10			
"	11		Training carried on: Hard Frost:	
NORDAUSQUES	12		Battn: marched to NORDAUSQUES and went into Billets, under orders to be ready to move at 12 hours notice. A + B. Coys: proceeded to QUEMY RANGE to fire on the 13th but were recalled to Billets at mid-day in readiness to move with the Battn: at one hours notice.	O.O. 94
"	13			

10th Sherwood Foresters

Army Form C. 2118.

Instructions regarding War Diaries and Intelligence Summaries are contained in F. S. Regs., Part II. and the Staff Manual respectively. Title pages will be prepared in manuscript.

WAR DIARY
or
INTELLIGENCE SUMMARY.
(Erase heading not required.)

Place	Date	Hour	Summary of Events and Information — MAP REF: HAZEBROUCK 5a. – LENS 11 — DECEMBER 1917	Remarks and references to Appendices
NORDAUSQUES	14		Battn. moved out at 3.45PM and proceeded to WIZERNES. Entrained there at 10.45PM, detrained at BAPAUME 11 am. 15 mins and marched to Billets at BARASTRE (HUTS) from 4pm. 14 mins. to 2pm. 15 mins. The Battn: marched 22 miles and spent 11 hours in train. One man only absent. Weather v. cold & fine.	O.O. 95
BARASTRE	15			
"	16		Under Orders to be ready to move at 2 hours notice. V. cold.	
"	17		H. Snow: O/C. Coy Commanders to view front line but cancelled. Coys worked in huts in morning. Short Route March in afternoon.	
"	18		Training proceeded with, and Companies exercised in the attack.	
	19		Bde. Scheme of Attack carried out by 2 Battns at a time. 10 Bn S.F. & R.S. Staff working together. WARNING ORDER received at 4pm, Bde in readiness to proceed to forward area in 20 mins.	
"	20		Occupied OLD ENGLISH line at BUTLERS CROSS, HAVRINCOURT.	
LINE	21		Took over front line K.17b. – K.11 c. (DEMICOURT 1/10000) and relieved 15th & 7th Lond. Regt.	
	22, 23, 24		In line. Hostile activity very slight, except for heavy bombardment on morning 24th with gas shells on Right of Battn. Sector. Col. KING returned to Battn. night 23/24.	
HAVRINCOURT	25/26		Relieved on night 25/26 by 7 Bn. BORDER Regt. Two Coys. went into TANK – TANK SUPPORT TR. Battn. Hqrs. & B. D. Coys. in cellars HAVRINCOURT.	
BUTLERS X	30/31		Battn. relieved by 10 Lond. Fus. and moved to OLD ENGLISH LINE on BUTLERS CROSS.	O.O. 99

H. J. King Lt Col Comdg

A5834 Wt. W4973 M687 750,000 8/16 D. D. & L. Ltd. Forms/C.2118/13.

Instructions regarding War Diaries and Intelligence Summaries are contained in F. S. Regs., Part II. and the Staff Manual respectively. Title pages will be prepared in manuscript.

WAR DIARY
or
INTELLIGENCE SUMMARY.
(Erase heading not required.)

Army Form C. 2118.

10th Sherwood Foresters

Vol 2

Place	Date	Hour	Summary of Events and Information — Map Refce DEMICOURT 1/10000 — January 1917	Remarks and references to Appendices
BUTLERS X	1		Battn. O.O. No. 100 circulated dealing with movement of the Battn. in case of a Hostile attack, whilst the Battn. was in BUTLERS CROSS.	B.O.O. 100
Front Line	3/4		Proceeded to relieve 3 Coys. 17 Middx. Regt. and ~~1 R. Berks Regt.~~ 1 Coy 1 R. Berks + 2 Coy 1 Kings Regt.	B.O.O. 101
			The Relief was much interfered with by a Hostile Raid on Right and Left of Battn. front. SCOTT POST was captured at 5.30 pm from the 17 MIDDX. and VALGRIN and Bridge Head POST on the extreme left were also lost about the same time. Attempts were made unsuccessfully by the 1 R. BERKS and 17 MIDDX to recapture these posts at about 10 pm and relief was not complete until 2 am Jany 3rd.	
-"-	4/5		On the night 4/5 Jany the 52 Inf. Bde extended their front to the left to K 10. a. 80. 25, this move altered the dispositions of the Battn, and on this night the following movements were made:- B. Coy extended their front to the LEFT and held the front line from K. 10. a. 80. 25 to within 300 yds of CAVAL, D. Coy being on their LEFT and holding to junction of CROSS AVENUE and Trench, with the 8 S. STAFFS. on their LEFT: A. Coy going into Support at WHITE HALL and C. Coy in CROSS AVENUE.	B.O.O. 102
			During this Period in the Line the enemy were not active, with the exception of bursts of artillery fire at intervals by day and night.	
-"-	9/10		The Battn. was relieved by the 7 Border Regt. night Jany 9/10 and went into Bde. Reserve at HERMIES, taking over the defences of this Village.	B.O.O. 103
	10/11		Working on HERMIES defences: from Jany 1/9 there was heavy snow and frost but a thaw set in on the 9th. Cases of Trench feet from Jany 1/11 = one.	

A5834 Wt. W4973/M687 750,000 8/16 D. D. & L. Ltd. Forms/C.2118/13.

Army Form C. 2118.

Instructions regarding War Diaries and Intelligence Summaries are contained in F. S. Regs., Part II. and the Staff Manual respectively. Title pages will be prepared in manuscript.

WAR DIARY
or
INTELLIGENCE SUMMARY.
(Erase heading not required.)

10th Sherwood Foresters

Place	Date	Hour	Summary of Events and Information	Remarks and references to Appendices
			MAP REF.: 1/10000 DEMICOURT. January 1917	
HERMIES	12/15		Battn: occupied in defence works at HERMIES.	
	16/18		On night 15/16, the Battn. relieved the 7th Border Regt in the Right Sub. Sector. With the exception of a Hostile T.M. Bombardment on night of 18 and early morning of 19, the activity of the enemy was very slight. The trenches were very wet and in a bad state.	
PHIPPS CAMP.	19/24		Battn. was relieved in the front line by 9th W. Ridings. Entraining at HERMIES it went into Huts at PHIPPS CAMP (O.6c.&d)	
			First two days in Camp were spent in cleaning up and refitting, the Battn. having been in trenches since December 20th.	
LONDON TRENCH.	25/26		This night the 51st Bde relieved the 50th Bde in the line. The Battn. relieved the 7th Yorks. Regt. in the Support Line. During the stay in Support all available men were on work parties nightly.	
	28		2 Lt. J.W. EASTWOOD killed accidentally whilst handling a German Shell near Camp.	
FRONT LINE.	31/1		Battn. moved into Right Sector of Bde front relieving the 7th Border Regt. on night Jany 31/Feby 1st.	

[illegible] Lt Col
Comdg. 10th Sherwood Foresters

A5834 Wt. W4973 M687 750,000 8/16 D. D. & L. Ltd. Forms/C.2118/13.

For War Diary January 1918 10th Sherwood Foresters

Officers Joined during the month

2nd Lieut J G Ferguson rejoined 17/1/18
" L Collins Joined 18/1/18
" H W Ward " "
" H Street " "
" G F Dexter " "
" W B Taylor " 30/1/18

Officers left during month

Major F W Daniel DSO MC To CO course Aldershot 6/1/18
Lieut R Wing To England (for Indian Army) 7/1/18
2nd Lieut J T Eastwood Killed 28/1/18
" N. Jones. To England Sick 4/1/18

P.T.O.

Other Ranks

Strength Increase

During month 48

Strength Decrease

Battle Casualties 16

Wastage 81

97

Instructions regarding War Diaries and Intelligence Summaries are contained in F. S. Regs., Part II. and the Staff Manual respectively. Title pages will be prepared in manuscript.

WAR DIARY
or
INTELLIGENCE SUMMARY.
(Erase heading not required.)

Army Form C. 2118.

16 Sherwood Foresters

WO 95/2

Place	Date	Hour	Summary of Events and Information February 1918	Remarks and references to Appendices
			MAP Refce. DEMICOURT. 1/10000 BOURSIES. 1/10000	
1	1/4		Quiet night after good Relief. Battn. started work on Strong points in front line and made good progress. Two Companies in Front Line and two Companies in Support. At 7 am. on the morning of the 2nd inst. after a heavy T.M. bombardment the enemy raided a listening post in the front of the Battn. on the LEFT. They were driven off with casualties	O.O. 108
	4/6		During this period Hostile Artillery were very active on the whole Brigade Front, bombarding heavily with artillery and T.M's for short intervals, chiefly from 5.30 AM – 8 AM. on the 5th inst, but no raids were attempted	
	6		Battn relieved on night 6/7 by 12 Manchester Regt. and moved into DIV. Reserve at HERMIES. Relief complete 1 AM, and men in HERMIES by 5 AM. 7 inst	
	7		Rest. and Clean up.	
	8		Draft of 3 Off. and 109 O.R. arrived from 17 S. FORESTERS (Battn. splitting).	
	9		8 Bn. S. Staffs. Regt. was this day disbanded, off. and men being sent to other Service Battns of the Regt. Maj. W.G. GIBSON MC and an N.C.O and 24 men of the Band representing the Battn at the final Dinner. Heavy Hostile T.M. bombardment of front line of DIV on our LEFT from 5.45 AM – 6.45 AM. Battn occupied on defence works HERMIES.	86 / 3
	10 11		Battn: occupied in improving HERMIES defences	
	12/13		Moved forward into Bde Reserve BOURSIES 1/10000 Battn H.Q. K.13 d. 7.3. B and C Coys in FAGAN AVENUE and A and D. Coys. in SLAGG St. area	O.O. 109

A5834 Wt. W4973/M687 750,000 8/16 D. D. & L. Ltd. Forms/C.2118/13.

Army Form C. 2118.

WAR DIARY
or
INTELLIGENCE SUMMARY.
(Erase heading not required.)

Instructions regarding War Diaries and Intelligence Summaries are contained in F. S. Regs., Part II. and the Staff Manual respectively. Title pages will be prepared in manuscript.

10th Sherwood Foresters

February 1918

Place	Date	Hour	Summary of Events and Information	Remarks and references to Appendices
			MAP Refce. BOURSIES 1/10000	
K.13.d	14		Reorganisation of front line: A + D Coys. moved back to J.35.d (SLAG HEAP) in the evening. Battn. in Bde Support: 2 Coys J.35.d. 2 Coys K.15.c. Battn. Hqrs LISCLOCHER LANE K.13.d.	
	15		Hostile activity very slight, except for T.M. activity nightly on FRONT LINE. DRAFT of 50 O.R. joined at Transport Lines.	
	16		V. clear day, Hostile artillery v active on front and rear of Bde. Sector.	
	17		Hostile Artillery still active. E.A. active at night. Bombs dropped on CANAL.	
	18		Relieve the 7 Bn. BORDER Regt. front line: one Coy. R + one Coy. L. of Canal. Two Companies in Support.	O.O. 110
K.9.c	19		Relief completed by 8.30pm, without Casualties. Enemy Snipers active, one man killed.	
	20		Enemy Snipers and Trench Mortars very active. Casualties from these causes 1 O.R. killed. 2 O.R. wounded.	
	21		Enemy Artillery very active at times in Support lines. SCOTT and STONE POSTS heavily bombarded by our artillery + T.M.s at 5 AM + 5.20 AM on	
	22		morning of 22nd. A great deal of work has been done by the Battalion during this tour in the Trenches. KELLETT and NUGENT much improved.	
			Returned from leave Lieut. FERGUSON 21/2/18	
			2 " GELL 22/2/18	
			2 " ATTFIELD 22/2/18	

A5834 Wt. W4973 M687 750,000 8/16 D. D. & L. Ltd. Forms/C.2118/13.

Army Form C. 2118.

WAR DIARY
or
INTELLIGENCE SUMMARY.
(Erase heading not required.)

Instructions regarding War Diaries and Intelligence Summaries are contained in F. S. Regs., Part II. and the Staff Manual respectively. Title pages will be prepared in manuscript.

10 Sherwood Foresters

Place	Date	Hour	Summary of Events and Information — Map Rfa BOURSIES 1/10000 — February 1918	Remarks and references to Appendices
K.Q.C.	23/24		Night twenty third/twenty fourth attempted to procure identification from SARK or PUPPY TRENCH, artillery and TM bombardment for five minutes, then patrol went out from A. Coy to reconnoitre both positions. Found SARK empty and garrison of PUPPY "standing to". Bombardment appeared to have been unsuccessful.	
			2 Lieut G. J. THORPE } " G. V. REED } posted from 17 Batt: arrived and were posted to A. Coy	
	24/25		Relieved by 10 Bn. Lanc. Fusiliers; Relief Completed by 9.30 pm. Batt. HQ and C.D. Coys moved into Camp at J. 34 d. A+B. Coys going into O.B. Line at K 32. HAVRINCOURT.	
	26-27		Maj GIBSON, proceeded on leave 27 inst. About this time 2 more LEWIS guns were issued to Batt: a Batt. HQrs L.G. Section formed. A further 2 guns were received on Feby 28 inst. Making 20 in possession of the Batt. at the end of this month	LEWIS GUNS
	28		Extract from London Gazette dated 12/2/18, undermentioned to be Temp. Captains:	
			30 Oct. 1917. T/Lieut. F. B. JOYCE. M.C (A/Capt)	
			T/Lieut. R. D. NEVITT.	

[signature]
Lt. Col. Comdg
10 Bn. SHERWOOD FORESTERS

A5834 Wt. W4973/M687 750,000 8/16 D. D. & L. Ltd. Forms/C.2118/13.

51st Inf.Bde.
17th Div.

10th BATTN. THE SHERWOOD FORESTERS (NOTTINGHAMSHIRE (AND DERBYSHIRE REGIMENT).

M A R C H

1 9 1 8

Army Form C. 2118.

WAR DIARY
or
INTELLIGENCE SUMMARY.
(Erase heading not required.)

Instructions regarding War Diaries and Intelligence Summaries are contained in F. S. Regs., Part II. and the Staff Manual respectively. Title pages will be prepared in manuscript.

MAP REF. 57c. FRANCE " BOURSIES 1/5000.

10TH SHERWOOD FORESTERS.

51/17

Place	Date	Hour	Summary of Events and Information	Remarks and references to Appendices
2 Coys + B.H.Q. Camp. J. 34 b. 2 Coys O.B.L. K-32	MAR. 1st 1918.		O.C.'s Coys. reconnoitred Right Sector of Brigade preparatory to relief. T/Major C. H. Page as second-in-command visited HQ and arranged details of relief. Capt. S. S. Mosley assumed duties of Adjutant (Feb 27th) vice Major Page. Change in weather – snow. Capt. R. O. Hewitt rejoined from hospital, posted to B. Coy.	
H.Q. K.15.d.	2/3	6pm to 6pm	Relieved 7th East Yorks in Right Sector – 1 Coy Front Line (Shingler), 1 Coy Support (Seal). HQ K15d and 2 Coys Reserve (Lowden, Joseph). 2nd Lt. F. W. Hanford joined. Good relief – complete by 9.45 p.m.	S.D. 13
	3/4	6pm to 6pm	Owing to bad weather, activity much below normal with the exception of M.G. fire at night.	
	4/5	6pm to 6pm	Very Quiet – Sleety, wet all day.	
	5/6	6pm to 6pm	Improved weather condition – Increased activity. – 58th Brigade reconnoitred line in view of relief. Heavy shelling most of night S. of Battalion, very intense at 5.30 a.m. At 3.30 a.m. a practice was carried out by Brigade taking up defensive positions. Good results – Battalion was in position in ½ hour.	S.O. 14
	6/7	"	~~Forces for Relief of Front & Support Lines~~ – During morning of 7th heavy bombardment about Ribecourt – continued later in day & during the night – 2nd Lt. H.E. MERRETT joined Batt. from Hospital. Lt. R. H. PAGE from Musketry School.	(Cancelled)
	7/8	"	Improved weather condition. Enemy bombardment of Hermies + Havrincourt – Quiet night – Two Coys in Res. relieved 2 Forward Coys.	S.O. 15
	8/9	"	Period normal – Enemy shelled Havrincourt with Gas Shells during day. Summer Time comes in force 9th at 11 o'clock.	
	9/10	"	Quiet on our sector except during the night at 7 pm during a raid by naval division. Heavy bombardment on Right at 2 a.m. (10th)	
	10/11		Quiet – nothing to report.	

A5834 Wt. W4973/M687 750,000 8/16 D. D. & L. Ltd. Forms/C.2118/13.

Instructions regarding War Diaries and Intelligence Summaries are contained in F. S. Regs., Part II. and the Staff Manual respectively. Title pages will be prepared in manuscript.

WAR DIARY
or
INTELLIGENCE SUMMARY.
(Erase heading not required.)

MAP REF. 57C

10th Sherwood Foresters

Place	Date	Hour	Summary of Events and Information	Remarks and references to Appendices
As Before	MAR 11/12	6pm to 6pm	Continuous enemy shelling during evening until 2am Pos & Back areas. Projector gas sent over by us on N. of canal 4 am (12th). Continuous shelling during the day on both sides. 2nd Lt Collins rejoined from Artillery (attd)	
	12/13	6pm to 6pm	6pm Enemy bombardment K.9 & K.10.	
	13–17		Nothing of note to report with the exception of heavy harassing fire each morning from 12 midnt until 6 a.m.	
	17/18	"	Battalion was relieved by 12 Manchesters – Quiet relief – complete by 8.25 pm. Moved into billets at BERTINCOURT – Total casualties for tour (15 days) 1 man killed.	O.O. 116.
"	18/19	"	Rain early morning – Shelling of village by enemy with H.V. Shrapnel.	
BERTINCOURT.	20 X		Enemy offensive commenced with bombardment at 5 AM. Battn moved forward to SLAG HEAP HEBBURN. 12 Noon Maj. GIBSON and C.D. Coys ordered to proceed at once & assist in defence of HERMIES at 3pm. Major PAGE and remainder of Battn followed and by 5pm. Battn was situated as follows: Batt. HQ. N.W. Corner of HERMIES on DOIGNIES Rd. Two Companies in trenches from DOIGNIES Rd to VELU – HERMIES Rly. Two Companies in Support on Railway Bank.	
HERMIES	21 X		Enemy attacked left FLANK several times during the day but were repulsed during the afternoon 7 BORDERS sent up to reinforce the defences, which now consisted of the following UNITS: RIGHT 7 LINCOLNS and elements of SEAFORTH BATTN. CENTRE 10 SHERWOOD FORESTERS LEFT 7 BORDER Regt. 6 guns M.M. Gun Coy.	

[signature] Lt Col

A5834 Wt. W4973/M687 750,000 8/16 D. D. & L. Ltd. Forms/C.2118/13.

Instructions regarding War Diaries and Intelligence Summaries are contained in F. S. Regs., Part II. and the Staff Manual respectively. Title pages will be prepared in manuscript.

WAR DIARY
or
INTELLIGENCE SUMMARY.
(Erase heading not required.)

10 Bn SHER FORESTERS

MAP Refce 57c — MARCH 18

Place	Date	Hour	Summary of Events and Information	Remarks and references to Appendices
HERMIES	22	X	At 1pm received orders that HERMIES was to be evacuated [illegible] the BORDERS & LINCOLNS [illegible] under the 10 SHER FORESTERS [illegible] the [illegible] to take up a position S of HERMIES [illegible] the [illegible] of these two Bns. By this time the enemy were heavily engaging the [illegible] of the LEFT DIV, slowly driving them in. The withdrawal was carried out in good order, the Bde passing through the 63 DIV holding the [illegible] line at BERTINCOURT. Masses of the enemy were now appearing on the high ground from HAVRINCOURT to VELU WOOD, and [illegible] the retreating troops as they passed along the HAVRINCOURT - BERTINCOURT VALLEY were [illegible] heavy and caused numerous casualties. Capt R. [illegible] WILSON was killed near here about 4pm. Bn assembled at [illegible] between 9PM - 12 midnight and [illegible] TRANSLOY Rd.	
ROCQUIGNY	23	X	5 Am Moved forward and took up line on SAILLY SAILLISEL - ROCQUIGNY [illegible] LINCOLN (RIGHT) & BORDERS (CENTRE) 10 SHER FORESTERS (LEFT). This [illegible] was made to support the 47 DIV and 52 [illegible] [illegible] in front of ROCQUIGNY and [illegible] RIGHT [illegible] Enemy heavily attacked ROCQUIGNY at about NOON and [illegible] fell back, at the same time the 9 DIV on the RIGHT withdrew. 10 SHER FORESTERS held on to line of TRENCHES S of ROCQUIGNY until the other two Bns of the Bde had retired, and then withdrew across country to MARTINPUICH arriving there about midnight.	

[illegible signature]

A5834 Wt. W4973 M687 750,000 8/16 D. D. & L. Ltd. Forms/C.2118/13.

Instructions regarding War Diaries and Intelligence Summaries are contained in F. S. Regs., Part II. and the Staff Manual respectively. Title pages will be prepared in manuscript.

WAR DIARY
or
INTELLIGENCE SUMMARY.
(Erase heading not required.) 10 SHER FORESTERS

Place	Date	Hour	Summary of Events and Information — MAP. ALBERT. 1/40000 — March. 1918	Remarks and references to Appendices
MARTINPUICH	24	4 Am	Moved at 4 Am cross country to MONTAUBON and took up a position [illegible] of the town in old trenches, with elements of 9 DIV and 2 Cavalry Bde on RIGHT. During the morning owing to our own artillery fire were obliged to withdraw to a line [illegible] through MONTAUBON from about S. 27 central – S. 27 c. central (RIGHT) 10 Bn. SHERWOOD FORESTERS, (CENTRE) 7 LINCOLNS (LEFT) 7 BORDERS. During [illegible] the DIV. on RIGHT was being attacked at intervals, and enemy were seen to be massing in large numbers in [illegible] MAMETZ WOOD. SHELLED heavily from [illegible] at 5.30 pm the Bde withdrew to the FRICOURT LINE and at 4 AM on 25 [illegible] withdrawal covered by M.M.G [illegible] TANK [illegible] was continued to HENENCOURT,	
FRICOURT	25/26		where the Battn arrived at 9 Am on morning of 25 [illegible]. Moved at 7 pm to MILLENCOURT via SENLIS ~~Support the 52 Inf Bde~~ ~~ENEMY having broken through at MEAULTE, and reported [illegible] in BUIRE and DERNANCOURT.~~	
~~MILLENCOURT~~	27	[illegible]	~~4th ANZACS came through about 11 Am to reinforce the 9 DIV who were being heavily pressed. Batt. was withdrawn from the Village. At 2 pm and took up a position and dug in in Artillery formation around the NORTH outskirts of MILLENCOURT. S. of MILLENCOURT – SENLIS Rd, in readiness to Counter attack~~	[illegible]
BOUZENCOURT		8 pm	Received orders to relieve the 35 Inf Bde, holding the line W. 27 a – W. 27 c. and at 10.30 pm moved [illegible]. Owing [illegible] [illegible] the line the Battn. dug themselves in [illegible], three Coys in front line one in support, with 7 Borders on RIGHT FLANK.	
	28		The Enemy action on our front ANZACS on RIGHT repulsed a heavy attack	

A5834 Wt. W4973/M687 750,000 8/16 D. D. & L. Ltd. Forms/C.2118/13.

WAR DIARY
or
INTELLIGENCE SUMMARY.
(Erase heading not required.)

Instructions regarding War Diaries and Intelligence Summaries are contained in F. S. Regs., Part II. and the Staff Manual respectively. Title pages will be prepared in manuscript.

10 Bn SHER FORESTERS

Place	Date	Hour	Summary of Events and Information — MAP ALBERT 1/40000 — MARCH 1918	Remarks and references to Appendices
BOUZENCOURT	29		Quiet day. Battn relieved by 1st Lan Fusiliers at 11 pm and moved into HENENCOURT	
	30/31		Rest in HENENCOURT, ~~[illegible]~~	
			Casualties from March 19 – 31: K. W. M.	
			Officers 2 5 1	
			RAMC (attached) – 2 –	
			Other Ranks 24 120 32	

[illegible] Lt Col
Cmdg 10th Sherwood Foresters

A5834 Wt. W4973 M687 750,000 8/16 D. D. & L. Ltd. Forms/C.2118/13.

10th Sherwood Foresters diary
March 1918

Date "20"	should be "21"
" "21"	" " "22"
" 22	" " 23
" 23	" " 24

H B Davies

18.7.25.

17th Division.
51st Infantry Brigade

WAR DIARY

10th BATTALION

THE NOTTS & DERBY REGIMENT

APRIL 1918

Army Form C. 2118.

WAR DIARY
or
INTELLIGENCE SUMMARY.

(Erase heading not required.)

Instructions regarding War Diaries and Intelligence Summaries are contained in F. S. Regs., Part II. and the Staff Manual respectively. Title pages will be prepared in manuscript.

10th Sherwood Foresters — April 1918 — Vol 32

LENS 11

Place	Date	Hour	Summary of Events and Information	Remarks and references to Appendices
In front of ALBERT	1		Relieved 7 Bn E. YORKS, in Support to front line N of ALBERT	
WARLOY	2/3		Relieved by 7. R. SUSSEX Regt 36 Bde. (12 DIV) and marched to WARLOY where the Battn. went into Billets	
MIRVAUX	4		Marched to MIRVAUX, moved out at 9.45 AM. arrived at 2.30 pm.	
"	5		Under Orders to move to MONTONVILLERS, move cancelled owing to hostile activity in front of ALBERT "STOOD TO" in billets all day.	
MILLONVILLERS	6		Marched to MILLONVILLERS and went into BILLETS. Draft of 216 O.R. (R.W. Fusiliers) joined Battn.	
DOMART	7/8		at 9 AM. moved out and marched to DOMART. Re organisation commenced	
"	9/10		Draft of 231 O.R. from ENGLAND, (mostly 19 year olds) joined Battn: night 8/9 Range practice commenced 9 ins. Fighting Strength Battn. approx. 27 off. 1100 OR.	
TALMAS	11		At 12 NOON, Battn. marched out and arrived at TALMAS. at 5.30 pm and went into Billets, received orders at midnight to move to LEALVILLERS area early in	
ACHEUX	12		morning of 12 ins. Moved out at 7.45 AM, marched through LEALVILLERS, arriving at ACHEUX 2 pm and went into Billets. Bde at one hour's notice to move. Draft of 81 O.R. arrived evening of 11 ins, from Base.	
"	13		ACHEUX. 5 off. and 400 OR. in Work Party. New Rear Defences.	

[signature] Lt Col

Instructions regarding War Diaries and Intelligence Summaries are contained in F. S. Regs., Part II. and the Staff Manual respectively. Title pages will be prepared in manuscript.

WAR DIARY
or
INTELLIGENCE SUMMARY.

(Erase heading not required.) 10th Bn. Sherwood Foresters.

Army Form C. 2118.

Place	Date	Hour	Summary of Events and Information LENS. 11 (Sheet) April 1918.	Remarks and references to Appendices
	14th		✓	
MESNIL:	15.		Relieved 4th Beds. Regt. in front line – MESNIL. 50th Inf. Bde. on LEFT and 7th Bn. LINC. Regt. on RIGHT. Battn. commanded by Maj. DANIEL DSO with Maj. PAGE as 2nd/c & adjutant. Comdg. officer and Adjutant were left out for this tour. Line held by the Battn. included the N.E. section of AVELUY WOOD and was held by an OUTPOST LINE, MAIN LINE of RESISTANCE, and SUPPORT LINE, Companies distributed in depth. C. Coy holding the OUTPOST LINE.	
"	16		Heavily shelled at intervals, at night all Ranks engaged in deepening and strengthening posns. and completing the digging of SUPPORT LINE.	
	17/19 } 20 }		Enemy Artillery active both by day and night, Casualties somewhat heavy particularly in main Line of Resistance.	
"	21/		After shelling Outpost Line severely all day, enemy opened heavy barrage with 5.9's and T.Ms. on OutPost Line and front of Main Line of Resistance. No communication with Outpost Post since 9 AM, at which time a PRIORITY message was being sent down from C. Coy when the wire was cut by shell fire. At 6 pm: Ptes MOAKES & MASON reported at Bn. H.Q., having got through from the Outpost Coy. They reported (i) that their Coy. had been heavily shelled all day and had suffered severe Casualties (ii) that Capt. Joyce had, just before they left, sent up the S.O.S. and that the enemy appeared to have come down both sides of Railway Bank and that the Outpost Line was probably now (6pm) in the hands of the enemy. As the SOS from Capt. Joyce had not been observed a Report was immediately sent on the wire and by Runner, the artillery responding within about four minutes. On the 21st the part of the Outpost Line affected by these operations was held by two platoons of 'C' Coy, roughly 78 strong with four officers, Capt. F.B. JOYCE M.C., Lieut. T.C. NUGENT and 2nd Lieut. G.L. THORPE.	[illegible initials]

A5834 Wt. W4973 M687 750,000 8/16 D. D. & L. Ltd. Forms/C.2118/13.

Instructions regarding War Diaries and Intelligence Summaries are contained in F. S. Regs., Part II. and the Staff Manual respectively. Title pages will be prepared in manuscript.

WAR DIARY
or
INTELLIGENCE SUMMARY.

(*Erase heading not required.*)

Army Form C. 2118.

10th Bn. Sherwood Foresters.

Place	Date	Hour	Summary of Events and Information	Remarks and references to Appendices
			Map. LENS (Sheet 11) April 1918	
MESNIL	21/		Patrol from 'A' Coy were immediately sent forward to try and gather further information and if possible get in touch with Capt. JOYCE. From 8 pm – 1 AM/22nd various reports were received at Battn. Hqrs. either by patrols or wounded men, and at 1 AM it appeared that the enemy had occupied our posts along the Railway, was holding huts between the Main Line of Resistance and the Railway and was probably digging in in the low ground immediately N. of the Railway Line; and that the Garrison of C. Coy was either killed, wounded or captured. At 1.50 AM. 22nd orders were received from the Bde. to counter attack and recapture the lost Posts in conjunction with the 10 Bn. W. YORKS on our LEFT. Artillery were to open a Barrage ~~at~~ at ZERO (4.30 AM) and the attacking troops to move forward at ZERO + 5. Company Cdrs and their officers had already been warned previous to the receipt of these Orders, and at a Conference at Battn. Hqrs. it was decided that 'B' Coy supported by 2 platoons of 'D' Coy commanded by 2Lt. MERRITT and 2Lt WYATT, one section of 2Lt. MERRITT's platoon to move forward immediately the attack commenced driving out the enemy and burn the huts. This operation was successfully performed by 2Lt. MERRITT and Cpl. CONNOR, assisted by 5. O.R. The main counter attack having proceeded forward about 100 yds was enfiladed by very heavy M.G. fire and forced to return to the line of assembly having suffered about seventy casualties including 2Lt. G.A. KITCHING, wounded, who was eventually killed while attempting to crawl back the same morning. Lieut L. JACQUES was in command of B Coy. during the attack.	

A5834 Wt. W4973 M687 750,000 8/16 D. D. & L. Ltd. Forms/C.2118/13.

10TH. SHERWOOD FORESTERS.

JOINED DURING MONTH OF APRIL 1918.

2/Lieut.	G. E. Baggott	Joined	19/4/18.
2/Lieut.	R. W. Larkam	"	"
2/Lieut,	J. Beech	"	24/4/18.
2/Lieut.	W. Stevenson	"	"
2/Lieut.	R. Catto	"	"
	and 612 O.R.		

STRUCK OFF DURING THE MONTH OF APRIL 1918.

2/Lieut.	A. Peterkin	Pronounced "B2"	29/3/18.
2/Lieut.	C. W. S. Cree	To England Sick	13/3/18.
Lieut.	A. B. Selby	ditto.	28/3/18.
2/Lieut.	H. R. Dodds	ditto.	29/3/18.
Captain.	F. B. Joyce M.C.	Missing	21/4/18.
Lieut.	T. C. Nugent	Missing	"
2/Lieut.	G. L. Thorpe	Missing	"
2/Lieut.	G. A. Kitching	Killed in Action	22/4/18.
	and 365 O.R.		

HONOURS REWARDS AWARDED DURING MONTH OF APRIL 1918

Major	C. H. Page	-	Distinguished Service Order.
Capt.	J. N. Knight	-	Military Cross.
Lieut	L. Jacques	-	Military Cross,
Lieut	R. A. Barker	-	Military Cross.
14481 Sgt.	Scaife	S. -	Military Medal.
13015 "	Huckerby	H. -	Military Medal.
32806 Pte.	Lamb	S. -	Bar to Military Medal.
58915 "	Sawyer	J. -	Military Medal.
20547 L/C.	Flint	S. -	Military Medal.

Instructions regarding War Diaries and Intelligence Summaries are contained in F. S. Regs., Part II. and the Staff Manual respectively. Title pages will be prepared in manuscript.

WAR DIARY
or
INTELLIGENCE SUMMARY.

(Erase heading not required.) 10 Bn. Sherwood Foresters.

Army Form C. 2118.

Place	Date	Hour	Summary of Events and Information	Remarks and references to Appendices
			Maps. LENS (Sheet 11) April 1918.	
MESNIL	23		Enemy quiet. Div. on our Right attacked at 7.30 pm in conjunction with Div. on their RIGHT. Attack made little progress.	
"	24		Relieved by 7th Bn Border Regt. Relief complete by 11.30 P.M. Battn. in relief occupying the Banks on the ENGLEBELMER - MARTINSART Rd. and coming into Bde. Reserve at Q 26.c	
			Casualties during tour in the line were:-	
			Officers K. 1 W. – M. 3 } at least 29 of the killed were casualties of the Counter attack.	
			O.R. 19 86 109	
"	25		Lt. Col. KING DSO rejoined and took over command of the Battn. O.R. on Work Parties nightly on Intermediate Line.	
"	27/28		Quiet.	
"	29		Relieved by 7th Bn. E. YORKS. relief complete. Battn. on relief moved to MILLENCOURT - ENGLEBELMER LINE. Advanced Battn. of Bde in Reserve.	
"	30		Quiet.	
			Following Honours and Awards were awarded to the Battn. vide DIV RO 790 for the share the Battn. took in the Retreat from HERMIES and the Rear guard fighting at that time	
			Major C. H. PAGE D.S.O. — 14481 Sgt. SCAIFE S. M.M.	
			Capt. J. N. KNIGHT M.C. — 13015 " HUCKERBY H. M.M.	
			Lieut. L. JACQUES M.C. — 39806 Pte LAMB S. Bar to M.M.	
			58915 " SAWYER J. M.M.	
			20547 L/Cpl. FLINT S. M.M.	[illegible signature]

A5834 Wt. W4973 M687 750,000 8/16 D. D. & L. Ltd. Forms/C.2118/13.

Army Form C. 2118.

Instructions regarding War Diaries and Intelligence Summaries are contained in F. S. Regs., Part II. and the Staff Manual respectively. Title pages will be prepared in manuscript.

WAR DIARY
or
INTELLIGENCE SUMMARY.
(Erase heading not required.) 10 Bn Sherwood Foresters.

Vol 33

L33

Place	Date	Hour	MAP. 57D.(SE)1/40000 - LENS.(Sh 11) Summary of Events and Information MAY 1918	Remarks and references to Appendices
ENGLEBELMER	1/3		Bde in Reserve. Battn. forward.	
	4		Battn. Relieved the 10 Bn LANC. Fusiliers in the MESNIL sector. Relief complete. 3 AM. 5th inst. A and D. Coys. held the Outpost Line with B and C in Support.	
	7		Capts BREEKENRIDGE and WHITEHOUSE. 77 DIV. U.S.A. army joined for three days instruction	
	8		Pte. SHAW. (No: 204558) D Coy disappeared from the Outpost Line between 9 AM - noon, no trace of him could be found. Line here about 300 yds. from the enemy.	
	9		Relieved by DRAKE Battn. of 63 (R.N.) DIV. relief complete by 12.30 AM. Battn. marched to ACHEUX WOOD and bivouacked until 6 AM. 6 AM 9th inst. Battn. marched to BOIS CREFTEL in TOUTENCOURT and went into Camp. During this tour in the trenches the enemy were abnormally quiet. Casualties for the four days were very light.	
	10		After bathing the Battn. moved to Camp W. of LEALVILLERS.	
	11		Work Parties 400 strong sent daily to Contruct Support Line near BEAUSSART.	
	12		SUNDAY: Work Parties as usual.	
	14 } 15 }		Field Firing by 3, A and C. Coys. On 14th inst, Gen. BYNG. Comdg: 3rd Army witnessed shooting.	
	16		Training and Battn. Drill.	
	17		Battn. held Sports Meeting: at which DIV. Commander and G.O.C. Bde. were present.	
	18		Bde. Moved to TALMAS, left LEALVILLERS at 6 AM, Full marching order. Packs having re-issued to all Battns. of the Bde.	

A5834 Wt. W4973 M687 750,000 8/16 D. D. & L. Ltd. Forms/C.2118/13.

Instructions regarding War Diaries and Intelligence Summaries are contained in F. S. Regs., Part II. and the Staff Manual respectively. Title pages will be prepared in manuscript.

WAR DIARY
or
INTELLIGENCE SUMMARY.

Army Form C. 2118.

(Erase heading not required.) 10 Bn. Sherwood Foresters

Place	Date	Hour	Summary of Events and Information — Map. 57.D. (SE) 1/40000. May 1918	Remarks and references to Appendices
BEAUQUESNES	20.		Bde. moved from TALMAS to BEAUQUESNES.	
"	21		Bde. inspected by Army Corps Commander Maj. General SHUTE. Bde was complimented for its smart turn out and for the work it had done from March 21st – April 1st.	
"	23		Bde. Sports held on BEAUQUESNES – PUCHVILLERS Road. Battn. won Tug of War, 1 Mile Race and wrestling on mule back.	
"	24		Training continued and preparations to move up to relieve 12th DIV. begun.	
ACHEUX	25		Moved into Camps at ACHEUX	
"	26		Moved into Billets at ACHEUX	
"	27		Moved out of ACHEUX, and bivouacked in open ground in P.15 and P.16.	
	28, 29, 30		Hostile Artillery very active, chiefly by night. Comdg. officer (Lt. Col. KING D.S.O.) left for Div. Wing. Bdr. Gen. BOND, proceeded to ENGLAND. Lt. Col. DUDGEON. D.S.O. M.C. assumed command of 51st Inf. Bde.	
	31		Battn. relieved 6 Bn. Dorset Regt. in Support of Left Sector of Front Line. Left in AUCHONVILLERS	

F W Daniel
Major
Comdg. 10 Bn. Sherwood Foresters
31/5/18

A5834 Wt. W4973/M687 750,000 8/16 D. D. & L. Ltd. Forms/C.2118/13.

Instructions regarding War Diaries and Intelligence Summaries are contained in F. S. Regs., Part II. and the Staff Manual respectively. Title pages will be prepared in manuscript.

WAR DIARY
or
INTELLIGENCE SUMMARY.

(Erase heading not required.)

Army Form C. 2118.

10 Notts & Derby

MAP. 57D. SE.

10 Bn. Sherwood Foresters — June. 1918.

Place	Date	Hour	Summary of Events and Information	Remarks and references to Appendices
AUCHON-VILLERS	1/3		Battn. working on defences of AUCHONVILLERS.	
	4		2.30 AM. Enemy raided Bde on our RIGHT. Captured 2 off and 13 O.R. Very heavy bombardment on entire DIV. front preceded Raid.	
	7		Relieved 7 Bn. Border Regt. and took over Left Battn. Sectn of front line. New Zealand DIV (4 Corps) on immediate LEFT. Relief complete by 3 a.m.	
	8.		7 Bn. E YORKS and 6 Bn. DORSETS, raided the CRATER on RIGHT of BEAUMONT HAMEL after intense Bombardment by V Corps Artillery, and penetrated 500 yds into Enemy Line. (Zero hour 10.5 pm) 4 M.gs. and 30 prisoners. Enemy suffered heavy Casualties. Battn. assisted the operation by Rifle grenade, Rifle and L.G. fire.	
	9		Quiet.	
	10		2 Lieut BLEEKLEY wounded. Artillery (enemy) more active than usual.	
	11		2 Lieut W. STEVENSON. wounded when out on Patrol, and unable to get back to our lines, fell into the hands of the enemy	
	12/13		Front particularly quiet.	
	14		Dispositions of Bde changed this day. Battn. took over the whole Bde front system holding the line thinly by platoon posts, Border Regt holding AUCHONVILLERS and 7 Lincolns in PURPLE LINE.	
	15		Warned at 1 AM that enemy attack was expected. Nothing happened.	
	16		Enemy shelled front line heavily for fifteen minutes.	
	17		Relieved by 52 Inf. Bde. Battn moved back to BROWN LINE in front of FORCEVILLE.	

A5834 Wt. W4973 M687 750,000 8/16 D. D. & L. Ltd. Forms/C.2118/13.

Army Form C. 2118.

WAR DIARY
or
INTELLIGENCE SUMMARY.
(*Erase heading not required.*)

Instructions regarding War Diaries and Intelligence Summaries are contained in F. S. Regs., Part II. and the Staff Manual respectively. Title pages will be prepared in manuscript.

Map 57 d. S.E. — 10th Bn. Sherwood Foresters

Place	Date	Hour	Summary of Events and Information — June 1918	Remarks and references to Appendices
P. 15 b.d.	18		Work Parties daily of 150 O.R. on PURPLE LINE.	
	19		Heavy Rain.	
	20/22		Work parties continued. Good weather.	
HERISSART	23		Battn was relieved by the 2nd Battn Royal Irish Regiment and marched during the evening to HERISSART, when D Coy & HQ were billeted in the village, & the other three Coys encamped just outside the village. Battn now in GHQ reserve.	
	24.		The day was devoted to cleaning up, and reorganization under the new scheme ie 3 sections in each platoon instead of four, one section being a double Lewis Gun section.	
	25.		A full days training. The commanding officer inspected the battn on early morning parade.	
	26.		Training continued.	
	27.		Parades from 6am to 10am, followed by Bde Horse Show, in which the battn took several prizes, winning the Company Commanders Jumping. The Mule Race. Four-in-hand Mules Driving Competition. etc.	
	28/29		Training and shooting on the range.	
	30.		Orders had been given for the Battn to move up in front of HARPONVILLE to relieve the 7th Border Regiment, who were there for finding working parties; but these were cancelled about 10am. A church parade was held on the Battn parade ground at 3pm.	
			Casualties for the month of June:- Officers:- 2/Lt W. Beakley, wounded 10/6/18; " W. Stevenson wounded & missing 11/6/18. O.R. killed 9. wounded 31. missing 2.	[signature] Major Cmdg

A5834 Wt. W4973 M687 750,000 8/16 D. D. & L. Ltd. Forms/C.2118/13.

Army Form C. 2118.

10 Notts & Derby Regt

WAR DIARY
or
INTELLIGENCE SUMMARY.
(Erase heading not required.)

Instructions regarding War Diaries and Intelligence Summaries are contained in F. S. Regs., Part II. and the Staff Manual respectively. Title pages will be prepared in manuscript.

Map 57.D SE

10th Battn Sherwood Foresters — July 1918

Place	Date	Hour	Summary of Events and Information	Remarks and references to Appendices
Hérissart	1/3		Training continued. Outpost schemes, battle practices and musketry on the range	
	4th		Battalion Scheme.	
"	5th		Range, firing with Lewis guns & rifles.	
	6th		Tactical & strategical exercises carried on.	
"	7th		A combined church parade with the 7th Lincolnshire Regt in the morning.	
RUBEMPRE			In the afternoon the Divisional Horse Show took place. Practice assembly took place at 11-30pm, we passed the starting at 12-50pm in correct time.	
HERISSART	8th		We returned from the battle positions, arriving back in HERISSART by 12 noon. Officers then reconnoitred the way into, & the positions in the line.	
"	9th		Left HERISSART at 6-15AM to relieve the Cambridgeshire Regt. We spent the day in the fields near HARPONVILLE, & completed the relief at 12 midnight without incident.	
FRONT LINE. AVELUY SECTOR	10th		A very quiet day. Very little hostile activity. Work on the trenches carried on.	
	11th		Raid by the 35th Divn on our left. Identification obtained. Very heavy shelling by hostile artillery.	
"	12th		Quiet day; work on the trenches continued.	
"	13th		Took over 4 posts in AVELUY WOOD from the Border Regt. Enemy activity increased considerably during the night.	
"	14th		Increased activity in the air, otherwise a quiet day.	

A5834 Wt. W4973 M687 750,000 8/16 D. D. & L. Ltd. Forms/C.2118/13.

Army Form C. 2118.

Instructions regarding War Diaries and Intelligence Summaries are contained in F. S. Regs., Part II. and the Staff Manual respectively. Title pages will be prepared in manuscript.

WAR DIARY
or
INTELLIGENCE SUMMARY.
(Erase heading not required.)

Map 57D.SE

Place	Date	Hour	Summary of Events and Information — 1/7th Battn Sherwood Foresters — July 1918	Remarks and references to Appendices
FRONT LINE	15th		Enemy much more active during the day. We were relieved by the 7th LINCOLNSHIRE REGT after which we took up positions in the PURPLE SYSTEM	
"	16/18		Working parties provided to work on the trenches in the front line system. Increased activity in the air.	
"	19th		Quiet day, working parties carried on. The new system of a 3 Brigade frontage ~~[illegible]~~ commenced. Raid by 63rd Div on our left in front of BEAUMONT HAMEL. Identification obtained	
"	20/21		Quiet day, work in front line continued.	
"	22nd		We relieved the LINCOLNSHIRE REGT who were in the front line. 2 Coys relieving in the afternoon, & 2 relieving by night. Relief completed by 12-20 AM	
"	23rd		Quiet day, work carried on	
"	24th		Raid carried out on the right by the 47th Div. 2 Prisoners captured. AMERICAN Officers & men attached to us for instruction	
"	25th		Very heavy bombardment of the enemies line N of ALBERT. Our artillery very active throughout the day.	
"	26th		Enemy attempted a raid on one of posts in 'A' Coy: line, but failed completely suffering heavy casualties. Two men missing from A Coy.	M[illegible] Coll

Instructions regarding War Diaries and Intelligence Summaries are contained in F. S. Regs., Part II. and the Staff Manual respectively. Title pages will be prepared in manuscript.

WAR DIARY
or
INTELLIGENCE SUMMARY.
(Erase heading not required.)

Army Form C. 2118.

MAR 5710 SE

Place	Date	Hour	Summary of Events and Information	Remarks and references to Appendices
			The 10th Batt. the Sherwood Foresters — July 1918	
"	27th		Very quiet day, rain throughout the whole 24 hours, trenches became extremely bad.	
"	28th		We were relieved by the 7th Border Regt after which we took up positions vacated by the 7th Lincolnshire Regt 3 Coys in the LOTHIAN SYSTEM 1 Coy in PURPLE SYSTEM. A day of very heavy artillery activity on both sides. We carried out 2 very heavy shoots on AVELUY WOOD. 3 American platoons were attached one to A B & D Coys	
LOTHIAN SYSTEM	29th		AVELUY WOOD was shelled twice during the day with heavy concentration of artillery. The 'shoots' began at 2PM & at 2.50pm, each lasting 20 minutes. The Enemy retaliation was only very slight.	
	30th		A sham attack took place on the front of the 17th Divn at 9AM. All field-guns, trench mortars, machine guns & Corps heavy artillery coming into action. The enemy retaliation was by no means heavy. At 1-15pm & 6-15pm AVELUY WOOD was again shelled heavily without any retaliation on the part of the Enemy. Between 9-45pm & 1-30am NAB VALLEY was subject to a heavy gas concentration.	
"	31st		A quiet day. Aveluy Wood was bombarded for 2 periods of 20 minutes no retaliation. The three American platoons attached to us for instruction returned in the evening and were replaced by 2 platoons which were attached to A and B Coys.	Maj. LEES, Lt. TAYLOR Killed

[signature] Lt Col
commanding 10th Batt
The Sherwood Foresters.

A5834 Wt. W4973 M687 750,000 8/16 D. D. & L. Ltd. Forms/C.2118/13.

51st Bde.
~~17th~~ Div.

<u>10th BATTALION</u>,

<u>SHERWOOD FORESTERS</u>,

<u>A U G U S T 1 9 1 8</u>.

Instructions regarding War Diaries and Intelligence Summaries are contained in F. S. Regs., Part II. and the Staff Manual respectively. Title pages will be prepared in manuscript.

Army Form C. 2118.

51/17

WAR DIARY
or
INTELLIGENCE SUMMARY.
(Erase heading not required.)

10th Sherwood Foresters

August 1918

Place	Date	Hour	Summary of Events and Information	Remarks and references to Appendices
MARTINSART.	Aug 1st		Battn. in support in left subsector of Div. (AVELUY) Front – had been relieved on previous night from reserve. Major E.B. LEES + 2/Lt. W. TAYLOR. killed at 8. pm. by a gas shell.	
"	2nd.		7th Lincolnshire Regt. raided with no success. Enemy withdrew during the night & was followed up by 7th Border Regt. We did not move.	
"	3rd. 4th. 5th.		Quiet days in the support system.	
"	6th.		Battn. relieved by 15th Welsh Regt (38th Div) + moved to camp in TOUTENCOURT WOOD	
TOUTENCOURT.	7th.		arrived in camp at 6.a.m. Rested all day.	
"	8th.		Urgent move to DAOURS by march route – leaving at 3.20 pm. The whole battn. billetted in the CHATEAU. Big British offensive.	
DAOURS.	9th.		Left at 7.50 pm + marched to VAUX where battn. bivouaced. Battle surplus left at DAOURS.	
VAUX	10th 11th		Quiet days rest.	
"	12th.		Hurried move at 3.15. pm into front line at PROYART. 51st Bde relieved 11th Bde 3rd Div. A.I.F. Men had teas at CERISY en route; transport remained at CERISY.	
In the line.	13th 14th		Fairly quiet days.	

Army Form C. 2118.

WAR DIARY
or
INTELLIGENCE SUMMARY.
(Erase heading not required.)

Instructions regarding War Diaries and Intelligence Summaries are contained in F. S. Regs., Part II. and the Staff Manual respectively. Title pages will be prepared in manuscript.

10th Sherwood Foresters

Place	Date	Hour	Summary of Events and Information — August 1918	Remarks and references to Appendices
In the line.	15th.		Heavy enemy gas bombardment started at 12.15 a.m. + lasted for three hours. 'D' Coy all casualties + most of 'B' Coy. Total casualties in the battalion were 13 Offrs + 423 OR including the following officers Lieut Col. H.T. King D.S.O. Capts G. F. March M.C., A. Kerr, Lieuts Barnes, 2nd Lieuts Collins - Phillipson - Merrett - Woonton - Ferguson - Ward - Williams - Ormerod, + Lieut Ousler (R.A.M.C. attd).	
			Major T.W. Daniel DSO M.C took over command of the battn at 3.15 p.m. Small operation at 10. pm was successful - Three advanced posts being taken + consolidated by the battn.	
"	16th.		Battn relieved by 57th Bn. 5th Div. A.I.F, + marched to FOUILLOY. Battle surplus rejoined.	
FOUILLOY	17th.		Marched in the evening at 8.30 pm. to VECQUEMONT. Capt R.O. NEVITT. came from Bde H.Q. + took over duties of adjutant.	
VECQUEMONT	18th.		Marched at 10 pm. from VECQUEMONT to HERISSART.	
HERISSART	19th.		Rested at HERISSART - Capt Clarke 7th Lincolnshire Regt joined Bn also a draft 3 officers + 170 o.Ranks	
"	20th.		Moved from Herissart to Toutencourt at 11 pm.	
	21st.		Marched at 1 pm from Toutencourt and bivouaced at Hedauville	
Hedauville	22nd.		Remained at Hedauville - worked on reorganisation of Battalion - raised three companies only.	
	24		— ditto	

A5834 Wt. W4973 M687 750,000 8/16 D. D. & L. Ltd. Forms/C.2118/13.

Army Form C. 2118.

I.6

WAR DIARY
or
INTELLIGENCE SUMMARY.
(*Erase heading not required.*)

Instructions regarding War Diaries and Intelligence Summaries are contained in F. S. Regs., Part II. and the Staff Manual respectively. Title pages will be prepared in manuscript.

10th Sherwood Foresters

August 1918

Place	Date	Hour	Summary of Events and Information	Remarks and references to Appendices
Hedauville	24th		Moved from Hedauville at 1-30pm via Mailly Maillet and took up position W of Courcelette	
Field	25th		Moved in support to Lincolns & Borders who took Courcelette and pushed on to the E of the ALBERT - BAPAUME road. Casualties 2Lt Smith killed, Lieut Catto, Lt Steel Lt Thomas & Capt John RAMC wounded	
"	26th		50th Bde went through 51st Bde and advanced on Flers. Bn collected two prisoners and two M. Gs	
	27th		Lt Hodding rejoined Battn from Brigade and took command of "C" Coy from Lieut Steel	
	28th		Moved Bn H.Q. to seven elms - Bn told to rest as much as possible - Night relieved W. Yorks in the line in front of Flers, - Lieut Williamson wounded	
	29th		Attacked and took Flers & Gueudecourt, very few prisoners the Boche being in a hurry to get away, - got a few M. Gs -	
	30th		Moved on to Le Transloy - found plenty of opposition from M. Gs - being finally held up about 1000 yards in front of Le Transloy - relieved at night by 50th Bde (Duke of Wellingtons) and returned to Div reserve	
	31st		Rest and reorganise being held in readiness to move up again at very short notice.	

[Signature illegible]
Lt Col
Cmdg 10th Sherwood Foresters

A5834 Wt. W4973 M687 750,000 8/16 D. D. & L. Ltd. Forms/C.2118/13.

Instructions regarding War Diaries and Intelligence Summaries are contained in F. S. Regs., Part II. and the Staff Manual respectively. Title Pages will be prepared in manuscript.

WAR DIARY
or
INTELLIGENCE SUMMARY
(Erase heading not required.)

Army Form C. 2118.

10th Sherwood Foresters

Place	Date	Hour	Summary of Events and Information August 1918	Remarks and references to Appendices
			Casualties	
Officers			Killed – 2/Lt A Smith 26 8/18	
			Died of wounds (2as) Lieut B G Barnes 19 8/18. 2/Lt H E Merritt 15 8/18	
			Wounded (8as) Lt Col H I King DSO. – Capt G F March MC 2/Lt F G Ferguson	
			2/Lt W J Williams – 2/Lt H E Ormerod. 2/Lt W J Wootton – 2/Lt G M Phillipson	
			2/Lt H W Ward. – Capt A Kerr – Lt Ivo Owsley. U.S. M C (attached)	
			2/Lt T Collins all on 15 8/18	
			Wounded Lieut 26 8/18 F Steel – Lieut 28 8/18 D B Williamson – 2/Lt 26 8/18 R Catto – 2/Lt 26 8/18 S A Thomas	
			2nd Lt 14 8/18 E Ellis – Wounded at duty Capt J R John 27 8/18 RAMC attached	
Other Ranks			Killed 33	
			Died of wounds 44	
			Wounded 431	
			Missing 7	
			Wounded at duty 4	
			519	

2449 Wt. W14957/M90 750,000 1/16 J.B.C. & A. Forms/C.2118/12.

17/51

Army Form C. 2118.

Instructions regarding War Diaries and Intelligence Summaries are contained in F. S. Regs., Part II. and the Staff Manual respectively. Title Pages will be prepared in manuscript.

WAR DIARY
or
INTELLIGENCE SUMMARY

(Erase heading not required.)

10th Sherwood Foresters

September 1918.

Place	Date	Hour	Summary of Events and Information	Remarks and references to Appendices
Field	1/9/18		In Divisional Reserve at Eaucourt-l'Abbaye; received orders to be ready to move into support at 4.30 am. – moved at 8 am. to N 35 b – map 57. C. S.W.	
Flers	2nd		Moved at 8 am. to FLERS, billeted till 7 pm and moved on to Gun pits in N.35.b. – 11 Casualties, 2 killed 9 wounded with one shell.	
Rocquigny	3rd		Moved at 11 am. to Rocquigny trench system, Bn still in support and stayed the night in this position.	
Line	4th		Moved 10 am. to O.36. – Bn H.Q. O.35.d. – midnight moved forward to take over whole of Divisional front from East & West Yorks. – Bn H.Q. Ytres station. Capt John RAMC & Lieut Harrison wounded. No other casualties.	
Line	5th		Remained in the line holding whole of Divisional front, with Lincolns and Borders in support, who later moved up, attacked, and captured [illegible] trench assisted by one platoon of "B" Coy. (Lt Harrison)	

2449 Wt. W14957/M90 750,000 1/16 J.B.C. & A. Forms/C.2118/12.

Army Form C. 2118.

Instructions regarding War Diaries and Intelligence Summaries are contained in F. S. Regs., Part II. and the Staff Manual respectively. Title Pages will be prepared in manuscript.

WAR DIARY
or
INTELLIGENCE SUMMARY

(Erase heading not required.) 10th Sherwood Foresters

Place	Date	Hour	Summary of Events and Information September 1918	Remarks and references to Appendices
Line	6th.		At 9. pm. relieved by Lancashire Fusiliers (52nd Bde) and marched back to Rocquigny where we became Divisional reserve	
Rocquigny	7th.		Moved at 5-30 pm nearer the line to an old camp recently used by the Bosche at Vallulant wood - camp very dirty and badly smashed.	
Vallulant wood	8th.		Spent the day resting and reorganising Battalion received a draft, including some good N.C.Os and specialists. R.S.M. Renons joined with these reinforcements. "D" Coy was formed again and Capt Jacques assumed command.	
Vallulant wood	9th.		1-30 am. Received warning order to be ready to move at 10 minutes notice, the Battalion moving off at 10.30 am. into the MOUETTES trench system, & at 8 pm moved forward again via DESART Wood and took over the support line in Q.32 from the 6th Dorset Regt., it was a very wet dark night, DESART Wood	

2449 Wt. W14957/M90 750,000 1/16 J.B.C. & A. Forms/C.2118/12.

Army Form C. 2118.

WAR DIARY
or
INTELLIGENCE SUMMARY
(Erase heading not required.)

Instructions regarding War Diaries and Intelligence Summaries are contained in F. S. Regs., Part II. and the Staff Manual respectively. Title Pages will be prepared in manuscript.

10th Sherwood Foresters

September 1918

Place	Date	Hour	Summary of Events and Information	Remarks and references to Appendices
	9th		being heavily shelled with gas & 5.9in shells.	
Line Q.32.	10th		Remained in the same position in support	
Line	11th		At 8.30pm the Division being relieved by the 38th Div. the Battalion being relieved in a well arranged manner by the Royal Welsh Fusiliers, and marched back to an old British Nissen Hut Camp at LECHELLE	
LECHELLE	12th		Battalion rested, were paid, cleaned up saw the tiny huts at night and were made very comfortable by the following day.	
LECHELLE	13th		P.T. musketry & a little drill, fitted equipment and prepared generally for CO inspection the following day - G.O.C. Bde happened an accident from his horse.	
- do	14th		C.O's inspection in the morning, played Bde at football in the afternoon and won 5-3.	

2449 Wt. W14957/M90 750,000 1/16 J.B.C. & A. Forms/C.2118/12.

Army Form C. 2118.

Instructions regarding War Diaries and Intelligence Summaries are contained in F. S. Regs., Part II. and the Staff Manual respectively. Title Pages will be prepared in manuscript.

WAR DIARY
or
INTELLIGENCE SUMMARY
(Erase heading not required.)

10th Sherwood Foresters

September 1918

Place	Date	Hour	Summary of Events and Information	Remarks and references to Appendices
LECHELLE	15th		At 10.45 am. Battalion were paraded for an open air service, G.O.C. Division being present and admired general appearance of the Battalion. C.O. attended a Bde conference at 4 pm. Platoons played football in the evening.	
LECHELLE	16th		Carried on with training and general preparations to return to the line	
LECHELLE	17th		Completed Bn with all the necessary equipment ready for moving. At 8.30 pm the Battalion moved off to its place of assembly in the FINS RIDGE trench system W.16. - Bn H.Q at W.15.b.5.8.	
Line	18th		Bn moved off in artillery formation at 5.24 am to the first objective - LOWLAND SUPPORT - HEATHER SUPPORT, trench system at 6.40 am. the Battalion moved forward again to the line of the railway from X 7 c.2.0. - X 7. c.0.8. and at 7.43. am advanced through the 50th Bde, and moved	

2449 Wt. W14957/M90 750,000 1/16 J.B.C. & A. Forms/C.2118/12.

Instructions regarding War Diaries and Intelligence Summaries are contained in F. S. Regs., Part II. and the Staff Manual respectively. Title Pages will be prepared in manuscript.

WAR DIARY
or
INTELLIGENCE SUMMARY
(Erase heading not required.)

Army Form C. 2118.

10th Sherwood Foresters

September 1918

Place	Date	Hour	Summary of Events and Information	Remarks and references to Appendices
Line	18th		closely to a very fine barrage seized BEET trench which was the final objective. D Coy (Capt Jacques MC) was on the right flank, B Coy (Lieut Skeggs) on the left. A Coy (Capt Brandt) right support, & C Coy (Lieut Hope) in reserve. D Coy took FIVES trench - a noted strong point without a casualty & got 75 prisoners, & reached their final objective with little loss capturing the entire garrison. B Coy was equally successful on the left flank & captured numerous prisoners. A Coy was then moved to the left flank & were successful in assisting the Border Regt who were held up by MG fire from the Sunken road in X 8 b 4 9, routing the enemy & capturing 100 prisoners from a dugout. C Coy stopped in [illegible] trench. Touch was maintained throughout the attack with the 7th Border Regt, & the 9th K.O.Y.L.I. (21st Div) on the right. Approximate number of prisoners - 250; 15 Machine Guns & two Field Guns; the latter were captured by D Coy about 200x in front of their final objective - During the whole advance casualties were only 30 ORs	

2449 Wt. W14957/M90 750,000 1/16 J.B.C. & A. Forms/C.2118/12.

Army Form C. 2118.

Instructions regarding War Diaries and Intelligence Summaries are contained in F. S. Regs., Part II. and the Staff Manual respectively. Title Pages will be prepared in manuscript.

WAR DIARY
or
INTELLIGENCE SUMMARY

(Erase heading not required.)

10th Sherwood Forester

Place	Date	Hour	Summary of Events and Information — September 1918	Remarks and references to Appendices
Line	18th		Bn H.Q. were established with the 7th Border Regt in a dugout at X 1 a 5.0. At 1-30 pm the enemy put down a heavy M.G. barrage & bombed the Borders out of their front line & commenced to push out B. Coy. Lieut Steggall & 2nd Lieut Tuck were killed while gallantly rallying their men. 2/Lieut Greenwood of A Coy who was in close support immediately formed up his platoon & regained the whole of the lost trench, killing 25 of the enemy and capturing two together with 6 M.Gs. This fine piece of work saved a critical situation; at 8.15 pm the enemy again commenced bombing down the front line of the Borders but was held up when the Borders had become more organised; throughout the night enemy M.Gs were very active, & 2/Lieut Langham was killed.	
Line	19th		Both sides were very active with Artillery & Bn H.Q. was shelled continuously; The Bn was relieved by the 4th Kings Liverpool Regt (33rd Div) which was complete by 11-45 pm & marched out to the trench system at W.16.	[initials]

2449 Wt. W14957/M90 750,000 1/16 J.B.C. & A. Forms/C.2118/12.

Instructions regarding War Diaries and Intelligence Summaries are contained in F. S. Regs., Part II. and the Staff Manual respectively. Title Pages will be prepared in manuscript.

WAR DIARY
or
INTELLIGENCE SUMMARY

(Erase heading not required.)

Army Form C. 2118.

10th Sherwood Foresters

September 1918

Place	Date	Hour	Summary of Events and Information	Remarks and references to Appendices
Line	20th		The Bn rested and reorganised, ~~at 7.30pm~~ S.O.	
Line	21st		Completed and ready once again the Bn moved at 7.30pm to the forward positions and relieved the 10th W Yorkshire Regt in Lancashire trench & Somme Alley - still holding all GAUCHE WOOD with Bn H.Q. in its previous place at X 1 d. 5.0; Relief complete by 11-30pm.	
Line	22nd		Battalion holding Gauche Wood; nothing of importance happened.	
Line	23rd		——— do ———	
Line	24th		Still holding GAUCHE WOOD enemy shelled Bn H.Q. area with 8 inch & 5.9s plenty of work was done by the Bn preparatory to further operations later	
Line	25th		Things got generally lively and parts of the line were shelled intermittently throughout the day; The 6th Leicesters (21st Div) relieved the Battalion at night; relief complete	

2449 Wt. W14957/M90 750,000 1/16 J.B.C. & A. Forms/C.2118/12.

Instructions regarding War Diaries and Intelligence Summaries are contained in F. S. Regs., Part II. and the Staff Manual respectively. Title Pages will be prepared in manuscript.

WAR DIARY
or
INTELLIGENCE SUMMARY
(Erase heading not required.)

10th Sherwood Foresters

Army Form C. 2118.

Place	Date	Hour	Summary of Events and Information September 1918	Remarks and references to Appendices
Line	25th		By 1 a.m. and after halting for hot tea near HEUDECOURT the Battn marched back to a good camp in MANANCOURT for rest. Casualties during operations were 9 Offs & 180 O.R. Killed :- Lieut Steggall 2Lieut Tack 2Lieut Langham; Wounded :- 2Lieut Greenwood, 2Lieut Sears, 2Lieut Burrows, 2Lieut Garton, 2Lieut Leighton, 2Lieut Windsor.	
MANANCOURT	26th		Rest and general cleanup. Battalion were paid and saw the Army Muffins at night	
MANANCOURT	27th		Started parades at 9 am; reorganisation. Lt Col Daniel DSO, MC, proceeded on leave. Major Clarke M.C, D.C.M, took over command. 10 Officer reinforcements arrived.	
MANANCOURT	28th		Bde parade at 11 am for Divine Service. Major Gen Robertson C.B. C.M.G. being present and presented medal ribbons to officers N.C.Os & men.	[illegible initials]

Army Form C. 2118.

Instructions regarding War Diaries and Intelligence Summaries are contained in F. S. Regs., Part II. and the Staff Manual respectively. Title Pages will be prepared in manuscript.

WAR DIARY
or
INTELLIGENCE SUMMARY

(Erase heading not required.)

10th Sherwood Foresters

Place	Date	Hour	Summary of Events and Information September 1918	Remarks and references to Appendices
[illegible]	29th		[illegible]	
[illegible]	30th		[illegible]	

2449 Wt. W14957/M90 750,000 1/16 J.B.C. & A. Forms/C.2118/12.

16

Army Form C. 2118.

WAR DIARY
or
INTELLIGENCE SUMMARY.
(*Erase heading not required.*)

Instructions regarding War Diaries and Intelligence Summaries are contained in F. S. Regs., Part II. and the Staff Manual respectively. Title pages will be prepared in manuscript.

10th Sherwood Foresters

Place	Date	Hour	Summary of Events and Information	Remarks and references to Appendices
			Ref Map 57B + 57C. SE — October 1918.	
Manancourt	1/10/18		In rest at Manancourt. Reorganisation + Training in morning. Games in afternoon	
do.	2/10/18		Training continued. Lewis Gun practice on range.	
do.	3/10/18		do do Rifle + revolver competitions on the Range in the afternoon. Very good application shooting.	
do.	4/10/18		Training continued. Football match in afternoon against 7th Lincolns. Result Sherwood Foresters 5 Lincolns 0.	
do.	5/10/18		Received orders at 11/30 am to move. Left Manancourt at 12.30 and marched to W12a area west of Gouzeaucourt arriving at 14/30 pm.	
Gouzeaucourt	6/10/18 7/10/18		Training as usual in morning. Games in afternoon.	
Hindenburg Line.	8/10/18		Moved at 2 am to HINDENBURG LINE via GOUZEAUCOURT, GONNELIEU, BANTEUX and BANTOUZELLE arriving at 0500 hrs, so following up 21st Divn. At 13.30 hrs we moved forward to trench system at M35 b and d, west of Mont Couvez Farm where we stayed the night.	
Mont Couvez Farm	9/10/18		At 0450 hrs. 51st Brigade moved forward + passed through the 21st Divn. 7th Lincolns + 7th Borders in front line, 10th Sherwood Foresters in support, passing through MALINCOURT, SELVIGNY and CAULLERY, reaching MONTIGNY the 3rd objective at 1800 hrs. Casualties 2 killed 17 wounded. During the night Lincolns + Borders held the line of Railway in J32 and J33. Sherwood Foresters in support in the village of MONTIGNY. In the early morning the 50th Bde passed through + pushed forward	

A5834 Wt. W4973/M687 750,000 8/16 D. D. & L. Ltd. Forms/C.2118/13.

Army Form C. 2118.

Instructions regarding War Diaries and Intelligence Summaries are contained in F. S. Regs., Part II. and the Staff Manual respectively. Title pages will be prepared in manuscript.

WAR DIARY
or
INTELLIGENCE SUMMARY.
(Erase heading not required.)

10th Sherwood Foresters

Place	Date	Hour	Summary of Events and Information — Ref Map 57B NE — October 1918	Remarks and references to Appendices
Montigny	10th 11th		In Divisional Reserve. Reorganisation in morning. As much rest as possible obtained.	
Inchy	12th		Left MONTIGNY at 1230 hrs. and moved to INCHY in support of 52nd Bde. Lincolns + Borders located in INCHY. Sherwood Foresters J18 b. Bn H.Q. at J23 b5.4. We were then placed at disposal of GOC 52nd Bde who ordered the Battn to move up in support to Ravine in J12 b and d. Bn H.Q. with A and D Coys in Ravine. B and C Coys remaining in J8 a. in artillery formation. At 18 hrs Battn moved + took over front line from 52nd Bde who had been heavily counter attacked and driven back to the line of the river. We had great difficulty in taking over owing to the night being very dark and wet, the bridges over the river being smashed + heavy M.G fire.	
	12th		We took up positions on EAST side of River from K1 d 0.5 to K8 a 1.8 thence on West side of river K8 a 0.7 with the Lincolns on our right Borders in support + Middlesex on left with whom we got in touch. This movement entailed several casualties. 2/Lt Whyatt killed, Henderson + Spencer wounded. Capt Barker was seriously wounded at 1000 hrs and died in F.A. at about 1900 hrs. Upon application the artillery strafed the village + quietened the Enemy's fire.	
Line	13th		Enemy very active, MGs and snipers firing from windows and high buildings in village of NEUVILLY, causing numerous casualties.	

A5834 Wt. W4973/M687 750,000 8/16 D. D. & L. Ltd. Forms/C.2118/13.

Instructions regarding War Diaries and Intelligence Summaries are contained in F.S. Regs., Part II. and the Staff Manual respectively. Title pages will be prepared in manuscript.

WAR DIARY
or
INTELLIGENCE SUMMARY.
(Erase heading not required.)

Army Form C. 2118.

10th Sherwood Foresters

October 1918.

Place	Date	Hour	Summary of Events and Information	Remarks and references to Appendices
Line	14th		Bn H.Q. moved to J11 d 35.00. From reports from front line Enemy were moving in twos and threes out of village, but later, scouts and patrols trying to work through village found it was still held in force.	
	15th		Enemy less active. Fairly quiet day. Relieved at night by 6th Dorsets afterwards marching back to MONTIGNY.	
			Lt Col Daniel DSO MC returned from leave.	
Montigny	16th		Spent the day resting and reorganising the Battn. Draft received from base of 7 officers 32 O.R.	
do	17th		Training & refitting.	
do	18th		Usual daily training. Baths. Played the 7th Borders at football in afternoon & won 3-0.	
			All officers of Brigade attended a lecture by the G.O.C. Brigade at 1430 hrs on the forthcoming operations.	
do	19th		Usual daily training. Baths. Preparations for returning to the line. At 1920 hrs Battalion went forward to Assembly Positions in J12 d on the west of the NEUVILLY Ridge.	
Line	20th		At zero 0200 hrs. the Battn moved forward crossing the river SELLE by footbridge in support to the 50th Bde & formed up on their 2nd objective running from E 26 d 5.3 to K 3 a 6.3 (the railway) in platoon columns A & C Coys leading B & D Coys in support 250 yds in rear. 7th Lincolns on right & 1st East Surreys of 5th Divn on left. Bn H.Q. moved to K 2 D 05.70. At 0350 hrs the Battn going through the 50th Bde went forward & captured the	

A5834 Wt. W4973/M687 750,000 8/16 D. D & L. Ltd. Forms/C.2118/13.

Instructions regarding War Diaries and Intelligence Summaries are contained in F. S. Regs., Part II. and the Staff Manual respectively. Title pages will be prepared in manuscript.

WAR DIARY
or
INTELLIGENCE SUMMARY.
(Erase heading not required.)

Army Form C. 2118.

10th Sherwood Foresters

October 1918

Place	Date	Hour	Summary of Events and Information	Remarks and references to Appendices
Line	20th	(Cld)	the 3rd objective running from E27 b 3 7 to E 28 c 3 8.	
			At 06.54 hrs D Coy attacked the 4th objective, ridge running from E22 central to E 28 b 3 8, but meeting with heavy M.G fire had to come back. At 1600 hrs C Coy attacked and captured the 4th objective taking 50 of the 2nd Prussian Guard prisoners, including 5 officers & sustaining only a few casualties.	
			The Battn was first to gain its objectives. Throughout the weather was very bad, the night being very dark & raining heavily. Casualties 1 Officer & 13 O.R. killed. 4 Offrs & 52 O.R. wounded. 2/Lt Franklin killed. Bucklow & Roe wounded, and Lt Lynch & 2/Lt Brown wounded, at duty.	
Line	21st		Battalion consolidated. D Coy moved up into front line. Relieved in evening by 10th Lancashire Fusiliers of 52nd Bde and Battalion marched back to billets in INCHY.	
INCHY	22nd		Cleaning & reorganisation.	
"	23rd		51st Bde moved from INCHY at 0700 hrs by column of route the Battn going to E29a between AMERVAL and OVILLERS so following up the 21st Division who had continued the advance.	
E29a	24th		Battalion resting.	
do	25th		Battn moved back to billets in BEAUMONT at 0900 hrs.	
BEAUMONT	26th		17th Division relieved the 21st Divn in line. Battn moved up to	

A5834 Wt. W4973 M687 750,000 8/16 D. D. & L. Ltd. Forms/C.2118/13.

Instructions regarding War Diaries and Intelligence Summaries are contained in F. S. Regs., Part II. and the Staff Manual respectively. Title pages will be prepared in manuscript.

WAR DIARY
or
INTELLIGENCE SUMMARY.
(Erase heading not required.)

Army Form C. 2118.

10th Sherwood Foresters

October 1918

Place	Date	Hour	Summary of Events and Information	Remarks and references to Appendices
BEAUMONT	26th		to VENDEGIES in reserve and took over billets from 9th KOYLI's	
VENDEGIES	27th		Cleaning up. Overhauling of Lewis Guns and checking ammunition bombs etc. B Echelon located at OVILLERS	
"	28th		Lewis Gun & Kit inspection in morning. Football match in afternoon: Result Officers 4 NCOs 2.	
"	29th		17th Division relieved by 21st Division. 10th Sherwood Foresters relieved by the 15th DLI at 1330 hrs marched back to good rest billets at INCHY	
INCHY.	30th		Usual Coy daily training in morning. C.O. inspected billets at 0900 hrs. Inspection of 1st line transport at 1400 hrs by GOC, Bde.	
"	31st		Company training. Lewis Guns firing on range. All officers & NCOs attended a lecture by the Divl Gas Officer at 1530 hrs.	

[illegible]
Lieut Col
Commanding
10th Sherwood Foresters

A5834 Wt. W4973/M687 750,000 8/16 D. D. & L. Ltd. Forms/C.2118/13.

Army Form C. 2118.

Instructions regarding War Diaries and Intelligence Summaries are contained in F. S. Regs., Part II. and the Staff Manual respectively. Title pages will be prepared in manuscript.

WAR DIARY
or
INTELLIGENCE SUMMARY.
(Erase heading not required.)

10th Sherwood Foresters. Vol 39

Place	Date	Hour	Summary of Events and Information	Remarks and references to Appendices
			Ref Map 51 S.W. 1-20000. November 1918.	
INCHY.	1st		At rest. Company Training in morning. Parade service for Roman Catholics. The Battalion gave a Guard Mounting Demonstration to the 51st Brigade. The G.O.C. and all officers & N.C.O's of Brigade attended.	
INCHY.	2nd		C.O. attended a Battalion Commanders conference at Brigade H.Qrs at 11.00 hrs. The 17th Divn relieved the 21st Division in the line. The 51st Brigade relieved portions of 62nd & 110th Bde at POIX-du-NORD in support. The Battalion relieved the 1st Wilts. Bn. H.Qrs located near church. Battalion left Inchy at 16.45 hrs & reached Poix du Nord 22.00 hrs to billets.	
POIX-DU-NORD	3rd		C.O. Coy Commanders & 1 subaltern of each Coy reconnoitred the assembly positions in the early morning. Battalion moved to assembly positions near Ft GAIE FARM in evening. Bn H.Qrs in barn. Capt Kerr died of wounds 2/Lt Taylor, & R.S.M. wounded. O.R's 1 Killed 11 wounded.	
In the field	4th		The 52nd Bde in line 51st in support. At 05.30 hrs the 10th Sherwoods moved from assembly positions in platoon columns & advanced 500 yds in rear of 10th Lancs Fusiliers C Coy on right, A Coy in centre, B Coy on left, with D Coy in support. They met with heavy German barrage & sustained numerous casualties. Our barrage was good.	

A5834 Wt. W4973 M687 750,000 8/16 D. D. & L. Ltd. Forms/C.2118/13.

Army Form C. 2118.

Instructions regarding War Diaries and Intelligence Summaries are contained in F. S. Regs., Part II. and the Staff Manual respectively. Title pages will be prepared in manuscript.

WAR DIARY
or
INTELLIGENCE SUMMARY.
(Erase heading not required.)

10th Sherwood Foresters.

Place	Date	Hour	Summary of Events and Information	Remarks and references to Appendices
			Ref. Map 51 1/40000. November 1918.	
In Field.	4th	Contd.	At Zero (05.30 hrs) plus 185, the Battalion formed up on 1st Objective running from S 15 d 4.4 to S 15 b 4.9 & moved forward under a creeping barrage & captured the 2nd Objective from S 17 a 8.9 to S 17 c central without meeting much opposition. Two field guns were captured. Touch was maintained throughout with 7th Lincolns on right but the 1st Herts on left were held up and were some distance behind. At Zero plus 449 minutes the 7th East Yorks passed through but were held up by M.G. fire before gaining the 3rd objective. The Battalion consolidated. Bn. H. Qrs moved to S 11 C 5.0. Casualties 4 officers 98 O.R. 2/Lt. E.E. Wilson killed, Capt Arundel M.C. & Holding M.C. 2/Lt. Street wounded. [illegible] Lynch to C.C.S. owing to shellshock. Weather was very bad especially in morning.	
In Field.	5th		21st Divn. went through us & continued the advance in the early morning. The Battalion moved forward to S. 18 a central in support. Rained all night & day.	
Do.	6th		Battalion moved at 11.30 hrs by column of route to billet at La Tête Noire on Eastern outskirts of the Forêt de Mormal. Rain all day.	
La Tête Noire.	7		Moved to Aulnoye via Berlaimont to billets and at 18.15 hrs to the line at Limont Fontaine relieving the 64th Bde. ~~the Battn~~ 20 Reinforcements from Divl. Wing.	

A5834 Wt. W4973 M687 750,000 8/16 D. D. & L. Ltd. Forms/C.2118/13.

Army Form C. 2118.

Instructions regarding War Diaries and Intelligence Summaries are contained in F. S. Regs., Part II. and the Staff Manual respectively. Title pages will be prepared in manuscript.

WAR DIARY
or
INTELLIGENCE SUMMARY.
(Erase heading not required.)

10th Sherwood Foresters

November 1918.

Place	Date	Hour	Summary of Events and Information	Remarks and references to Appendices
In Line at LIMONT-FONTAINE.	8th		51st Brigade continued the advances at daybreak. Battalion in support. Brigade were held up on ~~line~~ road running from N to S in W 13 central. Two unsuccessful attacks were made here, in which ~~we~~ we did not participate. Bn HQrs located at V 17 c 3.5.	
Do.	9th		At 03.00 hrs the 52nd Brigade advanced through the 51st Bde without meeting opposition. Battalion then marched back to good Rest Billets at AULNOYE.	
Do.	10th		Cleaning & Reorganising. Major Clarke was President of an F.G.C.M.	
Do	11th		Armistice declared at 11.00 hrs. Very little excitement. Battalion paraded in afternoon when the C.O. spoke to & congratulated the men.	
Do	12th		~~Moor.~~ 51st Brigade moved back, the Battalion went to poor billets at Locquignol in the Forêt de Mormal	
Locquignol	13th		Battalion moved to good billets at Troisvilles. Long march which the men did well. Packs were brought in motor lorry. Draft received 5 officers, 1 R.S.M. & 67 O.Rs. 2/Lts Harrison, Rattray, Birch, Adkins & Chamberlain. R.S.M. Powell.	

A5834 Wt. W4973 M687 750,000 8/16 D. D. & L. Ltd. Forms/C.2118/13.

Army Form C. 2118.

WAR DIARY
or
INTELLIGENCE SUMMARY.
(*Erase heading not required.*)

Instructions regarding War Diaries and Intelligence Summaries are contained in F. S. Regs., Part II. and the Staff Manual respectively. Title pages will be prepared in manuscript.

10th Sherwood Foresters.

Place	Date	Hour	Summary of Events and Information	Remarks and references to Appendices
			Ref. Map. Valenciennes. 12. November 1918.	
Troisville	14th		Battalion parade at 09.00 hrs, Posting of drafts + re-organisation of Companies. C. Coy. reformed. Men on Headquarters sent to Companies. O.C. Coys. are 2/Lt Ross 'A', 2/Lt Fletcher 'B'. Lt Winckley 'C'. Capt Jacques 'D'.	
Do.	15th		Company Training & refitting in morning. Capt Brice E.W. rejoined to command 'B' Coy. Two drafts received. 263 O.Ranks	
Do.	16th		Company Training in morning. United Divine Thanksgiving Service at 11.00 hrs	
Do.	17th		Company Training. Draft of 3 officers + 12 O.Rs received 2/Lts. Hemsted, Drabble & Stafford.	
Do.	18th		G.O.C. Brigade inspected the Companies at Coy. Drill in morning. Lecture at 15.15 hrs on Demobilisation to Battalion. Strength of Battalion 28 officers 780 O.R's. 2/Lt Callingham to Hospital.	

Army Form C. 2118.

Instructions regarding War Diaries and Intelligence Summaries are contained in F. S. Regs., Part II. and the Staff Manual respectively. Title pages will be prepared in manuscript.

WAR DIARY
or
INTELLIGENCE SUMMARY.
(Erase heading not required.)

10th Sherwood Foresters.

Place	Date	Hour	Summary of Events and Information November 1918.	Remarks and references to Appendices
Troisvilles	19		Company Drill & Battalion Drill.	
			Lt. C. K. Hope, 2Lt. H. T. Brook & 6 O.R.s rejoined.	
Do.	20		Company Training & Battalion Drill in morning.	
Do.	21		Ceremonial Drill in Morning. Baths & fitting of Clothing	
			Lt. E. J. Lynch rejoined & 4. OR.s 2Lt. Fletcher to Hospital.	
Do.	22		Battalion Ceremonial Drill. G.O.C. Brigade inspected.	
			Lecture on Education by Bde. Education Officer.	
			Lt. Watson joined.	
Do	23.		Church Parade in 'Henry Muffins' Hall at 11.00 hrs.	
			Football in the afternoon.	
Do	24		Usual Parades & Games during the day	
Do	25.		G.O.C. Brigade attended Guard mounting at 12 noon. Usual Parades.	
Do.	26		Lt. Bennett went forward by Lorry to the new area by Abbeville with a billeting party.	
			The G.O.C. 17th Division inspected the Brigade at J.34.c.4.8. at 10.00 hrs.	
			Whole battn. transport were on parade.	
			Draft of 40 O.R. arrived.	

A5834 Wt. W4973 M687 750,000 8/16 D. D. & L. Ltd. Forms/C.2118/13.

Army Form C. 2118.

WAR DIARY
or
INTELLIGENCE SUMMARY.
(Erase heading not required.)

Instructions regarding War Diaries and Intelligence Summaries are contained in F. S. Regs., Part II. and the Staff Manual respectively. Title pages will be prepared in manuscript.

10th Sherwood Foresters

Place	Date	Hour	Summary of Events and Information	Remarks and references to Appendices
Troisvilles	27.		The G.O.C. Brigade inspected billets at 12 noon.	
Do	28.		Capt G.F. March M.C., Lieut A.L. Dent, Sec Lieuts J.K.L. Roberts, A.H. Ladd, & A.C. Kendrick, & 42 O.R. joined the Battn.	
			The Battn Education Officer delivered lectures in the morning.	
Do	29.		11 men left the Battn. to proceed to England as miners.	
			Usual Parades & Education lectures.	
Do.	30.		The Battn. went for a seven kilometre route march in the morning.	
			Games in the afternoon.	

[illegible] Lt Col
10th Sherwood Foresters

A5834 Wt. W4973/M687 750,000 8/16 D. D. & L. Ltd. Forms/C.2118/13.

Instructions regarding War Diaries and Intelligence Summaries are contained in F. S. Regs., Part II. and the Staff Manual respectively. Title pages will be prepared in manuscript.

WAR DIARY
or
INTELLIGENCE SUMMARY.
(Erase heading not required.)

Army Form C. 2118.

10

Place	Date Dec	Hour	Summary of Events and Information	Remarks and references to Appendices
Troisvilles	1st		Capt R. O. Nevitt assumed command of 'C' Coy, T/Capt G. F. March M.C. took over duties of adjutant. 2/Lt. R. Catto rejoined the Battn from England. 50 men left for England as miners at 08.30 hrs. C of E. Parade in 'Merry Muffins' Theatre at 09.15 hrs.	
do	2nd		Training programme carried out in the morning. 1st round of the Bde Soccer Football Competition in the afternoon, results A Coy lost to C Coy Lincolns 3–4. B Coy a bye. C Coy beat Trench Mortars 13–0. D Coy beat D Coy Borders 4–1. 80 O.R. proceeded to ENGLAND to work in the coal mines	
do.	3rd		No parades, the day was spent in cleaning up for H.M. the King's visit on the following day	
"	4th		Battn paraded at 08.00 hrs and marched to cross roads in J.30.b where the Div was formed up on either side of the road to welcome H.M. The King. 80 miners proceeded to ENGLAND in the morning.	
"	5th		Training programme carried out.	
"	6th		No parades, men cleaned up for the march the following day	
"	7th		The Battn moved from TROISVILLE by march route to MASNIERES, and were billeted there for the night. Dinners were cooked at a mid day halt	
HERMIES.	8th		The Battn marched to HERMIES in the morning. Passing through FLESQUIERES where our front line was situated from Dec – March 1918. The camp at HERMIES	

A5834 Wt. W4973 M687 750,000 8/16 D. D. & L. Ltd. Forms/C.2118/13.

Army Form C. 2118.

WAR DIARY
or
INTELLIGENCE SUMMARY
(Erase heading not required.)

Instructions regarding War Diaries and Intelligence Summaries are contained in F. S. Regs., Part II. and the Staff Manual respectively. Title Pages will be prepared in manuscript.

Place	Date	Hour	Summary of Events and Information	Remarks and references to Appendices
HERMIES	Dec	8.	was situated almost on the identical ground, where the Battn made its last stand before ~~[illegible]~~ withdrawing in March last.	
HERMIES	"	9th	Battn marched to FAVREUIL and was accommodated in old huts for the night.	
FAVREUIL	"	10th	Battn marched to ALBERT and was encamped just outside the remains of the town for the night. The camp was in the same field as that in which our front line was dug at the finish of the withdrawal last March.	
ALBERT	"	11th	Battn marched to PONT NOYELLES and was billeted there for the night.	
PONT NOYELLES	"	12th	Battn marched via AMIENS to FOURDRINOY where it was billeted for the night.	
FOURDRINOY	"	13th	Battn marched ~~from~~ to billets in BAILLEUL & BELLIFONTAINE. The B.G.C. & C.O. congratulated the Battn on the way they carried out the march more especially as 3 out of the 7 days were very wet indeed.	
BAILLEUL	"	14th	Battn rested. D. Coy moved from BELLIFONTAINE to GRANDSART.	
"	"	15th	The day was devoted to cleaning up.	
"	"	16	Again devoted to cleaning up.	
"	"	17th	Ordinary parades carried out. A Bde Ploughing match took place, the Battn won the following prizes, 1st prize best [illegible] bed. 2nd prize best pair of horses 1st prize best groomed horses 1st prize best kept harness. D. Coy moved to EPAGNETTE.	
"	"	18th	Battn. H.Q. & A Coy moved to EPAGNETTE	
EPAGNETTE	"	19	Ordinary parades carried out.	
"	"	20th	do	
"	"	21st	do Bde cross country run in afternoon. Bn won. Cpl & Tasker first man home.	

2449 Wt. W14957/M90 750,000 1/16 J.B.C. & A. Forms/C.2118/12.

Instructions regarding War Diaries and Intelligence Summaries are contained in F. S. Regs., Part II. and the Staff Manual respectively. Title Pages will be prepared in manuscript.

WAR DIARY
or
INTELLIGENCE SUMMARY
(Erase heading not required.)

Army Form C. 2118.

Place	Date	Hour	Summary of Events and Information	Remarks and references to Appendices
EPAGNE	18 Dec	22nd	B & C. Coys moved to PONT REMY.	
"	"	23rd 24th	Ordinary parades. Capt Brice & several other ranks proceeded to ENGLAND as pivotal men. A few remaining coalminers also went.	
"	"	25th	Xmas Day. Xmas dinners were eaten by Companies, they went off very well & were much appreciated by all ranks. They were followed by concerts & entertainments. The C.O. visited all the Battn during dinners.	
"	"	26th	The day was devoted to football & other recreation.	
"	"	27th	Ordinary parades. The Battn Education scheme was put into force & the men seemed to appreciate it. Opening lectures on elementary subjects were given by 2 Lt Kendrick & 2 Lt Pringle & on Agriculture by Capt Marsh. A singing class & reading circle were formed by B & C. Coys at PONT REMY.	
"	"	28th	C.Os kit inspection in the morning, football in the afternoon.	
"	"	29th	Church parades held at EPAGNE & PONT REMY.	
		30	Ordinary parades & Education scheme carried out.	
		31.	Ordinary Parades.	

T W Daniel Lt Col
10th Sherwood Foresters.

2449 Wt. W14957/M90 750,000 1/16 J.B.C. & A. Forms/C.2118/12.

Army Form C. ~~2118~~ 17

V 41

WAR DIARY
or
INTELLIGENCE SUMMARY
(Erase heading not required.)

Instructions regarding War Diaries and Intelligence Summaries are contained in F. S. Regs., Part II. and the Staff Manual respectively. Title Pages will be prepared in manuscript.

10th Sherwood Foresters

Place	Date	Hour	Summary of Events and Information January 1919	Remarks and references to Appendices
EPAGNETTE	1919 Jan 1st		General Holiday. Match between the Lincolns We won 2 to 1	
	2		General parades, & a lecture held at Epagne on Influence of Sports on Character, by Mr. Prior (Harrow School)	
	3		General Parades. & Education scheme carried out.	
	4		Kit Inspection by C.O.	
	5		Church parades at EPAGNETTE & at Pont REMY	
	6		Coy Parades & Education scheme carried out	
	7		Kit Inspection by Coys.	
	8		Education scheme, 2 coys ordinary parades & 2 Coys cleaning up for Generals inspection	
	9		Salvaging. Generals inspection of 2 Coys at EPAGNETTE Lecture by Mr Hemsted to 2 Coys at Pont-Remy.	
	10		Generals inspection of 2 Coys at Pont-Remy. Route march for 2 coys at EPAGNETTE	
	11		Ordinary Parades & Education scheme	
	12		Church parade at Epagnette & Pont-Remy.	
	13		Parades & Education Scheme	
	14		Route march by Coys	

[signature] Lt Col.

Instructions regarding War Diaries and Intelligence Summaries are contained in F. S. Regs., Part II. and the Staff Manual respectively. Title pages will be prepared in manuscript.

WAR DIARY
or
INTELLIGENCE SUMMARY.
(Erase heading not required.)

Army Form C. 2118.

10th Sherwood Foresters

January 1919

Place	Date	Hour	Summary of Events and Information	Remarks and references to Appendices
EPAGNETTE	1919 Jan 15		Practice for the presentation of Colours.	
	16		The presentation of Colours by Maj General Sir R. Robertson CB. CMG. Comdg 17 Division. + ribands to recipients of recent awards.	
	17		Ordinary parades + Education.	
	18		Route march by Coys.	
	19		Church parades at Epagnette + Pont Remy.	
	20		Route march + Education Scheme.	
	21		Ordinary parades + Education	
	22		Route march by Coys.	
	23		Ordinary parades + Education. Lecture given on "The French Revolution" at Eaucourt	
	24		Ordinary parades + Education.	
	25		Ordinary parades + Education	
	26		½ Battalion moved from Pont-Remy to Epagnette	
	27		Ordinary parades + Education	
	28		Route-march	
	29		Battalion marched to EAUCOURT to hear lecture given by Capt Monkton on "The problems of the peace conference."	
	30		Ordinary parades + Education	
	31		Battalion marched to EAUCOURT to hear lecture on "The War Office in War time" by Major G. N. [illegible] G.S.O. II 17 Division	

[illegible] Lt.

A5834 Wt. W4973 M687 750,000 8/16 D. D. & L. Ltd. Forms/C.2118/13.

Army Form C. 2118.

WAR DIARY
or
INTELLIGENCE SUMMARY.
(Erase heading not required.)

Instructions regarding War Diaries and Intelligence Summaries are contained in F. S. Regs., Part II. and the Staff Manual respectively. Title pages will be prepared in manuscript.

10th Bn Notts & Derby Regt.

Vol 42

Place	Date	Hour	Summary of Events and Information	Remarks and references to Appendices
		1919		
EPAGNETTE	Feb. 1.		Ordinary parades & Education.	
	2		Men all on Train Guards No Church parade. 2/Lts. E Harrison, T.L. Blackman, J.P. Brown & Lt. G.T. Watson & 22 O.R. to 17th Div. Rec: Cp for demobilization	
	3		Education & Train Guards	
	4		Games & Train Guard.	
	5		Education & Games.	
	6		Education & Route march. 2 O.R. proceeded to Div: Recept. Camp en route for England for demobilization	
	7		3 officers 2/Lts. F.C. Shaw, G.T. May, J Chamberlain & 17 O.R to 17th Div reception Camp en route for England demobilization	
	8		20 O.R. left on proceeding to 17th Div. Recep Camp for demobilization. Train guards for supply trains [illegible]. 2/Lt. J.K.L. Roberts left proceeding to join 2nd Bn Sherwood Foresters. Lt Col. T. W. DANIEL DSO. MC proceeded to the War office for a conference. Capt G F MARCH [illegible]	
	9		Church parade full by H.C. at 10.30 a.m. 4 O.R. proceeded to 17th Div Conc: Camp for demobilization.	
	10-11		Games & Education.	
	12.		Capt G.C. WINCKLEY M.C. & 2/Lt. S.S. ADKINS proceeded on 2 months leave to ENGLAND, pending joining to Regtl Depot for service in the Regular Army.	
	13.		Parades & education. The colours were taken to ABBEVILLE by 2/Lt. B.W. STAFFORD and colour party. Capt G.F. MARCH. MC & Capt. S. J. Rearsall accompanying them. Two photographs were taken at the French Barracks of the colours of the Regiments of the 51st Inf Bde together with the colours of a French Regt afterwards the officers entertained the French officers to lunch at the officers club at	

A5834 Wt. W4973/M687 750,000 8/16 D. D. & L. Ltd. Forms/C.2118/13.

Instructions regarding War Diaries and Intelligence Summaries are contained in F. S. Regs., Part II, and the Staff Manual respectively. Title pages will be prepared in manuscript.

WAR DIARY
or
INTELLIGENCE SUMMARY.
(Erase heading not required.)

Army Form C. 2118.

Place	Date Feb 1919	Hour	Summary of Events and Information	Remarks and references to Appendices
EPAGNETTE	13 (contd)		ABBEVILLE, and the N.C.O.s entertained the French N.C.O.s at a restaurant.	
	14-15		Ordinary parades and education.	
	16.		Church Parade in the Recreation Room.	
	17.		B.G.C. 51st Inf. Bde inspected the company composed of men for the Army of Occupation.	
	18		Ordinary parades in the morning. In the afternoon the battn won the final of the Bde competition in the Divisional inter Coy Association football competition, thus qualifying to represent the 51st Bde against the other Bdes in the Division. N.B. The strength of the Battn is now that of full Company — hence we only provide one team from the Battn.	
	19.		Ordinary parades and education in the morning. Capt. R.O. Hewitt rejoined from a course in ENGLAND, and Lt. G.V.H.C. BLACKWALL joined. In the evening a 51st Inf. Bde farewell dinner	

D. D. & L., London, E.C. (A7883) Wt. W803/M1672 350,000 4/17 Sch. 52a Forms/C/2118/14

Army Form C. 2118.

Instructions regarding War Diaries and Intelligence Summaries are contained in F. S. Regs., Part II, and the Staff Manual respectively. Title pages will be prepared in manuscript.

WAR DIARY
or
INTELLIGENCE SUMMARY.
(Erase heading not required.)

Place	Date FEB 1919	Hour	Summary of Events and Information	Remarks and references to Appendices
EPAGNETTE	19 (contd)		was held in ABBEVILLE. 47 officers were present.	
	20-21-22		Ordinary parades and education.	
	23		Church parade in the morning.	
	24-25		Ordinary parades.	
	26		Lt Col T.W. DANIEL DSO. M.C. rejoined from duty in ENGLAND.	
	27-28		Ordinary parades & education	

T.W. Daniel
Lt Col

D. D. & L., London, E.C.
(A7883) Wt. W593/M1672 350,000 1/17 Sch. 52a Forms/C/2118/14

4 14

Instructions regarding War Diaries and Intelligence Summaries are contained in F. S. Regs., Part II, and the Staff Manual respectively. Title pages will be prepared in manuscript.

WAR DIARY
or
INTELLIGENCE SUMMARY.
(*Erase heading not required.*)

Army Form C. 2118.

10th Sherwood Foresters

Vol 43

Place	Date	Hour	Summary of Events and Information	Remarks and references to Appendices
	March			
EPAGNETTE	1		The C.O. inspected kits during the morning.	
	2		No Church parades as all available N.C.O.s & men had to go on duty as guards of the Supply Trains.	
	3.		No parades as all the men were still away on train guards.	
	4		Company parades as detailed.	
	5.		Battalion provided supply train guards.	
	6.		Men on train guards, remainder paid by O.C. Coy.	
	7.		Company parades as detailed.	
	8.		Battalion provided supply train guards.	96
	9		Voluntary church service as men were away on train guards	F 3
	10		Company parades as detailed by O.C. Coy.	
	11		Company Route march.	
	12		1 hour Education men marched to ABBEVILLE for baths	
	13.		Education & musketry parades. Capt. L. Jacques M.C. returned to duty from 3rd Army Rifle School.	
	14		Company parades as detailed.	
	15		Kit & Rifle inspection by O.C. Coy. 2/Lt. A.L. Snowden returned from leave to U.K.	

D. D. & L., London, E.C.
(A7883) Wt. W803/M1672 350,000 4/17 Sch. 52a Forms/C/2118/14

Instructions regarding War Diaries and Intelligence Summaries are contained in F. S. Regs., Part II. and the Staff Manual respectively. Title pages will be prepared in manuscript.

WAR DIARY
or
INTELLIGENCE SUMMARY.
(Erase heading not required.)

Army Form C. 2118.

10 Sherwood Foresters.

Place	Date	Hour	Summary of Events and Information	Remarks and references to Appendices
	March			
Epagnette.	15		2/Lt. B.W. Stafford admitted to 36 C.C.S.	
	16		Church parade 10.30 hrs in Recreation Rooms followed by H.C. at 11.00 hrs. Collection, proceeds of which were given to the DOVER PATROL memorial Fund.	
			Bn Transport moved from PONT-REMY to EPAGNETTE.	
	17		Education & Rifle practice.	
	18.		Company parades as detailed.	
	19		Route march & R.E. fatigue.	
	20		Company parades & Education.	
	21		Company proceeded to PONT. REMY rifle range for Musketry practice. In afternoon they marched to ABBEVILLE for baths.	
	22		Lecture by Coy. Cmdr in Recreation room on Discipline.	
	23		Bn provided guards for Supply Trains. No parade service. Vol: Church service at 10.30 hrs in Recreation room. 51st L.T.M.B. absorbed into the battalion. 2/Lt H.J. Brook returned from U.K. Cow[illegible]	
	24		Coy found R.E. fatigue	

E.H. [illegible] Capt.
10 Sherwood Forest[illegible]

D. D. & L., London, E.C.
(A7883) Wt. W803/M1672 350,000 4/17 Sch. 52a Forms/C/2118/14

Instructions regarding War Diaries and Intelligence Summaries are contained in F. S. Regs., Part II, and the Staff Manual respectively. Title pages will be prepared in manuscript.

WAR DIARY
or
INTELLIGENCE SUMMARY.
(Erase heading not required.)

10 Sherwood Foresters. Army Form C. 2118.

Place	Date	Hour	Summary of Events and Information	Remarks and references to Appendices
	March			
Epagnette	24		Education & cleaning of equipment on account of bad weather	
	25		Lt. Col. Daniel D.S.O., M.C. & Lt. A.L. Dart proceeded to England on leave of absence. Capt L. Jacques M.C. proceeded to England for 2 months leave previous to joining Depot.	
	26		Education parades etc.	
	27			
	28			
COCQUEREL	29		Battn moved to COCQUEREL by march-route and was accommodated in billets.	
	30		No church parade as there was nowhere to have it.	
	31		Ordinary parades etc.	

[illegible signature] Capt
Commdg
10 Sherwood Foresters

Milton Keynes UK
Ingram Content Group UK Ltd.
UKHW050222160124
436090UK00006B/82